Critical Essays on
John Greenleaf Whittier

Critical Essays on John Greenleaf Whittier

Jayne K. Kribbs

G. K. Hall & Co. • **Boston, Massachusetts**

Copyright © 1980 by Jayne K. Kribbs

Library of Congress Cataloging in Publication Data

Main entry under title:
Critical essays on John Greenleaf Whittier.

(Critical essays on American literature)
Includes bibliographical references and index.
    1. Whittier, John Greenleaf, 1807-1892—Criticism
and interpretation—Addresses, essays, lectures.
I. Kribbs, Jayne K.   II.   Series.
PS3288.C7   811'.3   80-14207
ISBN   0-8161-8308-2

This publication is printed on permanent/durable acid free paper
MANUFACTURED IN THE UNITED STATES OF AMERICA

CRITICAL ESSAYS ON AMERICAN LITERATURE

This series seeks to publish the most important criticism on writers and topics in American literature. At the same time it aspires to represent the historical development of critical thought on a given topic. Both of these objectives are admirably met in Jayne Kribbs' collection of criticism on John Greenleaf Whittier. In the most substantial collection of criticism ever published on this author, she includes comment from such distinguished contemporaries of Whittier as Nathaniel Hawthorne, Orestes Brownson, and James Russell Lowell as well as essays from such modern scholars as Norman Foerster, Vernon Lewis Parrington, Howard Mumford Jones, Perry Miller, and Lewis Leary. Kribbs' introduction is itself an important assessment of the stages in Whittier's life and work and an overview of the major scholarly treatments of this important writer. We are confident that this collection will make a permanent and significant contribution to American literary scholarship.

JAMES NAGEL, GENERAL EDITOR

Northeastern University

FOR MY PARENTS

CONTENTS

ACKNOWLEDGMENTS

It is a pleasant duty to record my thanks to the staffs of the Paley Library of Temple University, the Van Pelt Library of the University of Pennsylvania, and the Library of Congress for their courteous help. I am grateful to Miss Priscilla J. Letterman, administrative assistant for the *World Shakespeare Bibliography* and the *American Literature* bibliography, for helping me track down articles on Whittier from some long neglected American periodicals; to Miss Maryann McLoughlin, my Temple University Research Assistant, for preparing the index, and for her unflagging persistence in searching out a number of extracts from Whittier's poetry; to Professor James Hessinger for his translations of several Latin and Greek passages; and to Ms. Carol Sullivan and Mr. Harry McCabe for their thoughtful comments on the manuscript. I am especially grateful to my editor, James Nagel, for his extraordinarily even-tempered forebearance, and to Professor John B. Pickard, not only for his well-reasoned scholarship, but also for his kind generosity in allowing me to reprint so much of it. Finally, I am especially indebted to Professor Glen A. Omans, Temple University, who read the introduction with great care and always gave me sound suggestions and warm encouragement.

INTRODUCTION

John Greenleaf Whittier was a Quaker, farmer, abolitionist, journalist, politician, and poet. Yet throughout a life defined first by fiery youthful ambitions for literary then political fame, then by a bitter struggle in the cause of abolition, and later by his undisputed popularity as an honored American institution, Whittier always cherished the family, religion, and soil that nurtured him. With something of reverence, Whittier found virtue and comfort in the simple pleasures of domestic affections, the serenity and quiet mercy of his Quaker faith, and in the elemental beauty of his rural New England landscape.

The Whittier family lived on a farm near Haverhill, Massachusetts, for almost 170 years before John Greenleaf was born on December 17, 1807. The boy grew up learning, not about what remained of the harsh New England Calvinistic beliefs in the wrathfulness of God, the Bible as His revealed word, the innate depravity of man, or selective salvation, but about the Quaker beliefs in the benevolence of God, the inner light, and the brotherhood of all men, beliefs that would guide him through life, influencing his art and literary philosophy. He would also remember the Merrimack River Valley with its lush green meadows, long unbroken range of hills, and the noisy, busy stream that ran near the ancestral home. He loved his "dear old landscape" but loathed the inevitable, strenuous farm labor necessary to keep the indifferent land alive. It became clear early that he was neither physically nor temperamentally suited to be a chore boy, and in some adolescent verse expressed his real ambition:

> "And must I always swing the flail,
> And help to fill the milking pail?
> I wish to go away to school;
> I do not wish to be a fool."[1]

There weren't many books in the Whittier home—the Bible, of course, *Pilgrim's Progress,* and the biographies and writings of such prominent Quakers as William Penn and George Fox. At age fourteen, he was introduced to the works of Robert Burns (about the first poetry he had ever heard, he once recalled) by a "pawky auld carle" of a Scotsman who wandered into the family homestead willing to exchange poetry for food, and he reached out for Shakespeare, Milton, Scott, Byron,

Coleridge, and Wordsworth.[2] His chance to go to school did not come, however, until some time after his older sister Mary, admiring his poems, secretly sent one to the Newburyport *Free Press*, then edited by the future abolitionist William Lloyd Garrison. Delighted with the piece, Garrison sought out Whittier, encouraged him in his writing, and urged his parents to cultivate the boy's talent by allowing him to have the opportunities of formal schooling. The rigorous demands of the New England farm required the boy's help, so it was with reluctance that tough-minded John Whittier gave his nineteen-year-old son permission to attend the newly formed Haverhill Academy. During his two terms there, Whittier boarded with the Abijah Thayer family, helping as he could around the editorial office of Thayer's *Gazette*, and earned his own tuition by making shoes, teaching school, and keeping account books for a local merchant. Both Garrison and Thayer wanted to support Whittier in his writing and broaden his reputation as a poet, so Garrison channeled his productions into a number of New England magazines, and the kindly Thayer proposed a separate edition of the Whittier poems from the *Gazette*. Without the required number of subscriptions to support the publication of the volume, Thayer reluctantly abandoned his scheme, and with that, the Haverhill poet abandoned his chances for a college education. The bleak prospect of returning to the debilitating strain of farm labor faced Whittier until Garrison again interceded by securing for him the editorship of the *American Manufacturer*, a staunchly pro-Clay Boston weekly. Despite the fact that he held the position for only seven months in 1829, Whittier, discovering that he had a knack for political journalism, dramatically fashioned the *Manufacturer* into a respected, important periodical. At the same time, he acquired the skills necessary in getting a paper out; by being "his own typesetter, proofreader, book reviewer, news analyst, poetry writer, and office boy,"[3] he developed the imaginative and mechanical expertise that prepared him to move into the editorship of the Haverhill *Gazette* in 1830 and, until 1832, Hartford's *New England Weekly Review*, Connecticut's most influential political paper.

During his residence in Hartford, he was not too busy to accept a place in a sophisticated literary circle that had at its center Lydia H. Sigourney, the popular sentimental versifier. The tall, somewhat handsome young editor with glowing black eyes was attractive to, and attracted by, many of the city's women who eagerly sought his attention. Although he never married, always pleading, if sometimes conveniently, poverty, precarious health, his Quaker faith, and care of his mother and sister, he had a number of relationships with women. His romantic interests were first stirred in his Academy days by Mary Emerson Smith, a non-Quaker distant cousin who finally wanted only to be his sister, and by Evelina Bray, who claimed in old age that she had once been engaged to Whittier and then jilted. In 1832, he met the woman he came closest to marrying—the Quaker, poet, and abolitionist, Elizabeth Lloyd; "the most beautiful woman I ever saw," he confessed at one time, and the only woman he ever loved. These women as well as poets and abolitionists like Lucy Hooper, "a noble girl—in heart as well as intellect," and Gail Hamilton, who called Whittier her "Dear Angel" and "Dear Little Darling," always maintained cordial, comfortable friendships with the poet, no matter what their spoken or unspoken feelings for him may have been.[5]

When he wasn't caught up in Hartford's social and political activities, he relentlessly cranked out poems, an average of one a week, on topics ranging from New England folklore and Indian legends to inequality and intemperance. At the same time, however, he grew to recognize his limitations as a poet, to see that his poetry, like that of so many scribblers at the time, lacked "character of thought"—it was "the tinsel and drapery of poetry, without the substance."[6] And with his poetry merely praised, rarely paid for, he knew that he had to trust other, perhaps less ephemeral, pursuits for distinction and profit. In an 1832 essay "The Nervous Man," a downcast Whittier grudgingly admitted that "Time has dealt hardly with my boyhood's muse. Poetry has been to me a beautiful delusion. It was something woven of my young fancies, and reality has destroyed it. I can, indeed, make rhymes, now, as mechanically as a mason piles one brick above another; but the glow of feeling, the hope, the ardor, the excitement has passed away forever."[7]

The reputation he earned as a skillful political editor and contact with the leaders of his party provided him with a new way to win the public recognition that he seemed to need. Not just political journalism but direct involvement in politics was to be the answer. He attended the National Republican Party convention in Massachusetts, and while still the editor of the *Weekly Review* was selected to be a Connecticut delegate to the National Republican Party Convention in Baltimore. However, the ill health that followed him throughout life prevented him from making the difficult journey from Hartford, forced him to relinquish his editorship and retreat to the seclusion of the farm to recuperate. From there he was soon well enough to take an active part in Essex County politics, to renew his contributions to political papers, and, after his father's death, to assume responsibility for the farm. Because of his unaffected Quaker honesty and his ability to turn a persuasive phrase, he quickly became popular in his district, and well-meaning friends convinced him to campaign for the Massachusetts seat in Congress. But at twenty-four, he was neither legally old enough nor physically able, so, disappointed and restless, he cast about again for

some kind of political activity. His Quaker sympathies were clearly
leaning toward the persecuted band of Abolitionists when he received
a letter from Garrison that may well have influenced his decision to
support the unpopular cause. "This, then, is a time for the philanthropist—any friend of his country, to put forth his energies, in order to let
the oppressed go free and to sustain the republic. . . . Whittier enlist!—
Your talents, zeal, influence—are all needed."[8] Whether Whittier's own
inclination or Garrison's passionate challenge formed his resolve to
join the Abolitionist movement, it is clear that the principles involved
in such a commitment were fundamental to his Quaker up-bringing that
insisted upon the equality of all men and the ideal of human freedom.
Liberty and slavery, peace and injustice, could never dwell in harmony;
the great crusade was indeed worthy. He marched forward with energy
and enthusiasm even though his partisan work would mean his estrange-
ment from a broad, primarily literary audience. His first blast of moral
indignation at the evils of slavery came in 1833 with the pamphlet
Justice and Expediency, a thoroughly researched, carefully documented,
and effectively argued appeal to the country's heart and conscience.
Published at his own expense from his thinly furnished pocket, the
essay thrust him immediately into national prominence and launched
his thirty-year devotion to the anti-slavery cause. Also in 1833 he became
a Massachusetts delegate to the National Anti-Slavery Convention in
Philadelphia. There he signed the Declaration of Sentiments, drafted
by Garrison, which argued for immediate, peaceful emancipation, an
end to the inter-state slave trade, and the complete abolition of slavery
in the District of Columbia. Whittier was to say years later that he
valued his name on this document more highly than on the title page
of any of his books.

The 1830s were exciting and turbulent years for Whittier. He was
elected to the Massachusetts legislature, appointed vice president of
the New England Abolition Society, and named board member and
later secretary of the Essex County Anti-Slavery Society and corresponding secretary for the American Anti-Slavery Society; in 1839 he left the
Whig Party and founded the Liberty Party. He became known as a
skillful lobbyist; he rained petitions on Congress; and he was highly
influential in political circles. But his work was never easy. More than
once at anti-slavery meetings in New England towns he was taunted
by angry crowds "noisy with turbulent respectability and unwashed
rascality," nettled by his unpopular cause. Once he was even hunted
by a mob and pelted with rotten eggs, stones, and debris. His health
became too fragile to endure the strain of activity swirling about him.
Incessant, wearing headaches and a generally delicate constitution
forced him to withdraw from the center of the fray in 1836. Broken
in body but not in spirit, he retreated to Amesbury with his mother

and sister Elizabeth after selling the Haverhill farm. "I am still," announced Whittier in 1840, "so far as my failing health admits of, ready to *do* and *suffer* if need be for abolitionism."[9]

From Amesbury for many years afterwards, with only an occasional stay in Boston, New York, or Philadelphia, he continued to expand the appeal of abolitionism. In passionate outbursts, he responded to the nation's strife. With some of his most stirring poetry, Whittier roused his countrymen to acknowledge the effects of man's injustice and begged them to end the ranklings of sectional prejudice and to free their "dusky brothers" from their evil oppressors for the sake of God and humanity. More than 100 in all, some of these poems, calculated frankly to agitate people's emotions, served little longer than their hour. A number of critics dismissed them as being loaded with too much passion or an excessive vehemence of feeling, while others thought them to be merely shallow emotional indulgence and empty rhythmical arrangements. He himself acknowledged that they had been dashed off "with no expectation that they would survive the occasions which called them forth: they were protests, alarm signals, trumpet-calls to action, words wrung from the writer's heart, forged at white heat, and of course lacking . . . finish and careful word-selection."[10] Nevertheless, several fine poems do emerge out of this rubble. "Massachusetts to Virginia" was written in 1843 to focus attention on the case of George Latimer, a fugitive slave from Virginia then on trial in Boston, and to condemn Virginia for denying the democratic spirit nurtured a century earlier by its wiser forebears. In the poem he boldly cautions Virginia to end the slave hunts in Massachusetts, and pleads with Massachusetts to hold firm in its desire for truth and freedom. With our southern brothers, he says, "We wage no war, we lift no arm, we fling no torch within."

> But for us and for our children, the vow which we have given
> For freedom and humanity is registered in heaven;
> No slave-hunt in our borders,—no pirate on our strand!
> No fetters in the Bay State,—no slave upon our land!

"Ichabod" originated with the author's surprise and disappointment at Daniel Webster's famous seventh of March, 1850, speech in support of the Fugitive Slave Bill. Whittier's invective is a withering blast of extraordinary power. Not rage but indignation, blended with grief and pity at the orator's betrayal, lies at the heart of the poem. Like the haloed angels tempted by Lucifer to evil and destruction by an excess of pride, Webster is

> So fallen! so lost! the light withdrawn
>   Which once he wore!
> The glory from his gray hairs gone
>   Forevermore!

And Whittier mourns the loss of all that was once good in the man, for "naught/ Save power remains."

> All else is gone; from those great eyes
> The soul has fled:
> When faith is lost, when honor dies,
> The man is dead!

Years later he looked back on the activities of those days before the Civil War and remembered not so much the ideals and expectations of the abolitionists but his often difficult role in jarring the public conscience. Through the torrent of hostilities, he remained "a dreamer born," a crusading poet who abandoned

> the Muses' haunts to turn
> The crank of an opinion-mill,
> Making his rustic reed of song
> A weapon in the war with wrong.[11]

Though the War would eventually reward his efforts, the peace-loving Quaker was dismayed by its inevitable approach. In Amesbury, still working for reform but far removed from the center of things, he began to "walk in pleasanter meadows," taking refuge in his nostalgia for the more carefree times of his boyhood, his love of nature in her endless possibilities, and in the quiet beauties of his religion. *Lays of My Home* (1843) reflects these interests, although the only work to endure from it is "The Ballad of Cassandra Southwick," the dramatic monologue of a woman persecuted by the Puritans. The book, more importantly, marks the beginning of a life-long friendship with fellow poet and astute editor James T. Fields and with the publishing company that, after a number of name changes, eventually became Houghton Mifflin. This company published in fairly rapid succession *Ballads, and Other Poems*, 1844, (many of which had already appeared in *Poems*, 1838, and *Lays of My Home*); *The Stranger in Lowell*, 1845, (a collection of eighteen essays, most of which appeared originally in the *Middlesex Standard* and were later reprinted in *Literary Recreations*, 1854); *Voices of Freedom*, 1846, (anti-slavery poems collected from several newspapers and published by some friends without the poet's consent); *The Supernaturalism of New England*, 1847, (reprinted essays devoted to folk legends and superstitions); *Poems*, 1849, (105 previously published works plus "Proem"); and *Leaves from Margaret Smith's Journal*, 1849, (an historical novel, Whittier's only attempt at sustained fiction).

From early in 1847 to late in 1857, Whittier sent nearly all his poetic output to the *National Era* in Washington, the official organ of the National and Foreign Anti-Slavery Society. The best remembered poems from this period are "Ichabod," "The Barefoot Boy," and "Maud Muller," source of Whittier's most quoted lines:

> For of all sad words of tongue or pen,
> The saddest are these: "It might have been!"

Although he continued to serve as a corresponding editor of the *Era* for almost three more years, he found it increasingly more advantageous to his pocket and popularity to join the "dignified company" and "discriminating audience" of the newly founded, decidedly literary *Atlantic Monthly*.[12] By doing so, he went a long way in mending the tear in his literary reputation made by his abolitionist work. Now he linked arms with New England master singers Emerson, Holmes, Lowell, and Longfellow. Even though he was a faithful contributor to the *Atlantic* until his death and many of his works display a keen and refined poetic sensibility, only three ballads have retained their power to charm: "Barbara Frietchie," "Skipper Ireson's Ride," and "Telling the Bees." "Barbara Frietchie," widely reprinted in northern periodicals after its first appearance in 1863 and once popular for its melodramatic quality and determined patriotism, can not be classed as first rate poetry. Today, more people seem to know the poem than recall its author. Surely we remember from our schooldays the words Dame Barbara spoke from her attic window:

> "Shoot, if you must, this old gray head,
> But spare your country's flag," she said.

A more substantial poem, considered to be the finest American ballad of the nineteenth century, is "Skipper Ireson's Ride," an adaptation into verse of a Massachusetts legend Whittier had learned as a young man. For reasons unclear to us as the ballad begins, "Old Floyd Ireson, for his hard heart," has been tarred and feathered by the women of Marblehead and is being carried out of town in a cart, humiliated and ridiculous:

> Body of turkey, head of owl,
> Wings a-droop like a rained-on fowl,
> Feathered and ruffled in every part.

Explanation for the degrading spectacle comes in the fourth stanza: Ireson left his crew to die on a sinking ship, and now their women take revenge on him—the "sharp-tongued spinsters, old wives gray," and "Girls in bloom of cheek and lips." The pathos that is evoked briefly as the women wait for their men "Over moaning and rainy sea" dissolves when the scene moves away from the racket and confusion of the narrow Marblehead streets to the open serenity of the Salem Road. The transition is made more striking by a shift in the narrative which allows

Ireson to speak for the first time. The shame and punishment he must now endure cannot compare with "the nameless horror" in his soul:

> "Waking or sleeping, I see a wreck,
> And hear a cry from a reeling deck!
> Hate and curse me,—I only dread
> The hand of God and the face of the dead!"

Touched by the wretched man's pain, the women "with soft relentings and rude excuse,/ Half scorn, half pity," release him to suffer his punishment from a higher authority. The ballad is superb in its harmonious blending of the well-known New England legend with a simplicity of diction, a carefully wrought dramatic structure, a well-modulated consistent tone, and a concentration on one central incident. And for once, Whittier did not slap on a moral.

He again skillfully manipulates narrative, scene, diction, and tone in "Telling the Bees," for Robert Penn Warren a "gentle little masterpiece of nostalgia."[13] The poem depends upon an Essex County superstition that when a person dies the household beehives must be draped with black cloth lest the bees, mourning the loss, seek a new home. The easy conversational tone of the first person narrator, a young man reliving a visit to the home of his love Mary after a year's absence, invites the reader to re-walk the path with him:

> Here is the place; right over the hill
>   Runs the path I took;
> You can see the gap in the old wall still,
>   And stepping-stones in the shallow brook.
>
> There is the house, with the gate red-barred,
>   And the poplars tall;
> And the barn's brown length, and the cattle-yard,
>   And the white horns tossing above the wall.[14]

The description is simple and unadorned; the scene is just as it was when the narrator made his first visits to Mary. The same sun still shines, the same roses nod in the breeze, the same brook sings, and the same sweet clover smell overwhelms the evening air. But this time, the beehives are being covered with black cloth by the "drearily singing" chore girl. Trembling, he moves closer and hears her woeful song which

> ever since
>   In my ear sounds on:—
> "Stay at home, pretty bees, fly not hence!
>   Mistress Mary is dead and gone!"

The poem ends with no need for an underlying statement. The elegaic tone, structural control, lyrical dramatic quality, and the simplicity of the diction are especially admirable since the poem is an expression of Whittier's bereavement at the loss of his mother. A wiser, more artistically mature author was beginning to emerge—little by little, he had learned his craft, blundered and stumbled his way, issuing now and then a rare flash of his particular genius. Now his poetry was becoming more full and mellow.

The death of his sister Elizabeth eight years later gave Whittier the inspiration and energy to write a poem dedicated to her memory, dedicated, in fact, to the memory of the entire Whittier household and to the "winter joys his boyhood knew." Snow-Bound, his longest work and certainly the most important of his genre poems, won immediate popular and critical acclaim, and over the years has remained the almost unanimous choice among critics as his most masterful production. Less than two months after it appeared in 1866, James T. Fields wrote to Whittier of its enormous success. "We can't keep the plaguey thing quiet. It goes and goes, and now, today, we are bankrupt again, not one being in crib. I fear it will be impossible to get along without printing another batch! I do indeed. Pity us!"[15] Whittier received $10,000 for his winter idyll, a considerable sum for those days, and for the first time in his life he was freed from financial worries. The simple directness of this rural snow picture is carefully woven together with the homely details and fond recollections of a bygone time. As the white air swirls a veil over the landscape and wraps the farm in solitude, the housemates gather around the cheery, crackling fire. Even though theirs is

> A solitude made more intense
> By dreary-voicëd elements,
> The shrieking of the mindless wind,
> The moaning tree-boughs swaying blind,
> And on the glass the unmeaning beat
> Of ghostly finger-tips of sleet,

they little care, for the elements cannot extinguish the fire's ruddy glow or their warm affection for each other. Peopling the rustic scene are members of the poet's family: his father, "A prompt, decisive man"; his mother, who as she works her spinning wheel, recalls "in her fitting phrase,/ So rich and picturesque and free,/ . . . The story of her early days"; Uncle Moses, "innocent of books" but "rich in lore of fields and brooks," "A simple, guileless, childlike man,/ Content to live where life began," who entertains the children with tales of his boyhood in the Merrimack Valley; Aunt Mercy, "The sweetest woman ever Fate/ Perverse denied a household mate," who tells of her girlhood with its huskings, apple-bees, sleigh rides, and summer sails; Mary, the older sister, with a "full, rich nature" who is "Impulsive, earnest, prompt to act, / And make her generous thought a fact"; and "Our youngest and our dearest," Elizabeth, who with "her large, sweet, asking eyes" charms the cold away.[16] Two others, obliged by the winter storm to make themselves guests, complete the scene. The district schoolmaster, George Haskell, "Brisk wielder of the birch and rule," often filled a space by the Whittier hearth. This night he seemed a "careless boy"—teasing the cat, singing songs, and telling stories. And, Harriet Livermore, a woman intense "In thought and act, in soul and sense," "A not unfeared, half-welcome guest," who rebuked "with her cultured phrase/ Our homeliness of words and ways." The fire growing dim, the clock indicating nine, Uncle Moses puts his pipe away, Mrs. Whittier her sewing; as everyone prepares for bed, wishes for warmth, health, and contentment go around. The following morning brings teamsters clearing the road, but a week will pass before the great outside world in the form of a village newspaper can disturb their snowy solitude. And thus

> The chill embargo of the snow
> Was melted in the genial glow;
> Wide swung again our ice-locked door,
> And all the world was ours once more!

Just as time must inevitably bring the world back to the farm, so must it also triumph over the family unit. Few friends now remain who can sit with the aging poet beside the homestead hearth, gather comfort from the "Flemish pictures of old days,"

> And stretch the hands of memory forth
> To warm them at the wood-fire's blaze!

Snow-Bound turns, as John B. Pickard points out, "on the poet's nostalgic recalling of the love and protection which his family once gave him, emphasizing his painful sense of present loss and hope for spiritual consolation. These emotions are primarily developed by a series of contrasts: of fire and snow, past and present, people and elements— which combine to form the larger theme of love and immortality struggling against pain and death." "So the poem moves in artistic transitions from the physical level of storm and fire to the psychological world of death and love, utilizing the wood fire as the dominant symbol."[17]

Whittier continued on the crest of his literary ability and the public's favorable estimation of his work with the publication in 1867 of The Tent on the Beach. The book was an even bigger immediate success than Snow-Bound, the first printing of 20,000 copies selling out in twenty days. Learning this, the surprised Whittier wrote to Fields: "Think of bagging in this Tent of ours an unsuspecting public at the rate of a thousand a day! This will never do. The swindle is awful. Barnum is a saint to us. I am bowed with a sense of guilt: ashamed to look an honest man in the face. But Nemesis is on our track; somebody will puncture our Tent yet, and it will collapse like a torn balloon. I know I shall have to catch it: my back tingles in anticipation."[18]

The poems in the volume are framed by a narrative which tells how the poet and his friends Bayard Taylor and Fields pitched a tent on an Atlantic beach for a few summer days and read poetic tales to each other around the evening campfire. Alternating with the stories are conversational and autobiographical interludes more engaging and imaginative than the stories themselves. In addition to Whittier's description of himself and delineations of his fellow poets, these sections are important for providing his most rounded view of the function of art. At one point, for example, Bayard Taylor suggests that

> Art no other sanction needs
> Than beauty for its own fair sake,

and that his old friend has, perhaps because of the too keen exercise of his conscience, yoked the free play of his imagination to "reason's rigid rule." Whittier agrees that his poetry has too often been moralistic and that this tendency has at times constricted his imaginative flights. But he insists that it is better to have a moral in poetry,

> Than bolder flights that know no check;
> Better to use the bit, than throw
>   The reins all loose on fancy's neck.
> The liberal range of Art should be
> The breadth of Christian liberty.

Despite continuing bouts with poor health, the poet lived 25 years longer and wrote voluminously, primarily occasional, personal, and religious verse. His fame was world-wide; his birthdays were celebrated nationally; and honors and praise were lavished upon him. In 1860 he was awarded M.A.'s from both Haverford and Harvard; in 1866 Harvard followed with an LL.D. He was made an overseer of Harvard from 1858 to 1871 and a trustee of Brown University from 1869 to his death. Many historical and literary societies sought his membership—the American Philosophical Society, the Massachusetts Historical Society, Western Reserve Historical Society, and others. Whittier College in Iowa was named after him as was a town in California. In the 1 December 1877 issue of the Boston *Literary World*, America's greatest literary figures paid their tributes in verse and prose to the author on his seventieth birthday. Longfellow led the elder singers with a sonnet, "The

Three Silences," invoking the "Hermit of Amesbury" as one

> whose daily life anticipates
> The life to come, and in whose thought the word
> The spiritual world preponderates.

William Lloyd Garrison described Whittier as being "catholic beyond the bounds of sect" and as having "a divine compassion over all." He had

> perfect chastity of thought and speech,
> And an uplifting moral power to bless
> And strengthen frailty through the inner light.

William Cullen Bryant acclaimed him as "a poet, whose life is as beautiful as his verse"; Harriet Beecher Stowe agreed that "He is the true poet whose *life* is a poem. . . . His life has been a consecration, his songs an inspiration, to all that is highest and best"; and George Bancroft knew him as "a New England man of the sharpest outline, and at the same time a cosmopolite militant, doing battle with spiritual weapons for liberty and humanity." Among the other authors recognizing Whittier's life and art were Bayard Taylor, Oliver Wendell Holmes, Lydia Maria Child, Richard Henry Dana, Thomas Wentworth Higginson, and Edmund Clarence Stedman. Several weeks later the publishers of the *Atlantic* held a banquet in his honor, with H. O. Houghton presiding, and Emerson, Longfellow, Holmes, Howells, Twain, Warner, Stoddard, and others joining in a chorus of praise for the poet. Hundreds of well-wishers sent birthday greetings, and admirers made pilgrimages to Amesbury from all over the country hoping only to catch a glimpse of the man whose poetry had so intimately touched their lives. All this kind attention moved Whittier to say that while he highly prized the love and good will of others, over-praise pained him like blame. "I know my own weakness and frailty, and I am humbled rather than exalted by homage which I do not deserve. As the swift years pass, the Eternal Realities seem taking the place of the shadows and illusions of time."[19]

All the praise and good will could not mitigate the poet's sense of loneliness at having outlived by many years all of his immediate family and most of his close friends. In a letter to Annie Fields he expressed a hope that he might pass his eighty-second birthday quietly, to be near the old home and the "unforgotten landscape of youth," and to muse by the same fireside where his family used to spend happy, peaceful days. With the marriage in 1876 of his niece and housekeeper, Elizabeth, Whittier began to spend much of his time at "Oak Knoll," the picturesque sixty-acre farm owned by cousins in Danvers, in Newburyport with other relatives, or in the White Mountains or on Lake Winnepesaukee. He was always welcomed at the Boston homes of the

Fields and Governor and Mrs. Clafin, or at Celia Thaxter's home on the Isle of Shoals. In 1888 he busied himself by reading proof of the seven-volume collected edition of his poetry and prose. Some of the poems, especially earlier ones, embarrassed him; he wanted to drown them "like so many unlikely kittens." His publisher would not hear of it, however, and at last he set about trying to improve as best he could "a little of the bad grammar and rhythmical blunders which have so long annoyed my friends who have graduated at Harvard instead of a district country school."[20] His last volume, *At Sundown*, appeared in 1890, privately printed at the author's expense for circulation among family and friends—an expression of his gratitude for all their warm affection and kind ministrations. While visiting the Hampton Falls, New Hampshire, home of a family friend, Whittier suffered a paralytic stroke from which he was unable to recover. He died there 7 September 1892.

American poems, pronounced Whittier when serving his literary apprenticeship, "are studded here and there with delicate sentiment and exquisite beauty but they lack the sternness of thought—the concentrated power—the over mastering grasp of imagination, which alone can fix the mighty conceptions of genius in the eternity of mind."[21] The poetical defects young Whittier points to here are the very ones that critics would later mark off in his own poetry. While they could heartily applaud his Quaker passion for plainness, his romanticistic devotion to an idealized pastoral life, the spontaneous, elemental power of his best verse, and his direct, clear meanings, they could just as easily accuse him of failing to rise above a certain monotony of metrical form, of giving in to emotional indulgence that yielded only the affectation of sentiment, and of spoiling a poem by tacking on a moral rather than allowing the message to speak out on its own. He was, his detractors held, a pernicious influence in the molding of American literary taste, with his stumbling verse, crude disjointed rhymes, worthless panaceas, and empty show of piety and respectability.

When Whittier's critical contemporaries could look beyond his towering reputation as the honest, peace-loving New England Quaker who upheld religion and tolerance in godless and intolerant times, they did not find a major poetic talent. Discerning authors like James Russell Lowell prized his poems for their "boldness," "sincerity," "spontaneity," "grace," and "tenderness," and commended Whittier for his "perfect truthfulness of conception," "warm, unaffected geniality of spirit," and "exquisite expression of high poetical feeling," yet concluded, if only implicitly, that he was not a first-rate poet. Edgar Allan Poe thought that he was a "fine versifier, so far as strength is regarded independently of modulation. . . . But in taste, and especially in imagination . . . he is ever remarkably deficient. His themes are never to our liking."[22] Nathaniel

Hawthorne admitted to liking Whittier well enough, but he had "no high opinion" of either his poetry or prose. Richard Henry Stoddard, one of his most sympathetic apologists, saw Whittier's poetry as pleasantly different from that of his contemporaries in its genuine, natural expression and simple native speech, yet "not of the rare kind that refuses to be forgotten."[23]

In 1964 Lewis E. Weeks, Jr. surveyed 100 years of Whittier scholarship in his essay "Whittier Criticism Over the Years"[24] and found that it necessarily falls into two periods divided by the author's death at the turn of the century. Critics during the first period, Weeks maintains, were at a disadvantage because they had only part of Whittier's total output to evaluate and because they were clearly aware of Whittier as an active personal force. His death provided critics with both the canon and objectivity they needed. Weeks' two divisions make for a convenient discussion, but, in fact, they oversimplify and devalue the movement of critical response to the poet's life and works. Because the vicissitudes of time and changing literary and critical modes have caused his reputation both to soar and to suffer considerably, it is more appropriate to discuss Whittier scholarship in terms of four periods of criticism rather than Weeks' two. The first period, from Garrison's first review of Whittier in 1826 to the end of the Civil War, found critics alternately praising his poems and condemning their many defects in style and execution. The second period, from the publication of *Snow-Bound* in 1866 to the second decade of the twentieth century, was the halcyon time for the poet's reputation, when critics defined it primarily with loving reminiscences, elegiac flights, and fond memorials. The third period, from the literary revolt of the 1920s to about mid-century, outgrew the hero worship as many critics dismissed Whittier as representative of the faded dignity and prudish gentility of a bygone era. And the fourth period, from the 1950s to the present, has begun a careful revaluation of Whittier's works and of his place against the backdrop of his age and in America's literary canon.

A number of critics in the first period promoted him as a modest, gentle Quaker whose poetry was thoroughly American in its union of purity, piety, domesticity, and patriotism. In particular, they approved of the didactic element in his poetry. In his didacticism, as well as in his persistent moralizing, Whittier did not stand apart from the dictates of his age which believed that poetry should touch its readers' deepest spiritual natures and shape their moral sentiments. J. G. Forman repeats a stock nineteenth-century idea when he insists in 1849 that "The highest ends and aim of genuine poetry" are "the advancement of truth or the good of humanity."[25] If it is to retain its vitality and survive its own day, poetry *must* sound a moral note, touch the common soul, comfort an aching heart, and spread the gospel of eternal love. Any departure from these functions, it was felt, is a violation of all that is acceptable in poetry. In short, the duty of "perfect" poetry is to serve Truth and Man, Decency and Morality rather than the concept of art for art's sake. The Quaker poet had little trouble understanding and serving these ideas. His vigorous, clear expression of the popular thought, his imaginative and descriptive powers, and his kindness and personal integrity, the reviewers concluded, will endear him forever in the national mind. "The future," envisioned Lowell, "will not fail to do justice to a man who has been so true to the present."[26]

Some critics in this period could not share Lowell's optimism, however. As the decades passed, they began to resent more and more Whittier's brand of open didacticism and assaulted him as the outspoken, strident propagandist who could not discipline his poetic talents into any consistent quality. His poems, especially those on anti-slavery themes, some charged, were uneven in quality because they had been spun out of a shallow imagination "irregularly excited and roused to fitful action."[27] Others assigned the unevenness and resulting diffuseness to Whittier's untutored facility for rhyming and his simple meter patterns. Critics like his friend William Sydney Thayer attributed this unevenness and diffuseness to the pressures of editorial and abolitionist work which, from time to time, caused him to grind out his poems and speed them off for publication without revisions.[28] According to H. Ballou, Whittier has a tendency to write too much—or as he put it more graciously, Whittier allows his Muse "to wander in her strain . . . after she has ended her song proper."[29] Consequently, his poems are full of declamatory excesses, clumsy grammatical and idiomatic errors, and inadmissible rhymes. They lack "tenderness and felicity," "grace and finished liveliness," and are badly organized, "frigid, very monotonous, and very commonplace."[30] In taking a satirical poke at the slapdash quality of Whittier's reform poetry, Augustine Duganne simply rewords a commonly shared critical view:

> Ah, Whittier! Fighting Friend! I like thy verse—
> Thy wholesale blessing and thy wholesale curse;
> I prize the spirit which exalts thy strain,
> And joy when truth impels thy blows amain;
> But, really, friend! I cannot help suspecting
> Though writing's good, there's merit in correcting.[31]

Orestes Brownson goes even further in his censure of the poet's work in an 1850 review that is colored by his personal biases rather than by any attempt at objective criticism. Whittier's poems, he declares flatly, are "our abomination. He is a Quaker, a Red Republican, a nonresistant, a revolutionist, all characters we hold in horror and detestation, and his poems are the echo of himself."[32]

The second period, beginning roughly with the publication of *Snow-Bound* in 1866 and ending in the second decade of the twentieth century, did the justice to Whittier that Lowell had intended by considering him one of America's most admired poets. From the results of an 1884 poll of its readership, the *Critic* published a list of America's "Forty Immortals," in which Whittier placed third after fellow New England poets Holmes and Lowell, and fared significantly better than Henry James and Mark Twain, who came in thirteenth and fourteenth, and Walt Whitman, who ranked a much less respectable twentieth. In an 1893 survey, the *Critic*'s readers put Whittier's *Poems* eighth in a list of "The Best Ten American Books," after such works as Emerson's *Essays*, Hawthorne's *The Scarlet Letter*, Stowe's *Uncle Tom's Cabin*, and Irving's *The Sketch Book*.

But the *Critic*'s ranking of Whittier on a comparative scale with the masters of the century does not fully register the profound impact he had upon the public. Oliver Wendell Holmes's comment to Whittier, for example, is typical of the extraordinary popular and critical response to his work: "I never rise from any of your poems without feeling the refreshment of their free and sweet atmosphere, . . . the morning air of a soul that breathes freely, and always the fragrance of a loving spirit."[33] His works rarely failed to awaken readers to the beauties of nature, to plumb the depths of their spiritual nature, to compel them to strive for social justice, and to direct them toward the rewards of proper ethical conduct. The power of Whittier's poetry to touch people's souls and to influence their moral behavior remained so strong into this second period, in fact, that Mary B. Clafin in all earnestness remarked that she "would rather give a man or a woman on the verge of a great moral lapse a marked copy of Whittier than any other book in our language."[34] The crusading reformer and philanthropic worker Dorothea L. Dix wrote to Whittier that his poem "At Last" "meant more than any minister's administration." She is said to have died with its words upon her lips and insisted that a copy of the poem be buried with her.[35]

Whittier's fame was indisputable. He was "the Poet Laureate of the Nation," "Our Rustic New England Bard," "the Poet of Nature," "the Poet of Hope and Immortality," and "the Poet of the Hearth." The simplicity and peace of his later life together with his unassuming manner and personal charm, and his rise from an uneducated farm boy to a distinguished national figure promoted the view that Whittier was a hero and saint. Literally hundreds of the poet's friends and acquaintances as well as perfect strangers rushed into print with their fond reminiscences of visits to Amesbury, personal and loving recollections of the poet's character, and affectionate memorials to his life and writing. Such reminiscences usually followed a pattern which began with a general sketch of Whittier's early life of hardship, then moved through selected anecdotes that demonstrated how virtuous he was, then quoted a few lines of his verse to show the quality of his thinking and the uniqueness of his wit, and ended with praise of his deep feeling for life.[36] The best representatives of this form include Harriet Prescott Spofford's "John Greenleaf Whittier at Amesbury" (*Critic*, 1 Nov. 1884, pp. 205–06), Mrs. Clafin's *Personal Recollections of John G. Whittier* (New York: Thomas Y. Crowell, 1893), Annie Fields' *Whittier: Notes of His Life and of His Friendships* (New York: Harper & Brothers, 1893), Robert S. Rantoul's "Some Reminiscences of the Poet Whittier" (*Essex Institute Historical Collections*, 37 [1901], 129–44), and Abby J. Woodman's *Reminiscences of John Greenleaf Whittier at Oak Knoll* (Salem: Essex Institute, 1908).

Two full-length biographies of this period adopt basically the same form as these reminiscences and puff Whittier out of all just proportion until he becomes something of an American myth. In Francis H. Underwood's *John Greenleaf Whittier: A Biography* (Boston: James R. Osgood and Co., 1884), he is the heroic, selfless, accomplished, saint-like man who lived his entire life with only the purest motives, and who, with great humility and dignity, wore his laurels as a major bard long before his death. B. O. Flower's *Whittier: Prophet, Seer, and Man* (Boston: Arena Pub. Co., 1896) builds upon the myth idea in its highly sentimentalized interpretation of Whittier as the "Barefoot Boy Who Was Also a Dreamer; a Prophet of Freedom . . . [and] a Modern Apostle of Lofty Spirituality."

However, a much more reasonable estimate of Whittier had been published earlier by William Sloane Kennedy in his *John Greenleaf Whittier: His Life, Genius, and Writings* (Boston: S. E. Cassino, 1882). Kennedy obviously admired the poet deeply and could write of the parallels between the man's life and works without lapsing into the larger-than-life and Horatio Alger-like images of Underwood and Flower. In fact, his affectionate portrait is tempered considerably by his sharp evaluation of Whittier's poetry. Most of it has been ruined by "three crazes": "the reform craze, the religious craze, and the rhyme craze." The worst of these, the one to which most of the shallowness, inelegance, and unoriginality can be assigned is the "art-chilling" effect of his Quakerism. George Rice Carpenter (*John Greenleaf Whittier* [Boston: Houghton, Mifflin, 1903]) agrees with Kennedy that much of his poetry is disfigured, but attributes it not to the numbing influences of his religion but to the creatively stifling atmosphere of the abolitionist movement. Nevertheless, Carpenter's treatment of the man is also largely sympathetic. Whittier was profoundly typical of the freedom-loving New England spirit because "the reforming element belonged to the essence of his nature." Richard Burton's position in his biography (*John Greenleaf Whittier* [Boston: Small, Maynard, 1901]) is not unlike both Kennedy's and Carpenter's, although he finds that the very facets of Whittier's character that weakened much of his work—the intensity of his religious and political convictions and his penchant for moralizing—made him a well-respected national poet. Burton discerns a clear progression in Whittier's life: his religious beliefs logically directed him into reform work, the reform work led to the didacticism, and the didacticism made him enormously popular. Thomas Wentworth Higginson (*John Greenleaf Whittier* [New York: Macmillan, 1902]) deemphasizes Whittier's religious and reform interests which, Higginson feels, were negative forces shaping his creative impulses, and emphasizes, rather, his love of nature, family, and humanity. Whittier "speaks for the masses in a kindred voice" and represents the best impulses of a purely democratic spirit. Bliss Perry (*John Greenleaf Whittier: A Sketch of His Life* [Boston: Houghton, Mifflin, 1907]), instead of insisting upon Whittier's abolitionist activity as the source of his limitations as a poet, argues that it provided the opportunity for Whittier to develop and sharpen his talents. However, Perry, at the same time, acknowledges that a number of the anti-slavery poems are little more than "a rhythmical rearrangement of matter that would have served equally well for a peroration by Wendell Phillips." And he cannot credit Whittier with being particularly original: he simply restated the eternal truths in the accepted poetical formulas of his day; he opened "no undreamed horizons to the imagination."[37] Whittier's authorized biographer and nephew, Samuel T. Pickard, recognizes, like Perry, that Whittier had to pass through the fires of reform in order to become an effective poet; the very force of his militancy strengthened his art. Pickard advances Whittier as the ardent reformer whose principles were honest and uncompromising. He was the genuine representative of New England, alive to nature in her various aspects, and happy in the company of family and friends. He was the model Quaker, politician, journalist, poet, and man.

To complete their sketches of Whittier, critics in this second period tried to rank him in relationship to the other New England writers. The author of a *London Quarterly Review* article (74 [1893], 224–44), for example, finds in him "an intensity of conviction, a white heat of enthusiasm, a trumpet-note of courage and faith" that had no parallel in the works of his contemporaries, yet as a man of letters, he lacked "the artist soul of Longfellow, the wit and fancy of Holmes, the keen satire and culture of Lowell." Carpenter insists that he was not "a learned reader, like Lowell, nor a philosophic reader like Emerson, nor indeed a wide reader in pure literature like Longfellow." Wendell Stafford shows that Whittier outranked the other poets only in his humanitarian reform work: "He was not the poet of nature—Bryant surpassed him there. He was not the poet of old-world culture and memories—there

Longfellow was easily his master. He was not the poet of varied gifts and manifold achievement—he was narrow beside Lowell. He was not the poet of mysticism—Emerson was there before him and will hold his throne long after he is gone. But he was the poet of human freedom, in a sense in which they never were, with a force and fire which none of them could ever hope to match."[38]

Most serious criticism of this second period, like that by Richard Henry Stoddard and Edmund Clarence Stedman, accepted Whittier's literature as the organic expression not only of his character and individuality but of his time, nation, and society as well. Attention, by and large, was focused more on a life justly spent and nobly lived than on the depth and significance of his thought and art. Critics celebrated his democratic spirit, his unwavering devotion to his religious and political convictions, and his earnest moral sense and personal influence. Yet, like the critics of the earlier period, they gave him a secondary position in American letters: "Whittier's descripive powers are always great, fresh, and simple but not deep. He is a genuine story teller, though 'mystic beauty, dreamy grace, rounded art, lofty imagination, are not his gifts.' "[39] If Whittier is not a superb poet and is "bald, crude, narrow, careless," he is, nevertheless, a fine poet who has "sincerity, simplicity, sinew, enthusiasm, spontaneity, and directness";[40] "if we cannot call him great we can at least call him good."[41]

When the third period began in the 1920s, critics were no longer confusing popular recognition with literary quality. Many of the country's young intellectuals were having difficulty reading Whittier sympathetically, for he did not give evidence of unique experience, new heights of vision, or a profound artistic conscience. As a result, the endless laudatory reminiscences, the pretty biographical fluffs, and the richly embellished mythologies of the second period gave way to the debunking and repudiation of the third. By 1934 Winfield Townley Scott[42] could neither stop the critics from batting Whittier's reputation about nor prevent them from thinking his poetry appropriate only for schoolchildren. Even as early as 1912 Trent and Erskine (*Great American Writers* [New York: Holt]) saw the extent of Whittier's critical decline and loss of popular appeal: "His hold upon unsophisticated readers who are docile to tradition and full of patriotism has doubtless continued fairly strong, and the teaching of American literature in the schools will undoubtedly help to maintain his reputation; but when all is said, one is left wondering how the sophisticated public of two generations hence will regard him." In a 1931 essay entitled "Fiction of the Eighties and Nineties," William Allen White explained that man's new "way of looking" has caused this precipitous decline in Whittier's reputation: "Truth has changed. Man's theory of beauty has changed. His manners and morals have changed. And so the parables of another generation, written to carry home its truth, its sense of beauty, its moral conventions, its tricks and manners, seem stale and stilted and outworn."[43] And with poetry flaunting its "ultra-modernity" and "superiority to the works of poets dead and gone,"[44] and with the establishment of realism and naturalism as vital literary forces, critics found it increasingly easier to attack what they saw as Whittier's outworn sentimentalism, his showy (empty, some said) display of the good, noble, and lofty, and his participation in a long since faded romantic tradition. His religious orthodoxy was repeatedly challenged by the disillusionment of an industrialized, impersonal society. In the face of the century's accelerated pace of social change and shifts to newer literary and critical methods, Whittier's sentimentality and moralizing became largely irrelevant, and his imperfectly formed philosophies on art and life seemed vaporous.

Critics were not without their appreciation of Whittier's moral hold upon his age and his basically gentle and compassionate nature, but they, nevertheless, regarded many of his works as too narrow, too conventional, too insulated, too didactic, or too optimistic. In *Quaker Militant*, Albert Mordell dismisses the poems written after *Snow-Bound* and *The Tent on the Beach* as historically insignificant. He claims that, if anything, they negatively influenced America's literary tastes by perpetuating the view that "the paramount requisites of great poetry were purity and piety." They have no vitality because they are "steeped in nineteenth-century respectability." He feels that such poems appeal not to literary critics and sophisticated thinkers but to readers of "ordinary mental caliber." Desmond Powell suggests that Whittier's limitations as a poet stem from his notions that "the devils of society" could be exorcised simply by pretending they don't exist, and that poetry should be "plaintive and sweet"—"charm the world away from its memory of bitter things."[45] Vernon Lewis Parrington points out that, even during his own lifetime, the rustic Quaker was something of an anachronism because he was "ill equipped to understand a materialistic philosophy of society." His economics, like his democracy, as spelled out in his *Songs of Labor*, "was of a by gone time, having no kinship with a scrambling free-soilism or a rapacious capitalism."[46]

These twentieth-century critics, then, naturally considered most of Whittier's poetry as bad. Powell notes that "He could not restrain his faculty for jogging verse. He could not concentrate his powers. He could not recognize a bad stanza even when it occurred between two good ones. He could spoil a lyric by tacking a moral on the end as readily as Bryant. He could accept the popular canons of taste, and thereby enervate his work, as thoroughly as Longfellow. He could rely on what he deemed to be the truth, rather than upon his ability to express it in terms of life and beauty, as completely as Lowell." In

Poets of America (New York: E. P. Dutton, 1925), Clement Wood calls Whittier "a blameless mediocrity" and dismisses him entirely in one clean swipe: "As a poet, Whittier was a hard-headed Quaker; his flight brushed the ground." Ludwig Lewisohn in *Expression in America* (New York: Harper's, 1932) scorns Whittier, Longfellow, Holmes, and Lowell as mere "underbrush" about Emerson, our "single soaring tree." And in *The Cambridge History of American Literature* (New York: G. P. Putnam's Sons, 1917–21) Trent and Erskine think of Whittier as "an industrious scribbler of rhymes" who is probably "no more than a poet of the third rank."

With the exception of Clement Wood, however, no critic in this third period was quite willing to repudiate the man utterly. In fact, as they chipped away at his reputation, they were all the while seeking ways to retrieve and preserve in him what they saw as distinctively American. Norman Foerster, for instance, believes that Whittier, perhaps more than any other nineteenth-century poet, enobled nature and found moral value in its beauty; clearly, he, not Bryant, is America's "child of the soil."[47] For Howard Mumford Jones, Whittier has little sense of form, "dramatic power" and "literary tact," and as a result, much of his poetry is "insipid," "moralistic," and "narrow." But because his anti-slavery poems served as such powerful weapons for sixty years of the nineteenth century, Whittier will always be "one of the last and greatest of our rhyming pamphleteers."[48] Like Jones, Trent and Erskine doubt Whittier's high genius but not his ability to stir the country with poetry that yet retains some moral value and vitality. Winfield Townley Scott agrees with them in feeling that in certain of his abolitionist poems Whittier attained a "strength of fervent expression" although, like Foerster, he suggests that Whittier's chief claim as a poet must rest with his instinctive fidelity to the New England landscape.

Even though these critics make cases for Whittier as a gifted nature poet and as passionate writer for social reform, they seem to be more concerned with his importance as an influential personality and historical figure. They feel that if he did not have finely wrought artistic principles and the strength of intellect and imagination to become a front ranking poet, he at least had an essential nobility and a sincere humanitarian nature that impressed the national conscience and lent credibility to his writings. This is the message of two biographies written during this period. Like so many of the nineteenth-century accounts, they sketch in the figure of a modest yet spirited Quaker whose dynamic influence in matters of great social concern helped to change the course of the nation. Whitman Bennett's *Whittier: Bard of Freedom* (Chapel Hill: Univ. of North Carolina Press, 1941) portrays a man significant in the molding of American history, a man whose selfless devotion to humanitarian reform gave direction to the country's search for social equality and whose poetry delivered ringing appeals to the country's soul. In Bennett's hands Whittier is the well-balanced, talented author with a natural gift for song and an unfeigned love for his fellow man. In *John Greenleaf Whittier: Friend of Man* (Boston: Houghton, Mifflin, 1949) John A. Pollard's intent, like Bennett's, is to show the author as an experienced politician-prophet-poet whose best, most memorable verse was written in the cause of freedom. Whittier was the zealous champion of human rights whose works breathed the message of brotherly love and offered spiritual consolation to a strife-torn nation. Both Bennett and Pollard agree that Whittier's life enhanced the value of his poetry.

When the fourth period of criticism began in the 1950s, the "sophisticated public" that Trent and Erskine mentioned in 1912 had all but forgotten Whittier; his memory was kept alive only for young people by the meager selection of his poems in high school and college anthologies. But also by mid-century a fourth generation of scholars emerged who believed that he deserved better treatment. With a just perspective, historical imagination, and sympathy that earlier critics did not always have, they sought to place him within the framework of a "storm-stunned" post-Civil War society that longed for a happier, less complicated time. In so doing, their criticism returns to the attitudes of Whittier's later contemporaries in its emphasis upon his strength as a balladist and a religious and lyric poet.

The source of his strength as a poet, they seem to agree, is his religion. He is at his best in works that stress beliefs in the necessity of love and righteousness, the sacredness of the "inner light," and the importance of an absolute trust in God. No American author, comments Howard Mumford Jones in "Whittier Reconsidered," can equal Whittier's "finely phrased ... trust in the goodness of God."[49] He is unsurpassed in poems like "The Eternal Goodness," "The Meeting," "At Last," and "Our Master" that voice his concept of the relation of God and man. The true durability of these poems, for Lewis Leary in *John Greenleaf Whittier*, is in the solace they give to "people, who, like him, wished no greater joy than devout resignation of their lives to a strength much beyond their own." Hyatt H. Waggoner suggests that today, as during his own time, Whittier is most satisfyingly read as a religious poet. Yet Waggoner points out that, paradoxically, "Whittier's poetry is often most effectively religious when it is not explicitly 'religious poetry' .... His poems of nature and reform are seldom memorable except when they are informed by a strongly religious feeling."[50] Not just the nature and reform poems, adds John B. Pickard in his *Introduction and Interpretation*, but many of the ballads and genre pieces as well openly reflect strong religious convictions—"his admiration for spiritual strength, his deep faith in the goodness of God, and his love of fellow man as a sharer in the divine essence."

Using an understanding of Whittier's Quaker cosmology and its reflection in his poetry as a beginning point, the three recent Whittier biographies tend to be critical and interpretive studies of Whittier's successes and failures as both man and poet. In this, they are superior to older biographies that dwelt too long on Whittier as the stormy abolitionist and political activist. In no case does a modern biographer again adopt the William Sloane Kennedy attitude that Whittier's "religious craze" destroyed his poetry.

His Quaker goodness, for Lewis Leary, was Whittier's most precious possession, filtering through and giving direction to everything he wrote. It lent his poetry a kind of artistic discipline that his temperament, talent, and time could not always provide. His achievements, if small, are genuine, if not subtle or complicated, then charged with an essential simplicity and untroubled wholesomeness. His poetry fulfilled his readers' expectations by reflecting their thoughts, awakening their emotions, and comforting their spirits. Leary feels that it attracted a wide audience because it rested "on a plateau just above ordinary language and never soared out of sight or plunged to depths beyond common vision." But Leary points out that though a comfortable poet to be with, Whittier is not without his shortcomings. He could not break away from the superficial morality that overran the newspaper verse of his time, and he could not recognize that Emerson's "meter-making thought" was an essential of good poetry. Leary goes on to show, as Gay Wilson Allen had done earlier,[51] that Whittier seldom strayed from the ballad form and the four-stress lines, usually rhymed octosyllabic couplets. He seemed rarely "to have groped— as Emerson, Whitman, or Tennyson did—to discover poetic techniques which would add dimensions to meanings." With only certain exceptions, Leary dismisses as inferior productions the abolitionist poems which Whittier's contemporaries found so blasphemous and seditious. What "cripples" them, he says, "are words and phrases so worn that they provide no friction; they are counters moved about in imitation of perception; they fail to attach themselves to things." Of the approximately 100 that he wrote, only "Ichabod," "Massachusetts to Virginia," "Letter from a Missionary . . . ," "The Henchman," and "Laus Deo" are worth pulling from obscurity. Still, Leary can conclude that Whittier has left an important legacy both as "a courageous and gentle man and as a gifted minor poet whom his countrymen may well remember with gratitude and pride."

John B. Pickard, Whittier's most vigorous modern advocate and great-grandnephew, certainly would not debate with Leary the poet's place in American letters. His *John Greenleaf Whittier: An Introduction and Interpretation* takes up, instead, a more perplexing problem: "are there valid literary reasons for continuing to examine Whittier's best poems on a mature level beyond his historical and cultural interest?" Pickard answers that, after one sees Whittier as a man for his own time, comes to grips with nineteenth-century standards of taste, and admits to the distressing flaws in much of his work, both the man and his best poems do indeed justify continued study. Pickard agrees with Harry Hayden Clark that Whittier moved through three main "centers of emphasis."[52] Until 1833, he was primarily a sectional romanticist—his poems showed promise but were too openly imitative of Burns, Byron, Sigourney, and Willis to retain any enduring vitality. From 1833 to the 1850s, he was largely a political activist—his abolitionist poems were strengthened by the force of their moral indignation and religious intensity and weakened by their "digressive tendency" and "derivative phrasing." And from the 1850s to his death, he was a religious humanist —his nature, genre, and religious poems exhibited flashes of poetic genius, but in them he often broke all the rules of good poetry with his "uninspired reworkings of trite ideas, repetitive tributes to personal friends, fondness for sentimentality and moralizing, and limited response to external beauty." Of the more than 300 poems preserved in the canon, Pickard finds only about 40 that are still readable, and of those, his ballads best represent his mature poetic achievement. Through them, Whittier became "one of America's finest creators of historical and traditional narrative." Fundamental to the very substance of his poetic achievement, concludes Pickard in reference to a comment that Whittier's poetry was "written first of all for his neighbors," was his preservation of what was distinctively *his* and his neighbors'—"*his* Quaker heritage, *his* Haverhill boyhood, *his* Merrimack scenery, *his* love of local superstitions and legends, and *his* interest in Colonial times."

Edward Wagenknecht's *John Greenleaf Whittier: A Portrait in Paradox* presents a much more complex and sensitive view of the man than most earlier biographers had been able to give.[53] Instead of perpetuating the Whittier-as-Quaker saint-and-hero legends, Wagenknecht describes a life marked by difficult paradoxes: Whittier lived celibate yet was a "passionate" man, strongly attracted to women; he was torn between the selfish pursuit of poetical fame and his sense of moral obligation to the anti-slavery movement; he, as Quaker, was a pacifist, yet, by circumstance, became a militant propagandist; and he saw beauty as a kind of grace—"the beauty of holiness, of purity, and of that inward grace which passeth show"—yet saw it also as a kind of "snare"—a "worldliness" that could turn people away from God and "the breadth of Christian liberty." The expression of these paradoxes in his verses gives them an individuality and a lasting importance in American letters. For Wagenknecht, the word that best indicates the nature of that individuality is "integrity," and on this point, the man and the poet were one. If Whittier is not one of America's greatest poets, says Wagenknecht finally, he has, at his best, "the rightness of the inevitable about him."

The central question modern critics consider again and again is not "Is Whittier a major poet?" but rather "How minor is he?" And further: "To what extent does he survive as a poet?" Their answers merge with those of past critics into a kind of synthesis. If he is not one of America's greatest poets, he has, nevertheless, "major minor" status. If he is no longer an influential voice in American letters, he is a just representative of an important time in our literary development. Their critical assessments are perhaps best summarized by Whittier himself in "My Namesake":

> Some blamed him, some believed him good
> The truth lay doubtless 'twixt the two;
> He reconciled as best he could
> Old faith and fancies new.

The most recent criticism indicates, however, that Whittier's stock is slowly rising, although it probably will not soon, if ever, rise beyond the general estimate established by more than 150 years of criticism. Where the twenty-first century puts Whittier on its literary measuring stick depends, of course, upon just how much its standards of measurement change. One can only speculate that even if Whittier is never given a major place in American letters, he will survive for perceptive readers as a spokesman for significant historical events and literary trends. And as such, he will always remain a dynamic, irreplaceable voice in our literature.

Notes

1. Quoted from Samuel T. Pickard, *Life and Letters of John Greenleaf Whittier* (Boston: Houghton, Mifflin, 1894), I, 46. All other citations of Whittier's verse are from *The Complete Poetical Works of John Greenleaf Whittier*, ed. Horace E. Scudder, Cambridge Edition (Boston: Houghton, Mifflin, 1894).

2. Whittier later would propose as models for himself those English and American authors who, as Robert Penn Warren puts it, wrote that "flood of contemporary trash . . . Felicia Hemans, Lydia Sigourney, N. P. Willis, the elder Dana, Lydia Maria Child, Bernard Barton, and John Pierpont." At one point Whittier could write that Longfellow's "A Psalm of Life" was worth more to him than "all the dreams of Shelley, Keats, and Wordsworth." See Warren's *John Greenleaf Whittier's Poetry: An Appraisal and Selection* (Minneapolis: Univ. of Minnesota Press, 1971), pp. 6–7, and "Whittier," *Sewanee Review*, 79 (1971), 88.

3. John B. Pickard, *John Greenleaf Whittier: An Introduction and Interpretation*, American Authors and Critics Series (New York: Holt, Rinehart and Winston, 1961), p. 14.

4. For much of his life Whittier remained active in newspaper work. In 1836

he again edited the *Gazette*; in 1837 was the acting editor of the *Emancipator and Anti-Slavery Record* (New York); editor of the *Pennsylvania Freeman* (Philadelphia) 1838–40, the *Middlesex Standard* (Lowell) 1844–45, the *Essex Transcript* (Amesbury and Salisbury) 1845–46; and was a contributing editor of the *National Era* (Washington) 1847–60.

5. Most Whittier biographers try to account for his lifelong bachelorhood by constructing lists of women with whom he was involved, and then by speculating, with varying degrees of perception and sensitivity, on the depth and significance of those involvements. See, for example, Albert Mordell's psychoanalytic study in *Quaker Militant: John Greenleaf Whittier* (Boston: Houghton, Mifflin, 1933) which pictures Whittier as the "sexually repressed agitator" and "sexless saint." Modern biographers offer the most rational and even-handed studies of his friendships and unfulfilled romances. See John B. Pickard's *John Greenleaf Whittier*, Lewis Leary's *John Greenleaf Whittier*, Twayne's U.S. Authors Series, No. 6 (New York: Twayne, 1961), and Edward Wagenknecht's *John Greenleaf Whittier: A Portrait in Paradox* (New York: Oxford Univ. Press, 1967).

6. From an essay entitled "American Literature," *American Manufacturer* (Boston), 16 July 1829. Quoted from Edwin Harrison Cady and Harry Hayden Clark, *Whittier on Writers and Writing* (Syracuse: Syracuse Univ. Press, 1950), p. 25.

7. Cady and Clark, p. 99.

8. Quoted from John B. Pickard, ed., *The Letters of John Greenleaf Whittier* (Cambridge: Belknap Press of Harvard Univ. Press, 1975), I, [111].

9. John B. Pickard, *Letters*, I, 419.

10. "Introduction," *Complete Poetical Works*, xxi-xxii.

11. From *The Tent on the Beach* (1867).

12. See Leary, pp. 64–65.

13. *John Greenleaf Whittier's Poetry*, p. 41.

14. In his standard biography of the author, Samuel T. Pickard writes that the scene described here is actually Whittier's birthplace near Haverhill. "There were beehives on the garden terrace near the well-sweep, occupied, perhaps, by the descendants of Thomas Whittier's bees. The approach to the house from over the northern shoulder of Job's Hill by a path that was in constant use in his boyhood, and is still in existence, is accurately described in the poem. The 'gap in the old wall' is still to be seen, and 'the stepping-stones in the shallow brook' are still in use. His sister's garden was down by the brookside in front of the house, and her daffodils are perpetuated, and may now be found in their season each year in that place. The red-barred gate, the poplars, the cattle-yard with 'the white horns tossing over the wall.'—these were all part of Whittier's boy life on the old farm. Even the touch of 'the sundown's blaze on her window-pane' is realistic. The only place from which the blaze of the setting sun could be seen reflected in the windows of the old mansion was from the path so perfectly described, and no doubt the poet had often noticed the phenomenon in his youth while approaching the house in this direction." *Life and Letters*, II, 414–15.

15. Quoted from Thomas Franklin Currier, *A Bibliography of John Greenleaf Whittier* (Cambridge: Harvard Univ. Press, 1937), p. 99.

16. Greenleaf and his older brother Matthew, the only Whittiers still alive when the poem was published, are not described in *Snow-Bound*. They are the boys asked by their father to dig a path to the barn and the "we" who, while snuggled in their beds,

> heard the loosened clapboards tost,
> The board-nails snapping in the frost;
> And on us, through the unplastered wall,
> Felt the light sifted snow-flakes fall.

17. "Imagistic and Structural Unity in 'Snow-Bound,'" *College English,* 21 (1960), 338–43.

18. John B. Pickard, *Letters,* III, 146.

19. Quoted from Samuel T. Pickard, *Life and Letters,* II, 639.

20. Quoted from Samuel T. Pickard, *Life and Letters,* II, 733.

21. Cady and Clark, p. 25.

22. "A Chapter on Autography," *Graham's Magazine,* Dec. 1841, p. 286.

23. "The Poetry of Whittier," *The Independent,* 22 Sept. 1892, p. 1314.

24. *Essex Institute Historical Collections,* 100 (1964), 159–82.

25. *National Era,* 1 Feb. 1849, p. 17. See also Andrew P. Peabody's review of *Home Ballads and Poems* in the *North American Review,* Jan. 1861, pp. 267–68. Whittier's strong moral sense and his reverence for the "true and noble" render him "worthy of his mission" as a poet.

26. From a review of *Home Ballads and Poems, Atlantic Monthly,* Nov. 1860, p. 639.

27. C. C. Felton, from a review of *Lays of My Home, and Other Poems, North American Review,* Oct. 1843, p. 509.

28. See Thayer's "John G. Whittier and His Writings," *North American Review,* July 1854, pp. 31–53.

29. "Whittier's Poems," *Universalist Quarterly,* April 1849, p. 147.

30. From an anonymous review of *Lays of My Home, and Other Poems, Southern Quarterly Review,* 4 (1843), 516.

31. *Parnassus in Pillory. A Satire. By Motley Manners, Esquire* (New York: Adriance, Sherman & Co., 1851), p. 70.

32. From a review of *Songs of Labor, and Other Poems, Brownson's Quarterly Review,* 7 (1850), 540.

33. Quoted from Samuel T. Pickard, *Life and Letters,* II, 667.

34. Quoted from Augustus T. Murray, "The Religious Faith of Whittier: An Interpretation," in his *A Selection from the Religious Poems of John Greenleaf Whittier* (Philadelphia: Friends' Book Store, 1934), p. 8.

35. Mordell, p. 297.

36. Karl Keller, "John Greenleaf Whittier," in *Fifteen American Authors Before 1900: Bibliographical Essays on Research and Criticism,* ed. Robert A. Rees and Earl N. Harbert (Madison: Univ. of Wisconsin Press, 1971), p. 365.

37. See also Perry's "Whittier for Today," *Atlantic Monthly,* Dec. 1907, pp. 851–59.

38. "Whittier: A Quaker Who Became a Martial Poet," in his *Speeches* (St. Johnsbury, VT: Arthur F. Stone, 1913), p. 184.

39. From an article by R. E. Prothero in *Longman's Magazine,* Dec. 1886, pp. 182–89, quoted from Weeks, p. 168.

40. John V. Cheney, "Whittier," *Chataquan,* Dec. 1892, p. 305.

41. T. Cuthbert Hadden, "The Quaker Poet," *Gentleman's Magazine* (London), Oct. 1892, p. 409.

42. "Poetry in American: A New Consideration of Whittier's Verse," *New England Quarterly*, 7 (1934), 258–75.

43. In *American Writers on American Literature*, ed. John Macy (New York: Liveright).

44. W. Harvey-Jellie, "A Forgotten Poet," *Dalhousie Review*, 19 (1939), 91.

45. "Whittier," *American Literature*, 9 (1937), 338.

46. "John G. Whittier: Puritan Quaker," in his *Main Currents in American Thought* (New York: Harcourt, Brace & World, 1927), II, 142.

47. "Whittier," in his *Nature in American Literature* (New York: Russell & Russell, 1923), p. 20.

48. In *American Literature*, ed. Percy Boynton (New York: Scribner's, 1918), p. 646.

49. *Essex Institute Historical Collections*, 93 (1957), 244.

50. "What I Had I Gave: Another Look at Whittier," *Essex Institute Historical Collections*, 95, (1959), 34. Waggoner uses substantially the same article as his introduction to the new Cambridge Edition of *The Poetical Works of Whittier* (Boston: Houghton, Mifflin, 1975).

51. "John Greenleaf Whittier," in his *American Prosody* (New York: American Book Co., 1935).

52. Harry Hayden Clark, ed., *Major American Poets* (New York: American Book Co., 1936). Clark uses some of his ideas in this book for "The Growth of Whittier's Mind—Three Phases," *Emerson Society Quarterly*, 50 (1968), 119–26.

53. Only Albert Mordell had anticipated Wagenknecht's conclusions when he suggested the possibility that Whittier's "nervous condition" and migraine headaches resulted, at least in part, from his sexual frustrations.

REVIEWS

[Review of *Lays of My Home, and Other Poems,* 1843]

C. C. Felton[*]

There is a little affectation in the title of this volume, which may be excused by the necessity that most authors imagine themselves to be suffering under, of inscribing on their productions some pithy or characteristic *legend*, like the *cartouches* of the Egyptian monuments. The poetry of Mr. Whittier has merits of a high order, though not, perhaps, quite so high as he seems to fancy, if we may judge by a little touch of egotism in the poem entitled "Memories":—

> "On life's rough blasts, for blame or praise,
> The school-boy's name has widely flown."

Mr. Whittier commands a vigorous and manly style. His expression is generally simple and to the point. Some passages in his poems are highly picturesque; and at times his imagery is bold and striking. But he is deficient in the sense of proportion. His pieces seem to be the chance sallies of a strong imagination, irregularly excited and roused to fitful action, rather than the well planned and artfully finished works of the accomplished poet. In his poems, thoughts frequently are but loosely connected with each other; indeed, the associating link is sometimes wholly imperceptible. At times, a poem continues long after the sense is completed; then again, the strain suddenly ceases, why or wherefore we know not. From this it happens, that the reader carries away from the perusal of his works a vague recollection of poetical phrases, but no image of an entire and perfected poem. Mr. Whittier is not yet completely master of English versification. With many passages of fine harmony, he has written more that are deformed by harshness, and forced turns of accentuation. The spirit of most of his pieces is highly to be commended; and yet the violence of the partisan introduces here and there a disagreeable discord. What right, for instance, has Mr. Whittier to speak in the virulent tone, which he sees fit to employ, against

[*]Reprinted from the *North American Review*, 57 (Oct. 1843), 509–10.

those clergymen who hold different opinions from his on the disputed question of capital punishment? There is no taste, no Christianity, and no poetry in all this: if Mr. Whittier supposes there is, he mistakes all three.

The most vigorous, finished, and the best conceived pieces in this volume are the "Norsemen," "Raphael," and "Massachusetts to Virginia." These three are worth all the rest of the volume together. The lines are musical almost without a fault; and the imagery and expression are noble and spirit-stirring. Had they been published by themselves, they would have placed the poet's name higher than the entire collection will raise it: for this is one of the cases, unfortunately not very rare in American poetry, where, in the phrase of Hesiod,

Νήπιοι, οὐδέ ἴσασιν ὅσῳ πλέον ἥμισν παντός.[1]

Note

1. "Fools! They know not how much more the half is than the whole." *Works & Days*, 40. [Ed. note.]

[Whittier's Poems: A Review of *Lays of My Home, and Other Poems,* 1843]

Anonymous*

Mr. Whittier is the writer of verses which it would be proper, in customary parlance, to describe as respectable. But in truth they rank in that class, which, we are told by unquestionable authority, is unendurable by gods, men or columns. The sin of mediocrity is at their doors. With tolerable smoothness of flow, and occasional energy of expression, Mr. Whittier's verses are distinguished by nothing so much as their wondrous frigidity. He is called the Quaker poet, and his poetry is the very pink of broad-brimism. It lacks, very equally, tenderness and felicity. Its chief, or only, merits, are plain good sense, general correctness, and a very fair and commendable appreciation of morals and propriety. Beyond this, the volume is a blank. It possesses neither originality nor warmth,—unless indeed, when the author falls into a fury (as he does) with Virginia,[1] and for no better reason that we can see, but because our very excellent senior sister thought proper to adopt certain measures to prevent philanthropic persons from the Bay State— Quakers, in all probability,—from stealing and carrying back the slaves which they (or their ancestors) had previously sold her. These proceedings of Virginia do make our poet worthy, and thus enable him to display—what otherwise we should scarcely have supposed him to possess— a due proportion of the *genus irritabile*. To confess a truth, we have been quite confounded by the perusal of this volume. Giving due credit to the lavish tongues of certain of the critics, and forgetting the monstrous penchant on the part of our Northern brethren, to mistake all their own geese as swans, we took for granted—in our own ignorance of Mr. Whittier's writings—that he was a genuine son of Phoebus,— blasted, in very tolerable degree, with the poetic fire. But this volume throws cold water on our former faith. It proves that our author's claim to the divine afflatus is exceedingly small. He makes verses, it is true,—

*Reprinted from the *Southern Quarterly Review*, 4 (Oct. 1843), 516–19.

very tolerable verses, as the world goes,—but sadly deficient in glow and inspiration.

Note

1. This reference is to the poem "Massachusetts to Virginia." Compare this reviewer's complaint with C. C. Felton's comments, p. 4, or with Paul Elmer More's assessment in "Whittier the Poet" (*Shelburne Essays*, 3rd ser. [New York: G. P. Putnam's Sons, 1909], pp. 33–34): "In 'Massachusetts to Virginia' this feeling of outrage calls forth one of the most stirring pieces of personification ever written, nor can I imagine a day when a man of Massachusetts shall be able to read it without a tingling of the blood, or a Virginian born hear it without a sense of unacknowledged shame. . . ." [Ed. note.]

["John Greenleaf Whittier," from a Review of Rufus W. Griswold's *The Poets and Poetry of America,* 1842]

Edwin Percy Whipple*

John Greenleaf Whittier is one of our most characteristic poets. Few excel him in warmth of temperament. Old John Dennis, the Gifford of Queen Anne's time, describes genius as caused "by a furious joy and pride of soul on the conception of an extraordinary hint. Many men have their hints, without their motions of fury and pride of soul, because they want fire enough to agitate their spirits; and these we call cold writers. Others, who have a great deal of fire, but have not excellent organs, feel the forementioned motions, without the extraordinary hints, and these we call fustian writers." Whittier has this "furious joy" and "pride of soul," even when the "hints" are not extraordinary; but he never falls into absolute rant and fustian. A common thought comes from his pen "rammed with life." He seems, in some of his lyrics, to pour out his blood with his lines. There is a rush of passion in his verse, which sweeps every thing along with it. His fancy and imagination can hardly keep pace with their fiery companion. His vehement sensibility will not allow the inventive faculties fully to complete what they may have commenced. The stormy qualities of his mind, acting at the suggestions of conscience, produce a kind of military morality which uses all the deadly arms of verbal warfare. When well intrenched in abstract right, he always assumes a hostile attitude towards the champions or practisers of abstract wrong. He aims to give his song "a rude martial tone,—a blow in every thought." His invective is merciless and undistinguishing; he almost screams with rage and indignation. Occasionally, the extreme bitterness and fierceness of his declamation degenerate into mere shrewishness and scolding. Of late, he has somewhat pruned the rank luxuriance of his style. The "Lines on the Death of Lucy Hooper," "Raphael," "Follen," "Memories," among the poems in his last published volume,[1] are indications that his mind is not without subtle imagination and deli-

*Reprinted from the *North American Review*, 58 (Jan. 1844), 1–39.

7

cate feeling, as well as truculent strength and fierce energy. There is much spiritual beauty in these little compositions. It is difficult to conceive how the man who can pour out such torrents of passionate feeling, and who evidently loves to see his words tipped with fire, can at the same time write such graceful and thoughtful stanzas as these:

"A beautiful and happy girl
   With step as soft as summer air,
And fresh young lip and brow of pearl,
Shadowed by many a careless curl,
   Of unconfined and flowing hair:
A seeming child in every thing,
   Save thoughtful brow and ripening charms,
As Nature wears the smile of Spring
   When sinking into Summer's arms.

.   .   .   .

"How thrills once more the lengthening chain
   Of memory at the thought of thee!
Old hopes, that long in dust have lain,
Old dreams, come thronging back again,
   And boyhood lives again in me;
I feel its glow upon my cheek,
   Its fulness of the heart is mine,
As when I learned to hear thee speak,
   Or raised my doubtful eye to thine.

"I hear again thy low replies,
   I feel thy arm within my own,
And timidly again uprise
The fringed lids of hazel eyes,
   With soft brown tresses overblown.
Ah! memories of sweet summer eves,
   Of moonlit wave and willowy way,
Of stars and flowers and dewy leaves,
   And smiles and tones more dear than they!
                [From "Memories."]

Whittier has the soul of a great poet, and we should not be surprised if he attained the height of excellence in his art. The faults of his mind, springing from excessive fluency and a too excitable sensibility, exaggerated as they have been by the necessities of hasty composition, have prevented him from displaying as yet the full power of his genius. It is by no means unlikely, that, when he has somewhat tamed the impetuosity of his feelings, and brooded with more quiet intensity over the large stores of poetry which lie chaotically in his nature, he may yet produce a work which will rival, and perhaps excel, the creations of his most distinguished contemporaries. He has that vigor, truthfulness, and manliness of character,—that freedom from conventional shackles,—that careless disregard of Mr. Prettyman's notion as to what constitutes the high, and Miss Betty's notion as to what constitutes the low,—that native energy and independence of nature,—which form the basis of the character of every great genius, and without which poetry is apt to be a mere echo of the drawing-room, and to idealize affectations instead of realities.

Note

1. *Lays of My Home and Other Poems* (Boston: William D. Ticknor, 1842). [Ed. note.]

["Supernaturalism": A Review of *The Supernaturalism of New England*, 1847]

Nathaniel Hawthorne[*]

Mr. Whittier's literary name has been little other than an accident of exertions directed to practical and unselfish purposes—a wayside flower, which he has hardly spared the time to gather. In the dedication of the little volume to his sister, he well expresses the feeling of relief, and almost self-reproachful enjoyment, with which he turns aside from his "long, harsh strife with strong-willed men," to converse with ghosts and witches, and all such legendary shadows. We doubt not, he will return to the battle of his life with so much the more vigor, for this brief relaxation; but we are bound to say that, if he could have more entirely thrown off the mental habit of a man writing under a stern sense of duty, he might have succeeded better in such a labor of love and idleness, as the present. In spite of himself, Mr. Whittier stoops to the theme with the austere dignity of a schoolmaster at his amusements; a condescension that may seem exaggerated, when we consider that the subject will probably retain a human interest, long after his more earnest efforts shall have lost their importance, in the progress of society.

In the first chapter of the book, there are some good remarks on the spiritual tendencies that lie beneath the earthy surface of the Yankee character. Such spirituality certainly does exist; but we cannot perceive that its indications are, or ever have been, so peculiar as to form any system that may come fairly under the title of New England Supernaturalism. The contrary is rather remarkably the fact; the forest life of the first settlers, and their intercourse with the Indians, have really engrafted nothing upon the mythology which they brought with them from England—at least, we know of nothing, although Mr. Whittier intimates that these circumstances did modify their English superstitions. We should naturally look for something duskier and grander in the ghostly legends of a wild country, than could be expected in a state of society where even dreams are covered with dust of old conven-

[*]Reprinted from *The Literary World*, 17 April 1847, pp. 247–48.

tionalisms. But, if there be any peculiarity, it is, that our superstitions have a more sordid, grimy, and material aspect, than they bore in the clime from which they were transplanted. A New England ghost does not elevate us into a spiritual region; he hints at no mysteries beyond the grave, nor seems to possess any valuable information on subjects of that nature. He throws aside even his shroud, puts on the coat and breeches of the times, and takes up the flesh-and-blood business of life, at the very point where he dropt it at his decease. He so mingles with daily life, that we scarcely perceive him to be a ghost at all. If he indeed comes from the spiritual world, it is because he has been ejected with disgrace, on account of the essential and inveterate earthiness of his substance.

This characteristic of a New England ghost story should by all means be retained; else the legend will lose its truth. Mr. Whittier has sometimes caught the just effect, but occasionally allows it to escape, by aiming at effects which are inconsistent with the one alluded to. He has made a fine ballad of the "New Wife and the Old;"—its only defect is, indeed, that he has made it too fine, at the sacrifice of the homeliness which was its essence. His style, in fact, throughout the volume, has not quite the simplicity that the theme requires; it sparkles a little too much. The proper tone for these legends is, of course, that of the fireside narrative, refined and clarified to whatever degree the writer pleases, but still as simple as the Bible—as simple as the babble of an old woman to her grandchild, as they sit in the smoky glow of a deep chimney-corner. Above all, the narrator should have faith, for the time being. If he cannot believe his ghost-story while he is telling it, he had better leave the task to somebody else. Now, Mr. Whittier never fails to express his incredulity either before or after the narrative, and often in the midst of it. It is a matter of conscience with him to do so.

One other criterion must be allowed us. Mr. Whittier has read too much. He talks too learnedly about the "Ahriman of the Parsee, the Pluto of the Roman mythology, the Devil of the Jew and the Christian, the Shitan of the Mussulman, the Machinito of the Indian;" and quotes some black letter mystic or modern poet on every page. There is nothing in his treatment of the subject that requires such an array of authorities, nor any such depth in the well of his philosophy, that we can descend into it only by a flight of steps, constructed out of old folio volumes.

But, how much easier it is to censure than to praise, even where the merits greatly outweigh the defects! We conclude, with the frank admission that we like the book, and look upon it as no unworthy contribution from a poet to that species of literature which only a poet should meddle with. We hope to see more of him, in this, or some other congenial sphere. There are many legends still to be gathered, especially along the sea-board of New England—and those, too, we think, more original, and more susceptible of poetic illustration, than these rural superstitions.

"Whittier's Poems"[1]

J. G. Forman[*]

Truth is the soul of poetry, and every departure from it is an offence against the highest laws of the poetic art. A pure imagination is as much offended by whatever is false in poetry, or untrue to nature, as a musical ear is by discordant sounds. The poet may attain the highest excellence in his art, and yet he is indebted to the outward and inward world for every form of beauty, and every true and holy sentiment he utters. His power is like that hidden influence by which the flowers extract their sweet perfumes and delicate tints from the earth and air in which they live. It is a divine gift. The poet lives in the outward world, and in the world of thought and spirit. As his eye is open to all forms of beauty in the one, his mind is open to the inspirations of the other, and from these his spirit distills, in the silent alembics of the soul, the highest forms of truth and beauty.

It does not follow that every composition, because it is metrical, contains true poetry. It may have the form without the soul, in which case it is but the shadow of poetry. Those who are captivated by beautiful images and a form of words, may not appreciate the distinction; but he who seeks the gem of truth, the soul of beauty, will not be deceived by the setting, or the gorgeous drapery in which it is displayed.

In forming an ideal standard by which poetry shall be judged, regard should be had to the object which consecrates it, or the end and aim for which it is written. Many volumes of poetry are given to the world which seem to have no object but to express certain feelings and emotions, of which the authors were the subjects—to narrate events of personal history, or to excite the sympathies and admiration of the reader, by some tale of love, or other fiction, the offspring of a sickly sentimentalism. There are few volumes of poetry published which have for their object the advancement of truth or the good of humanity. Yet it must be conceded, that these are the highest ends and aim of genuine poetry. There is much published, too, that possesses but a slight degree of originality, old thoughts in a new dress, and many similes but slightly

[*]Reprinted from *The National Era*, 1 Feb. 1849, p. 17.

changed, of which the original may be found in the poets of another age.

. . .

The poet, then, who does most for TRUTH and MAN, fulfils the highest mission of true poetry. His works shall live when those of Byron, and his host of imitators, shall be remembered only as bubbles on the waves of passion.

This is the standard by which ultimately true poetry shall be judged. By this standard must the author and his works be estimated, whose name stands at the head of this article. Here is a volume which the world may read, and grow better from the reading. The inspiration of its author comes through his Reason, his Conscience, and his Love of Man, and will be variously estimated, according as these are developed in the minds and character of those who read him. Wherever his utterances find their way into a true and upright soul, there will they meet with a response that shall strengthen the heart, and increase its love for God and Man—there will the name of WHITTIER be enshrined, and his memory be associated with the Right and True forevermore.

It is not our purpose, in this brief review, to go into a criticism of the comparative merits of Whittier as a poet. This is a work for abler pens. Like all others who possess superior excellences, he doubtless has his defects. There is one proof, however, that the former far surpasses the latter, which cannot fail to be appreciated by all. It is the widespread popularity of his poems, and the prominent place they already occupy in the literature of our country. It is of some of these excellences we would speak, and with the more confidence, because the great heart of Humanity, which is generally in the right place, is on his side.

Among the characteristics of Whittier's style, his *vigor, truthfulness,* and *simplicity,* are marked and striking. His descriptive powers are of a high order, though he displays them rather in presenting a strong outline, and the general features of a subject, than in giving minute details. His pictures, therefore, are most agreeable to the reader, and leave a strong impression on the mind, while something is left for the imagination to supply. The creative or imaginative faculty is probably less active than in some of his contemporaries, but in fidelity of description, and a delicate appreciation of all forms of beauty, he is unsurpassed. His poetry is the poetry of human life, of truth and pure sentiment, rather than of fiction. In his descriptions of New England scenery, of familiar landscapes, and the associations he connects with them, there is a tenderness and beauty that captivates the heart. He combines more of boldness and strength, with gentleness and delicacy of sentiment, than any author whom it has been our pleasure to read.

His descriptions of Indian life and character are remarkable for their strength and fidelity. Two of his longest poems are founded on incidents in the history of the Indian tribes that inhabited that portion of New England where Mr. Whittier has spent much of his early life. These are, the "Bridal of Pennacook" and "Mogg Megone." In both these poems a tragic interest is maintained throughout; the events, the scenes where they occurred, and the Indian character and mode of life, are brought before the mind with wonderful fidelity and power of description. There is no exaggeration, and no excess of imagery and verbiage encumbers these poems. The delineations are faithfully drawn, and the narratives given in language strong and vigorous, yet chaste, and flowing as a mountain stream. The style does not abound in similes, but when they do occur, they are always beautiful and perfect of their kind. The following is an instance. It is from "The Bridal of Pennacook," and refers to Passaconaway, an aged chief, and his only daughter, whose mother had died:

"A lone, stern man. Yet as sometimes
  The tempest-smitten tree receives
From one small root the sap which climbs
  Its topmost spray and crowning leaves,
So from his child the Sachem drew
  A life of Love and Hope, and felt
His cold and rugged nature through
  The softness and the warmth of her young being melt."

Another characteristic of Mr. Whittier is, the strong current of moral and religious sentiment that flows through all his poems. Occasionally, he indulges a vein of ridicule, as in "The Hunters of Men"; sometimes he uses a keen and powerful sarcasm, as in "The Response," and some other pieces; and again he burns with holy indignation, and utters the most writhing rebukes—but they are all for a good purpose, and sanctified by the end in view. These are called forth by the wrongs and sufferings of the oppressed and down-trodden slave, as though he would, by every means in his power, awaken his countrymen to a sense of the injustice and the shame of which we stand guilty before God and man. His sympathies are all on the side of Humanity. Oppression and cruelty find no apologist in him. His heart is in all the great reforms of the age. No poet of our times, or of any time, has accomplished more for Truth and Man than he. When the prisoner for debt was incarcerated in his gloomy cell, the companion of felons and the vile, and often for the crime of being poor, he was among the first to tell his wrongs in words that lingered on the public ear till the law was changed, in conformity to a better sentiment, to which he contributed largely by the influence of his poetry.

Through him the wrongs and cruelties inflicted on three millions of our brother men by the slaveholders of the South, find a ready and eloquent utterance, in "thoughts that breathe and words that burn."

.   .   .

Notwithstanding the influence of the slave power upon the literature of our country, on which its blighting influence has been felt, as upon everything else, the merits of Whittier, as a poet, must meet with universal acknowledgment, though it be yielded tardily by those who have no sympathy with the man. He has struck out a bolder path than any of his contemporaries, and seized upon greater and loftier themes than they. And this fact, itself, together with the vigor and beauty of his style, will give him a position in the front rank of American poets. With less of artistic skill than some of them, the greatness of his themes, and the outpourings of his generous spirit, will more than offset all his deficiencies. If he is not equal in the fertility and brilliancy of his imagination, he is unsurpassed in the simplicity, the beautiful flow and harmony, and the pure sentiment, of some of his miscellaneous poems. He possesses, too, a deep spirituality, and you feel that his mind is in intimate communion with the beautiful and true in all things.

.   .   .

Mr. Whittier's poems indicate a mind deeply imbued with the spirit of Christianity. He seems grieved that many of the Clergy should fall so far short of their true mission as to apologize for and uphold, by their influence, the iniquity of human slavery, and that they should be found the most strenuous advocates for the gallows, and lean to the side of revenge rather than to that of mercy. When several Clergymen put forth a pamphlet in favor of the Gallows, and a celebrated "Pastoral Letter" in regard to Slavery, it called forth an earnest appeal from Whittier, in each instance, that possessed more counteracting influence and power than all their efforts combined, and doubtless helped on the reform of these evils far more than they were able to retard it. In one of these appeals, he rejoices that he has lived to see the day when the spirit of the Gospel is beginning to leaven the hearts of the great masses of mankind.

> "Thank God! that I have lived to see the time
> When the great truth begins at last to find
> An utterance from the deep heart of mankind,
> Earnest and clear, that ALL REVENGE IS CRIME!

That man is holier than a creed—that all
   Restraint upon him must consult his good,
Hope's sunshine linger on his prison wall,
   And Love look in upon his solitude.["]
               [From "The Gallows."]

. . .

Mr. Whittier is a member of the religious Society of Friends, and those who know the faithful testimony which this people have always borne against Slavery and War, and all Revenge, will see what influences had aided in forming the character and principles of the poet. In all the descriptions which Mr. Whittier gives of Indian life and warfare, and in all his appeals to the patriotic achievements of our forefathers, he breathes not a sentiment that can be considered an approval of retaliation or war, in any form. His poetic fervor, and his love of liberty, have never carried him beyond his religious principles, while at the same time he makes use of the deeds of valor which our fathers did, in the name of Liberty, to awaken us to a sense of shame, in supporting a more inhuman and wrongful oppression than they were ever threatened with.

Some of the poems of Whittier are founded on events in the history of the Friends, but in none is there the least exhibition of bigotry or intolerance. He has too strong a repugnance to either, to fall into the same errors himself. The persecution of the Quakers is brought to our recollection, but not in such a way as to indicate a spirit of hatred towards those who were guilty of this wrong, or towards their descendants. The intolerance and bigotry of the priesthood, and the part they took in those persecutions, are made quite prominent, but not more so than was necessary to the truthfulness of his narrations. No one who reads him can fail to admire the beautiful ballad in which he recites the treatment of "Cassandra Southwick," and the fine poem entitled "Barclay of Ury." The beautiful spirit of meekness and submission which distinguished so many of the early Quakers forms a fine theme for Whittier's pen, while it enables us to frame an excuse for the extravagances of some who did not know so well how to bear the persecutions which they endured for conscience's sake. Some of his verses indicate a sympathy wide and deep enough to embrace the whole world of Humanity. He seems to connect himself with the destiny of his race, with which his and all other individual destinies are interwoven.

. . .

One valuable and interesting feature in the book remains to be noticed. It contains a fine steel engraving of the author, which will render it doubly dear to those who prize both the poet and the man. Those who have enjoyed his personal acquaintance say it is an excellent likeness. It is very much like the ideal image of the man we had formed from reading the productions of his mind, so far do we associate mental character with organization. It is a face full of *thought* and kindly sentiment. The features are finely chiseled, and the eye is full of calm, reflective passion. It is a face expressive of the finest sensibilities and feelings, in which gentleness and dignity of soul are harmoniously blended, indicating the warm and generous friend and the moral hero. In that thoughtful-looking eye, there dwells the perception and the love of beauty. The harmonies of the outward world—the beautiful in thought and deed, of love, religion, and the soul—are all reflected there. And then there arises above that face a head, of which the disciple of Gall and Spurzheim[3] might make a study. The Perceptive faculties and Language are full, but it is in the superior regions of the forehead that the strength and vigor of his mind are seen. There the Reflective powers stand out prominently, and Ideality swells its rounded form above the hollow temples, partially concealed beneath the hair. Then in the unusual height of the head you perceive the fulness of the moral region—of Benevolence, and Conscience, and Firmness—the Sentiments of Justice, Freedom, and Humanity. These are the sources of his moral power, and give direction to his mind. These were the "voices" that spoke to him during his visit to Washington, as his mind dwelt upon the scenes of the slave Capital, and which he has uttered again—

> "To thy duty now and ever!
> Dream no more of rest or stay;
> Give to Freedom's great endeavor
> All thou art and hast to-day:
> Thus above the city's murmur, saith a Voice, or seems to say."
> [From "At Washington."]

Another feature of his character, indicated in this likeness and in his poems, is an innate modesty. In this respect there is a striking contrast with the proverbial vanity and pride of authors and public men. He nowhere exhibits either of these qualities. You look in vain for anything like egotism in this book, and when you look on his face you see no expression of it there. Among his many excellences, is that of a meek and gentle spirit. When he advocates the cause of the wronged and the oppressed—when he speaks in the name of Right and Liberty— he is as bold as a lion; but when self is the subject of his verse, which is seldom, his vehemence is gone, and he writes as one who thinks humbly of himself. In his poem, he says—

"The rigor of a frozen clime,
The harshness of an untaught ear,
    The jarring words of one whose rhyme
    Best often Labor's hurried time,
Or Duty's rugged march through storm and strife, are here.
            .   .   .   .
    Yet here at least an earnest sense
Of human right and weal is shown;
    A hate of Tyranny intense,
    And hearty in its vehemence,
As if my brother's pain and sorrow were my own.

    Oh Freedom! if to me belong
Nor mighty Milton's gift divine,
    Nor Marvell's wit and graceful song,
    Still with a love as deep and strong
As theirs, I lay, like them, my best gifts on thy shrine!"
                              [From "Proem."]

                    .   .   .

Notes

    1. *Poems* (Boston: Benjamin B. Mussey & Co., 1849). [Ed. note.]
    2. Dr. Franz Joseph Gall (1758–1828) was a Viennese physician who orig-
inated the science of phrenology; Johann Gaspar Spurzheim (1776–1832), disciple
of Gall, sparked the popular imagination when he toured the United States lecturing
on this new science. Emerson thought him to be one of the world's great minds.
[Ed. note.]

"Whittier's Poems"[1]

H. Ballou*

It would seem that, of all classes of writers, those who attempt "the art divine" are the most likely to be misjudged on their first appearance. A thousand causes are always at work to magnify or to conceal their merit in the eyes of spectators, but more so at their entrance on the stage. So far as poetry is imitative, it is subject to the disadvantage that caricature, or extravagance, commonly takes the popular applause, before the modest truth. Indeed, with respect to poetry of all kinds, the taste with which people appreciate it, is far too subtile an element to be fixed, and too susceptible of intermixtures from abroad to remain pure under the least agitation. It is often discomposed by the very effort to judge truly; "come, let us sit in judgement," is a signal not more disquieting to the poor author, than to the finer sentiments of the arbiters themselves. Taste is liable to spontaneous fickleness through love of novelty, and is over ready to be affected by prejudice, fashion, attachment to particular interests, fondness for certain speculations or modes of thought, and by nearly every thing that is stirring in the world. Even the opinion of critics and connoisseurs, though more deliberately formed, is exposed, for this very reason perhaps, to still greater danger from some of these quarters; since conscious deliberation is apt to call up all one's prejudices, and to bring the artificial habits of one's mind foremost in play. Whether it be popular taste or professional opinion, it is, in both cases, swayed by so many adventitious circumstances, and by so many internal impulses, that a considerable time must pass, before the disturbing forces will subside, and the needle settle in its true and final direction.

We scarcely need say that these suggestions are verified by the history of criticism and popular favor, in this country as well as in other countries. Every one can recollect some three or four American poets, who, for a while, enjoyed a distinguished reputation among our reviewers and verse-readers, especially among those of certain classes, but who have already passed out of notice in every quarter. Many others were hailed at first as new stars, who turned out to be but shooting

*Reprinted from the *Universalist Quarterly*, 6 (April 1849), 142–60.

meteors, and in some cases but phosphorescent exhalations, or exhalations without the phosphorescence; while some, again, who were for a long time disregarded, except by a few, have since risen to a respectable standing in the public estimation.

So many instances of the kind have occurred within our own memory and observation, that we feel we ought to be cautious in making up, and especially in publishing, our judgement of any new candidate for the laurels. We certainly should not like to set down in these pages any blunder that might convict us of incompetence. The author of the volume before us is not one whose claims are now for the first time presented. In one way or another, he has been before the public so long, that the reviewer who, at this late day, pronounces a false or mistaken verdict in his case, cannot plead for indulgence on the ground that he was taken by surprise, but must abide his responsibility, as his decision is at least a deliberate one. He, as well as his author, is committed irretrievably to the issue.

With this fear before our eyes, and notwithstanding the wariness that has been taught us by the mistakes alluded to, we still must avow, in decided terms, our admiration of Mr. Whittier's genius. We must venture to name him as one of the two who should be ranked highest in the catalogue of American poets, if his rank may be determined by the more excellent half of his productions. We are aware that there are several others who excel him, if we regard merely the workmanship of the art. In this, he is now and then quite deficient, though not through want of capability, as many of his pieces show. Perhaps he undervalues artistic excellence; perhaps he deems it an acquisition not worth the time it would take from severer duties, or thinks it may be dispensed with in the presence of higher properties; a judgement, however, to which we should demur. Were his essential merits of a lower order, we should not so much regret blemishes in the workmanship. His lines, though in general very significant, are sometimes crude, sometimes filled out with verbiage to make up the measure; his rhymes do not always come within the conditions of what Walker calls the "allowable;"[2] and, in a very few instances, when the verse would not conform to the accent of his proper names, he has resorted to a Mohammed-like alternative, and made the accent, and even the syllabication, conform to the verse. But with all these occasional faults, as an artist, and with some others of a more general character, he has "the anointed eye," together with the heart and imagination, of a poet, in a greater degree than any of his American brethren with whom we are acquainted. We know not where, among them we could find the calm, clear depth of thought and feeling, through which he looks out on his objects, whether of external nature, or of human character and interests; and through which he sees every thing invested with a rich but chastened light, reflected from the inmost recesses of his soul. This we take to be the peculiar psychology of a poet. It is true, when that depth of soul is stirred up from the very bottom by the sense of wrong, it is at times like a volcano at sea, bursting through the waves in fierce eruption, and, at other times, like the ocean heaved by tempest, and running all before it. But in his usual moods, this power reveals itself only in the characters of alternate beauty and tenderness, earnestness and majesty. Nor is this profoundness of imagination and feeling his only distinction. We have seen this property so often ascribed to mere extravagance, or to the facility of making unnatural combinations, that the mention of it may be regarded as suspicious. But we know not where else we could find, among our countrymen, the perfect truthfulness of conception that lies under his imaginative coloring, together with his warm, unaffected geniality of spirit, tempered with just enough of pensiveness to give it a romantic charm,—all brought out in so natural a freshness of expression and imagery. We say this only of the better class of his poems, for there is great inequality among them.

It would be absurd perhaps, to attempt a parallel between him and the older poet, with whom we have associated him in rank. Indeed, their characteristics are so diverse as to admit of no regular parallel. Nevertheless, there are some points, we can hardly say of resemblance, but of equality and difference, that may be mentioned. We do this for the advantage it will give us in illustrating his character. By comparing it with a well-known standard, it will become the more distinct.

Both he and Bryant have the same truthfulness of conception, without which imagination but creates monsters, or draws caricatures, instead of heightening effects. Both have nearly an equal love of nature, but with the difference that the latter is nicer, and therefore more exclusive in selecting his objects. He is equally exact in his observations, at least of his favorite scenes, and perhaps even surpasses in point of acuteness; while Whittier takes in a wider, freer, and more varied range of objects. The wild, barren, and desolate, as well as the beautiful, reflect their latent, mysterious grace, when touched by his wand. We think also, that his communion with nature is more immediate. We come at his objects and scenery more directly; not barely seeing them, though ever so vividly and truly, as in Bryant, but we are present with them on the spot, seeming to breathe-in their freshness, to hear their music, to feel all their influences as we feel them in actual life; we have a living sympathy with every thing around us. This is one of the most infallible tests, the *crux experimenti*, of a poet's power. In the expression of feeling of whatever sort, we cannot but think Whittier the more genial, if compared either with Bryant, or with almost any of the rest. There is the pleasant warmth of the heart in his poetry, not because he strives to call it up, but because it comes there of itself. Occasionally, when roused to the last degree of vehemence, it may be that he now and then "o'ersteps the modesty of nature;" but with what effect? As a matter of fact, never has there been any thing sent forth that kindled, and fired, and bore the hearts of men along, as some of his anti-slavery pieces have done. This is proof, that if he offends, he "gloriously offends." Let a cold critic find what faults he may, still in those mighty torrents of mingled enthusiasm and poetry, Whittier has no equal, probably in the whole world.

There is another advantage that we are disposed to ascribe to him, though it may not be recognized among the peculiar properties of a poet: His charity, which is coexistensive with the liberality of Bryant, is underlaid, if we mistake not, with a more positive and definite religious faith; and this contributes indirectly, yet in a much greater degree than will be commonly believed, to give depth and vitality to his effusions. It is not out of place to mention this characteristic, here; for every thing that belongs to the man comes into action in the higher exercises of genius, and leaves its mark on the result. Whittier is always in earnest; a reserve of urgent purposes hovering in the background of his lightest pictures. This prevents him from ever descending to the sentimental, though no man deals more in sentiment. The motto, which he has taken from Coleridge, and inscribed on his title-page, was most happily chosen, as expressive of his own rigorous self-questioning:—

—"Was it right,
While my unnumbered brethren toiled and bled,
That I should dream away the entrusted hours
On rose-leaf bed, pampering the coward heart
With *feelings all too delicate for use?*"
[From "Reflections on Having Left a Place of Retirement."]

Even in his meditative and in his playful moods, he stands girded up for the great work of his life, bound by conscience to do battle against all wrong, and in behalf of all suffering. Bryant's heart is, perhaps, equally steadfast in the same cause; but he lacks the intense fervor that distinguishes the devotion of his fellow-laborer. The latter has the serene, philanthropy of a Channing, strangely united with the vehemence of one of the old prophets. We may add that both are truly American in their choice of subjects and of imagery; we think however, that Whittier is the more thoroughly so in his taste and manner, as well as richer in the variety of materials he has appropriated from his native land. With all his cosmopolitan philanthropy, his heart remains at home. As an artist, Bryant far surpasses him in every thing that relates to form. He is always careful to produce a symmetrical whole, and then to finish his verse by working it down to the last degree of consistence and harmony. He never suffers his Muse, as Whittier sometimes does, to wander in her strain, or sing on after she has ended her song proper.

It would do us injustice to suppose that we have aimed to furnish a regular sketch of Bryant. Our object was to take only such characteristics belonging to him as we thought would help, by comparison, to illustrate more fully those of our author. As to any question of general precedence between them, we do not attempt to determine it; a task which, were it practicable, we are sure neither would thank us for assuming. We have spoken of these two as, on the whole, the first among American poets. It will, of course, be understood that we do not mean to compare them with the great European masters, of the last generation, whose lives were devoted to their art, and whose genius placed them almost above the hope of competition.

It is very difficult to select, from such a writer as Whittier, specimens which, when thus cut out from their connection will represent him justly. An eminent lecturer has likened the practice, in another case, to extracting a fine eye, and presenting it on a surgeon's plate, that the spectators may see for themselves its kindling glance. Notwithstanding the disparagement, however, we cannot well dispense with the custom. A few extracts, garbled though they be, are necessary as the subject of some remarks we propose to offer.

Among his descriptions of natural scenery, let us take the first lines of his poem on the Merrimack,—premising that the point of view appears to be on some of the eminences of Salisbury, overlooking the Powow, and commanding a prospect of the Merrimack down to its mouth.

> "Stream of my fathers! sweetly still
> The sun-set rays thy valley fill;
> Poured slant wise down thy long defile,
> Wave, wood, and spire beneath them smile.
> I see the winding Powow fold
> The green hill in its belt of gold,
> And, following down its wavy line,
> Its sparkling waters blend with thine.
> There's not a tree upon thy side,
> Nor rock, which thy returning tide
> As yet hath left abrupt and stark
> Above thy evening water-mark;—
> No calm cove with its rocky hem,
> No isle whose emerald swells begem
> Thy broad smooth current; not a sail
> Bowed to the freshening ocean gale;
> No small boat with its busy oars,
> Nor gray wall sloping to thy shores;
> Nor farm-house with its maple shade

Or rigid poplar colonade,—
But lies distinct and full in sight,
Beneath this gush of sunset light." p. 75.

[From "The Merrimac."]

Goethe has pronounced strong "objectivity" to be one of the first requisites of a true poet. Nothing can exceed the clearness with which the general scene is here brought out to view, and shown in its appropriate light and shade. The several objects that fill up the outline do not seem to stand apart; they belong together, and are but features of one whole. There are many who can vividly present single points, or describe in fragments; but it is a different order of spirits who, by a sketch, can give a wide and diversified picture in its entireness, and keep it true to nature while they shed, over all, the coloring of their imagination. To this we must add another characteristic. Every thing here, though reposing in beautiful quiet, is full of life. A *materialistic* critic might seek to account for the effect, by the free play of the verse, the happy selection of particulars, &c. But all these do not reach down to the principle. They are themselves but an effect, and not the producing power. As our great orator has said, on another subject, "words and phrases may be marshalled in every way, but they cannot compass it."[3] It is the poet's sympathy with the scene, the mysterious power by which he diffuses himself, as it were, out over the whole, and feels as well as sees the several parts of which it is composed,—it is this that puts us in communication with his subject, at the same time that it selects his particulars for him, and attunes his verse. Wave, wood and spire smile beneath the sunset rays that are poured slant-wise down the long valley; the evening tide is returning; the sail bows to the freshening breeze from the ocean; the little boat plies its oars; all objects lie distinct in the golden light that gushes from the west. The poet seizes the whole in its living state,— in action. The same scene is afterwards presented, but at a later moment, and under a changed aspect:—

"But look!—the yellow light no more
Streams down on wave and verdant shore;
And clearly on the calm air swells
The twilight voice of distant bells.
From ocean's bosom, white and thin
The mists come slowly rolling in;
Hills, woods, the river's rocky rim,
Amidst the sea-like vapor swim,
While yonder lonely coast-light, set
Within its wave-washed minaret,
Half-quenched, a beamless star and pale,
Shines dimly through its cloudy veil." p. 77.

In these passages, and in others with which the volume abounds, we cannot but feel how directly the poet transfers his own impressions from the scenes of nature to ourselves. We receive them through him, as by magnetic communication; we take them in their first glow and warmth. This power of enchantment, when associated with truthfulness and entireness of conception, is a very rare gift; but it is a distinguishing property of all high poetic genius. We need not speak of the singular force with which it characterizes Shakespeare's occasional sketches of natural scenery, and all his allusions to external objects. In Milton, it seems to glorify almost every page. Among the great English masters, of the last generation, Byron stands unequalled in this respect. Burns possessed the complex faculty in remarkable intensity; Scott, in large degree, but in a much more diffuse form. Coleridge had no truthfulness of conception,—he lived too much on laudanum; and his very "objectivity," so far as he had it, was oppressed by his overweening egotism. Some give us, for nature, either a fairy world or a hob-goblin world. Then, again, in reading some of the first-rate versifiers, who are respectable too for truthfulness of outline, we who find occasion to complain that they seem to have studied, and measured, and even analyzed their objects scientifically, or wrought upon them with some philosophical alchemy, till all the freshness of them is gone. They give us preserved specimens, instead of the living, growing foliage; or, they give us nature at second-hand, after it has been exhausted of its native spirit in its passage through their own minds. This fault abounds in no less a poet than Wordsworth. His descriptions, always exact indeed, sometimes approach too nearly the character of mere enumerations, and still oftener want the free unconscious development that belongs to life; though, when he rises above his philosophical rules, he redeems himself,—nobly, now and then.

.   .   .

    They who have known Whittier only by his stormy lyrics, as those in the cause of Reform have been called, will be surprized to find the deepest and most genial sentiments pervading his poems. We naturally ask, What means it, that he who seemed to ride the blast like an eagle exulting in its might, is as domestic, as full of all gentle and quiet affections, as a dove! Yet the contrast need not surprize us, for we may detect the presence of these very qualities in his most vehement moods. The lightning that scorches, and the thunder that awes, are but manifestations of the same genial element that gives vitality to all living things. We are aware that it is too common to apologize for passionate violence in a good cause, by tracing back the abuse to its origin in some noble principle. This is not what we mean in his case. With him, the violence, or rather the vehemence, retains its original qualities still,

of which it is only a more intense form. His very indignation at his
country's misdeeds, bears the character of wounded patriotism, and
his withering scorn of the oppressor or of the recreant, appears but as
the spirit of outraged humanity. It is this pervading element that gives
his trumpet-like peals their force to stir the heart so thoroughly. When
the topic is changed, he passes into his accustomed serenity. He delights to linger around old associations and remembrances; the antique
has a peculiar spell upon him, Radical though he is; he loves the very
hearth-stones of his home, and is ever ready to appreciate all the forms
that have been sanctified by human life. Nor does there appear any
constraint, any thing unnatural, in this change of mood. We feel that
it is the same man in both phases, as we feel there is the same groundwork of character in John of the Apocalypse and in John the Evangelist.[4]

What we admire, in his utterances of sentiment and emotion, is the
air of reality that characterizes the whole. The feelings he expresses
are neither affected, nor got up for the occasion; they are such as belong
to the man in his own sound state of mind, and are not overcharged
nor desperately intensified. We give an example or two from his memorial to "Lucy Hooper," who died at Brooklyn, L. I.

> "They tell me, Lucy, thou art dead—
> . . . .
> Even as thou wert I see thee still;
> And,—save the absence of all ill
> And pain and weariness, which here
> Summoned the sigh or wrung the tear,—
> The same as when, two summers back,
> Beside our childhood's Merrimack,
> I saw thy dark eye wander o'er
> Stream, sunny upland, rocky shore,
> And heard thy low soft voice alone
> Midst lapse of water and the tone
> Of pine-leaves by the west-wind blown.
> There's not a charm of soul or brow,—
> Of all we know and lov'd in thee,—
> But lives in holier beauty, now
> Baptized in immortality. [p. 345.]

. . .

The geniality of his feelings is discernible also in the quality of
his humor,—serious, yet pleasant, without a spice of bitterness. We
recollect but one piece that is written throughout in this vein,—his
"Demon of the Study," though there are several passages in which the
latent shrewdness occasionally shines out on the surface, revealing

the depth of good-nature whence the smile arose. See his description of the young clergyman-tourist at the White Mountains:—

> " 'Twas in truth a study,
> To mark his spirit, alternating between
> A decent and professional gravity
> And an irreverent mirthfulness, which often
> Laughed in the face of his divinity,
> Plucked off the sacred ephod, quite unshrined
> The oracle, and for the pattern priest
> Left us the man."
>
> [p. 11.]

To review Whittier's Poems, without a notice of that remarkable and peculiar class of them which is directed against slavery, would be like playing "Othello," with the part of Othello left out "by particular request." In them he has taken a course distinctly his own, in which no one has followed him, as no one has had the strength of enthusiasm and imagination for the effort. In them we see the usually gentle, unobtrusive poet rapt into the mood of an old Hebrew Seer, and, with all his fine powers strung to their utmost tension, standing forth to shake the nation with his message. We sometimes feel, especially in reading his "Massachusetts to Virginia," as if there were a spell given him to summon the very elements into the struggle against the spreading curse of our land; the winds, the waters, hills and vallies, and the monumental shafts of granite, seem to bear a part in the conflict, as the old gods joined in the fight around Ilium. He has made conceivable a poetic machinery that would agree with the spirit of modern ages, as the mythological suited the genius of ancient times. At all events, to use his own expressive language, he "scatters the living coals of truth upon the nation's naked heart." This is the work which these poems have done,—which they are still doing. They may indeed be rough here and there, their imagery may now and then be too gigantic for an exquisite's reading, some of their lines may be overstrained, and others may almost break down in the intermittent rush of thought; but one thing nobody will deny: they do their work. And as the author does not pamper feelings that are "too delicate for use," he will be content with the effect, whatever be the critic's censure. We have heard it alleged that these wonder-working strains are eloquent rather than poetic. But this is plainly a mistake. The faults as well as excellences they have, are those of poetry. Or, if it be true that "action, godlike action," is something "higher than eloquence," we may say that there is, in them, an element higher than poetry, and that the poetic faults are no faults, or dwindle into insignificance, when viewed in this higher relation. We must not forget, however, that the distinguishing qualities of his genius are found here, intensified in some cases, and in others held in abeyance by stronger forces. Nor must we fail to remark that it is only of the better pieces even of this class, that we speak. There are some of them in which a sarcastic wit is attempted, but we think with little success and with a bad effect.

The anti-slavery poems have been so extensively read, that it seems rather gratuitous to quote examples. We take the following fragments from his "Massachusetts to Virginia;"—first observing that they were occasioned by some "indignation-meetings" in the latter state on the refusal of the former to give up Latimer, the fugitive slave. . . .

"The blast from Freedom's Northern hills, upon its Southern way,
Bears greeting to Virginia from Massachusetts-Bay:—
No word of haughty challenging, nor battle bugle's peal,
No steady tread of marching files, nor clang of horsemen's steel.
. . . .
"What means the Old Dominion? Hath she forgot the day
When o'er her conquered vallies swept the Briton's steel array,
How, side by side with sons of hers, the Massachusetts-men
Encountered Tarleton's charge of fire, and stout Cornwallis, then?

"Forgets she how the Bay-State, in answer to the call
Of her old House of Burgesses, spoke out from Faneuil Hall?
When, echoing back her Henry's cry, came pulsing on each breath
Of Northern winds, the thrilling cry of 'Liberty or death.'
. . . .
"We wage no war, we lift no arm, we fling no torch within
The fire-damps of the quaking mine beneath your soil of sin;
We leave ye with your bondmen, to wrestle while ye can
With the strong upward tendencies and Godlike soul of man.

"But, for us and for our children, the vow which we have given
For Freedom and Humanity, is registered in heaven:
'No slave-hunt in our borders! No pirate on our strand!
No fetters in the Bay-State! No slave upon our land!'"
                                                    [pp. 188, 191.]

                         . . .

We intended to conclude with some general views respecting the nature of true poetry, and with some strictures on certain theories which we have seen upon the subject. But, except in so far as they may be gathered from what we have incidentally said, they must be suppressed for want of room. We have only to add that, with a very high opinion of Whittier's genius, and with the fullest admiration of his own taste, we still must admit that he is quite unequal. He does not always sustain himself, through want of effort as it appears to us. There are pieces, too, in which we think the measure unfortunate. This is the case especially with those composed of triplets; since the monotonous recurrence of these does not allow sufficient scope for harmony of verse, or for variety of expression. And again: has he, at all times, confidence enough in himself to follow his own bent without being drawn aside by examples from abroad? We mean the question in no bad sense. Let him be assured, that there is no one in America, and no one at present in Europe, from whom he either needs, or can obtain, help, except in the way of general culture. As a poet, let him, above all things, preserve unsophisticated his rich fund of native gifts,—his manly truthfulness, his freshness of conception, his clear strong "objectivity," his immediate communion with nature, and his directness of expression. These are above all praise. Any refinement that should in the least impair these, would be false refinement, let it be sanctioned by whatsoever examples it may. If a little more polish be acquired in the course of practice, it will at least be no disadvantage, and a rigorous use of the pruning-knife may bring out a more beautiful growth; but let neither file nor knife touch the vital parts.

Notes

1. *Poems* (Boston: Benjamin B. Mussey & Co., 1849). [Ed note.]

2. James Walker (1794–1874), minister, editor of *The Christian Examiner* (1831–1839), Professor of Natural Religion, Moral Philosophy and Civil Polity at Harvard, and President of the College (1853–1860). [Ed. note.]

3. Surely this is Daniel Webster, although the quote was not immediately locatable in his *Complete Works*. [Ed. note.]

4. On the principles of some Biblical critics, might not a strong plea be made that the Whittier who wrote "Massachusetts to Virginia," and "Our Fellow-Countrymen in Chains," was not the Whittier who wrote "Lucy Hooper," and "The Merrimack"?

[Review of *Songs of Labor, and Other Poems*, 1850]

Orestes Brownson°

Mr. Whittier has some of the elements of a true poet, but his poems, though often marked by strength and tenderness, are our abomination. He is a Quaker, an infidel, an abolitionist, a philanthropist, a peace man, a Red Republican, a non-resistant, a revolutionist, all characters we hold in horror and detestation, and his poems are the echo of himself. God gave him noble gifts, every one of which he has used to undermine faith, to eradicate loyalty, to break down authority, and to establish the reign of anarchy, and all under the gentle mask of promoting love and good will, diffusing the Christian spirit, and defending the sacred cause of liberty. He approaches us in the gentle and winning form of an angel of light, and yet whether he means it or not, it is only to rob us of all that renders life worth possessing. If he believes himself doing the will of God, he is the most perfect dupe of the Evil One that Devil has ever been able to make. He is silly enough, after having denounced Pious the Ninth in the most savage manner, and canonized the assassins and ruffians who founded the Roman Republic, to think that he can pass with Catholics as not being their enemy, because, forsooth, he favored the Irish rebellion! Whoever denounces our Church or its illustrious chief is our enemy and we would much sooner hold the man who should seek to deprive us of life to be our friend, than the one who should undertake to deprive us of our religion. With this estimate of Mr. Whittier how can we praise his poems, or commend them to the public?[1]

Note

1. This review was written six years after Brownson's conversion to Catholicism and is interesting not so much because of what it says about Whittier but because it illustrates "the problem of writing objective literary criticism when strong personal feelings and beliefs are involved." (See Lewis E. Weeks, Jr. "Whittier Criticism Over the Years." *Essex Institute Historical Collections*, 100 [1964], 165.) [Ed. note.]

°Reprinted from *Brownson's Quarterly Review*, 7 (Oct. 1850), 540.

"John G. Whittier and His Writings"[1]

William Sydney Thayer*

In considering Whittier's merits as an author, it is quite manifest that we should mention, first, his intensity,—that vivid force of thought and expression which distinguishes his writings. His verses sometimes bear marks of extreme haste, but the imperfections which would result from this cause are in a great measure obviated by the strength and simplicity of his conceptions. He begins to write with so clear an apprehension of what he intends to say, that in many cases his poems come out at first heat with a roundness and perfection which would lead one to suppose that they had passed through the fires of revision. But at times this vehemence is overdone, and needs a restraint which longer consideration would have supplied. This vividness, which Whittier possesses in a greater degree than any other living author with whom we are acquainted, is in part a natural peculiarity of his mind, and in part arises from the urgent circumstances under which he wrote. His object was to produce an immediate effect upon the popular mind,—to stimulate his readers to immediate action,—and in consequence his productions have a business-like directness and cogency which do not belong to ordinary poetic effusions. Whittier's genius is essentially lyrical. It would be out of his power to write in a strain so purely imaginative as that of Keats "To a Grecian Urn," or other similar productions. Besides, mere devotion to the poetical art, mere exercise of the imagination for its own sake, seems inappropriate to him who considers, as he says,

> "Life all too earnest, and its time too short,
> For dreamy ease and Fancy's graceful sport."
>
> [From "To J.P."]

. . .

Like every other true lyric poet, Whittier does not lack his multitude of friendly critics, who advise him to concentrate his efforts upon some

*Reprinted from the *North American Review*, 79 (July 1854), 31–53.

32

great work, instead of dissipating his energy upon what they consider mere ephemerals,—to devote himself to some gigantic undertaking, which shall loom up like the Pyramids to tell posterity his fame. But in our opinion the author has unwittingly best consulted his genius and reputation in the course which he has adopted. His shortest productions are his happiest. There is no doubt that the writing of long poems is sanctioned by many eminent examples; but they are the least read of an author's works, and are known to most people only by certain favorite extracts. Readers in general look upon a great poem in the same light in which Leigh Hunt regarded a great mountain,—as a great impostor. The majority of the lovers of Homer and Dante and Virgil, in any given community, except schoolboys *qui amant misere*, might find accommodations in an omnibus of reasonable size. They are mistaken who measure the greatness of a poem by its length; for length is very little to be considered in estimating durability. Provided that a poem be vital in every part with true inspiration, and exhibit a perfect finish throughout, it matters very little for the permanency of its fame how many pages it covers.

. . .

The natural vehemence of Whittier's poetry has at times run into declamatory excess. This failing is discoverable principally in his earlier verses upon political and reformatory subjects, written while his judgement was still immature, and unduly influenced by his passions. Thus, upon reading the sentence of death passed on John L. Brown for assisting a female slave to escape, (which sentence was afterwards commuted), a series of stanzas were written, the first one of which makes the following insinuations against the clergy, addressing them in this style:—

> "Ho! thou who seekest late and long
>   A license from the Holy Book
> For brutal lust and Hell's red wrong,
>   Man of the pulpit, look!—
> Lift up those cold and atheist eyes,
>   This ripe fruit of thy teachings see;
> And tell us how to Heaven will rise
>   The incense of this sacrifice,—
> This blossom of the Gallows Tree!"
>   [From "The Sentence of John L. Brown."]

The poem entitled "Clerical Oppressors" was called forth by a meeting of the citizens of Charleston, which the clergy attended in a body, and has some good round invective, equally unfair, but rather more telling than that quoted above:—

"Pilate and Herod, friends!
Chief priests and rulers, as of old, combine!
Just God and holy! is that church, which lends
    Strength to the spoiler, Thine?"

. . .

A wider experience, and the more charitable judgement which generally accompanies increasing years, have had their effect in modifying
the tone of his recent verse. Without losing any of its fire, it shows in
a more chastened style and temperate spirit marks of a greater culture
and a more Christian forbearance. The exquisite sonnet, "Forgiveness,"
is an index of this change of feeling:—

"My heart was heavy, for its trust had been
    Abused, its kindness answered with foul wrong;
So, turning gloomily from my fellow-men,
    One summer Sabbath-day, I strolled among
The green mounds of the village burial-place;
    Where, pondering how all human love and hate
    Find one sad level,—and how, soon or late,
Wronged and wrong-doer, each with meekened face,
    And cold hands folded over a still heart,
Pass the green threshold of one common grave,
    Whither all footsteps tend, whence none depart,—
Awed for myself, and pitying my race,
Our common sorrow, like a mighty wave,
Swept all my pride away, and, trembling, I forgave."

A poem bearing the name of "Ichabod," provoked by the supposed
recreancy of a great statesman,[2] under circumstances which would have
once called forth all the denunciation of which the author was capable,
is an impressive example of the same kind.

. . .

The Quakerism in which Whittier was reared, and which he has
always professed, stands, as we have already said, in strange conflict
with the belligerent tone of many of his writings. We should hardly
have expected so rude and martial a strain from the quiet, drab-coated
professor of the mild tenets of his sect. Perhaps his tone is more in
accordance with the spirit of the early founders of the denominations,
than the comparatively uninteresting dulness of the modern type. Of
late years, the Quakers have lost their desire for propagandism, and have
become more accommodating and worldly-wise. But in early times,
no sect had so zealous and wide-awake champions as the Society of

Friends. George Fox, James Naylor, and even William Penn, show that their Quakerism had not wholly subdued their combative tendencies. The admirers of Whittier need not regret that he is not formed upon the more modern and respectable pattern.

We are naturally led, from the consideration of our author's Quakerism, to that strong religious fervor which is manifested in every part of his writings. So deeply rooted is it, and apparently so blended with his imaginative powers, that, in some of his productions, one can hardly tell which predominates. His religious views embrace a simple faith in the Quaker doctrine of the inward light, combined with an intense apprehension of the brotherhood of man.

. . .

The poems entitled "Follen," "Questions of Life," "My Soul and I," and others of a similar kind, are exquisite in their delicacy of thought and expression, and show a wrestling with some of the gravest and most perplexing questions that come under the consideration of meditative minds.

Whittier rarely writes without being so impressed with some strong feeling, that he cannot fail to awaken a corresponding emotion in his reader. Of this, his verses written in memory of his friends bear witness. We would refer emphatically to the "Lines to a Friend on the Death of his Sister," and to the perfect poem entitled "Gone." For the same reason, he writes with such energy, as not to give himself much concern about the customary ornaments of poetical diction. His imagery, when he introduces it, comes without an effort, as the natural accompaniment of his verse, never obtruding itself on the reader's attention, or seeming other than an essential part of the whole.

In the fine ballad of "Cassandra Southwick," (a young woman of Puritan times, who for non-conformity narrowly escaped being sold into slavery at Barbadoes,) he has happily described that transfiguration which nature seems to undergo in the eyes of one under the influence of some sudden and overpowering emotion. Immediately on leaving her prison-cell Cassandra exclaims:—

"Oh, at that hour the very earth seemed changed beneath my eye,
A holier wonder round me rose the blue walls of the sky,
A lovelier light on rock and hill, and stream and woodland lay,
And softer lapsed on sunnier sands the waters of the bay."

One peculiarity of Whittier's imagery is, that so much of it is drawn from the Bible. This book is so the common property of Christendom, that to resort to it for purposes of poetical illustration is as justifiable as to resort to the book of Nature. He shows a very great

familiarity with every part of holy writ, and an exceeding aptness in
its citation. Of a brother reformer and poet he speaks as

"Like Nehemiah, fighting as he wrought."
[From "To J.P."]

The conjunction of the clergy and laity against the Abolition agitation
he characterizes as

"Pilate and Herod friends!"

So the North complains to the South of supposed injustice and oppression:—

"What though Issachar be strong,
Ye may load his back with wrong,
Over much and over long."
[From "Texas."]

In "Margaret Smith's Journal" he says: "We also found grapes both
white and purple hanging down in clusters from the trees, over which
the vines did run, nigh upon as large as those which the Jews of old
plucked at Eschol." His graphic description will recall to every one
the picture in the old family Bible of the two Israelites staggering under
the weight of an enormous bunch of grapes. Other and perhaps better
instances might be readily selected.

The free and dexterous use of proper names is another characteristic
of our poet. With an affluence of these his extensive knowledge supplies
him, and he displays uncommon skill in weaving them harmoniously
into his verse. Even the long sesquipedalian Indian words present no
insuperable difficulties. There is something strangely impressive in the
effect of the introduction of a melodious or sonorous name, particularly
if it indicates a place of which we have no personal knowledge. The
imagination is touched in that vague and mysterious way in which it
delights, and the burden is put upon the reader of supplying the requi-
site beauty or sublimity to fill out the supposed conception of the
author. In this art Milton is the great master, and he had his originals
in the epic poets of antiquity, while Goldsmith furnishes a rather ludi-
crous instance in the well-known line,

"On Torno's cliffs or Pambamarea's side,"
[From "The Deserted Village."]

the locality of Pambamarea never having been precisely ascertained.

. . .

As a consequence of the seeming haste in which many of these poems are written, the author is betrayed into occasional inaccuracies of grammar and rhyme. Many of these, which we had observed in his earlier volumes, we are glad to see corrected in the revised collection. But some still remain. Speaking of the tendency of youth to look on the best side of everything, he says:—

> "Turning, with a power like Midas,
> All things into gold."
> [From "To - - - - with a Copy of Woolman's Journal."]

The first line is not in accordance with the idiom of the language, and even if it should be corrected by the addition of an apostrophe after Midas, it would remain clumsy. An obvious improvement would be to substitute

> "Turning with the power of Midas."

We have noticed several inadmissible rhymes,—"dawn" with "scorn," "curse" with ["]us," "war" with "saw" and "dray," &c.

Instances of anything resembling the use of other people's thoughts are seldom to be found in Whittier's poems. The following, from "The Chapel of the Hermits," is hardly a plagiarism:—

> "That all of good the Past hath had
> Remains to make our own time glad."

But Lowell's version is better:—

> "The Present moves attended
> By all of brave and excellent and fair,
> That made the old time splendid."[3]

In closing our notice of Whittier's poetry, we forbear extended remark upon the great variety of his metres, and his unusual success and facility in the management of them.

Whittier is a writer whose sentiments are thoroughly American;— not that he is always in harmony with the prevalent opinion of his countrymen, but that his productions are deeply imbued with the spirit of our institutions. They contain the genuine American doctrines of freedom and humanity, brought up to the latest and highest standard. His unmeasured sympathy for his kind has led him into a field new and entirely his own, and given him an unquestionable title to the name of an original author. It is the crowning and distinguishing glory of Wordsworth to have raised to notice the humblest objects of organic and inorganic life, and to have evolved from them latent beauties and significancies, which the many never could have discovered; and Whittier, by yielding to his own generous and ardent instincts, and following the slave, not in himself an inviting object, and with no claims upon the poet except those of a common humanity, through the various vicissitudes of his sad lot, has enlarged the domain of our sympathies and won for himself the benediction,—

> "Blessings be on him and eternal praise,
> Who gave us nobler hopes and nobler loves!"
> [From Wordsworth's "Personal Talk."]

Notes

1. A review of *Poems* (1849), *Margaret Smith's Journal* (1849), *Old Portraits and Modern Sketches* (1850), *Songs of Labor* (1850), and *Chapel of the Hermits, and Other Poems* (1853). [Ed. note.]

2. The poem is a biting retort to Daniel Webster's famous Seventh of March, 1850, speech in which he supported the Compromise and Fugitive Slave Law. [Ed. note.]

3. This extract could not be found in Lowell's *Collected Works*. [Ed. note.]

[A Review of *In War Time, and Other Poems,* 1863]

It is a curious illustration of the attraction of opposites, that, among our elder poets, the war we are waging finds its keenest expression in the Quaker Whittier. Here is, indeed, a soldier prisoner on parole in a drab coat, with no hope of exchange, but with a heart beating time to the tap of the drum. Mr. Whittier is, on the whole, the most American of our poets, and there is a fire of warlike patriotism in him that burns all the more intensely that it is smothered by his creed. But it is not as a singular antithesis of dogma and character that this peculiarity of his is interesting to us. The fact has more significance as illustrating how deep an impress the fathers of New England stamped upon the commonwealth they founded. Here is a descendant and member of the sect they chiefly persecuted, more deeply imbued with the spirit of the Puritans than even their own lineal representatives. The New-Englander is too strong for the sectarian, and the hereditary animosity softens to reverence, as the sincere man, looking back, conjures up the image of a sincerity as pure, though more stern, than his own. And yet the poetic sentiment of Whittier mislead him as far in admiration, as the pitiful snobbery of certain renegades perverts them to depreciation, of the Puritans. It is not in any sense true that these pious and earnest men brought with them to the New World the deliberate forethought of the democracy which was to develop itself from their institutions. They brought over its seed, but unconsciously, and it was the kindly nature of the soil and climate that was to give it the change to propagate and disperse itself. The same conditions have produced the same results also at the South, and nothing but slavery blocks the way to a perfect sympathy between the two sections.

Mr. Whittier is essentially a lyric poet, and the fervor of his temperament gives his pieces of that kind a remarkable force and effectiveness. Twenty years ago many of his poems were in the nature of *conciones ad populum*, vigorous stump-speeches in verse, appealing as much to

---

*Reprinted from the *North American Review*, 98 (Jan. 1864), 290–92.

the blood as the brain, and none the less convincing for that. By regular gradations ever since his tone has been softening and his range widening. As a poet he stands somewhere between Burns and Cowper, akin to the former in patriotic glow, and to the latter in intensity of religious anxiety verging sometimes on morbidness. His humanity, if it lack the humorous breadth of the one, has all the tenderness of the other. In love of outward nature he yields to neither. His delight in it is not a new sentiment or a literary tradition, but the genuine passion of a man born and bred in the country, who has not merely a visiting acquaintance with the landscape, but stands on terms of lifelong friendship with hill, stream, rock, and tree. In his descriptions he often catches the *expression* of rural scenery, a very different thing from the mere *looks*, with the trained eye of familiar intimacy. A somewhat shy and heremitical being we take him to be, and more a student of his own heart than of men. His characters, where he introduces such, are commonly abstractions, with little of the flesh and blood of real life in them, and this from want of experience rather than of sympathy; for many of his poems show him capable of friendship almost womanly in its purity and warmth. One quality which we especially value in him is the intense home-feeling which, without any conscious aim at being American, gives his poetry a flavor of the soil surprisingly refreshing. Without being narrowly provincial, he is the most indigenous of our poets. In these times, especially, his uncalculating love of country has a profound pathos in it. He does not flare the flag in our faces, but one feels the heart of a lover throbbing in his anxious verse.

Mr. Whittier, if the most fervid of our poets, is sometimes hurried away by this very quality, in itself an excellence, into being the most careless. He draws off his verse while the fermentation is yet going on, and before it has had time to compose itself and clarify into the ripe wine of expression. His rhymes are often faulty beyond the most provincial license even of Burns himself. Vigor without elegance will never achieve permanent success in poetry. We think, also, that he has too often of late suffered himself to be seduced from the true path to which his nature set up finger-posts for him at every corner, into metaphysical labyrinths whose clew he is unable to grasp. The real life of his genius smoulders into what the woodmen call a *smudge*, and gives evidence of itself in smoke instead of flame. Where he follows his truer instincts, he is often admirable in the highest sense, and never without the interest of natural thought and feeling naturally expressed.

[A Review of *Snow-Bound*. *A Winter Idyl*, 1866]

James Russell Lowell[*]

At the close of his poem Mr. Whittier utters a hope that it may recall some pleasant country memories to the overworked slaves of our great cities, and that he may deserve those thanks which are all the more grateful that they are rather divined by the receiver than directly expressed by the giver. The reviewer cannot aspire to all the merit of this confidential privacy and pleasing shyness of gratitude, but he may fairly lay claim to a part of it, inasmuch as, though obliged to speak his thanks publicly, he need not do it to the author's face. We are again indebted to Mr. Whittier, as we have so often before, for a very real and a very refined pleasure. The little volume before us has all his most characteristic merits. It is true to Nature and in local coloring, pure in sentiment, quietly deep in feeling, and full of those simple touches which show the poetic eye and the trained hand. Here is a New England interior glorified with something of that inward light which is apt to be rather warmer in the poet than the Quaker, but which, blending the qualities of both in Mr. Whittier, produces that kind of spiritual picturesqueness which gives so peculiar a charm to his verse. There is in this poem a warmth of affectionate memory and religious faith as touching as it is uncommon, and which would be altogether delightful if it did not remind us that the poet was growing old. Not that there is any other mark of senescence than the ripened sweetness of a life both publicly and privately well spent. There is fire enough, but it glows more equally and shines on sweeter scenes than in the poet's earlier verse. It is as if a brand from the camp-fire had kindled these logs on the old homestead's hearth, whose flickering benediction touches tremulously those dear heads of long ago that are now transfigured with a holier light. The father, the mother, the uncle, the schoolmaster, the uncanny guest, are all painted in warm and natural colors, with perfect truth of detail and yet with all the tenderness of memory. Of the family group the poet is the last on earth, and there is something

[*]Reprinted from the *North American Review*, 102 (April 1866), 631–32.

deeply touching in the pathetic sincerity of the affection which has outlived them all, looking back to before the parting, and forward to the assured reunion.

But aside from its poetic and personal interest, and the pleasure it must give to every one who loves pictures from the life, "Snow-Bound" has something of historical interest. It describes scenes and manners which the rapid changes of our national habits will soon have made as remote from us as if they were foreign or ancient. Already, alas! even in farm-houses, backlog and forestick are obsolescent words, and close mouthed stoves chill the spirit while they bake the flesh with their grim and undemonstrative hospitality. Already are the railroads displacing the companionable cheer of crackling walnut with the dogged self-complacency and sullen virtue of anthracite. Even where wood survives, he is too often shut in the dreary madhouse cell of an air-tight, round which one can no more fancy a social mug of flip circling than round a coffin. Let us be thankful that we can sit in Mr. Whittier's chimney-corner and believe that the blaze he has kindled for us shall still warm and cheer, when a wood fire is as faint a tradition in New as in Old England.

We have before had occasion to protest against Mr. Whittier's carelessness in accents and rhymes, as in pronouncing "ly′ceum," and joining in unhallowed matrimony such sounds as *awn* and *orn*, *ents* and *ence*. We would not have the Muse emulate the unidiomatic preciseness of a Normal schoolmistress, but we cannot help thinking that, if Mr. Whittier writes thus on principle, as we begin to suspect, he errs in forgetting that thought so refined as his can be fitly matched only with an equal refinement of expression, and loses something of its charm when cheated of it. We hope he will, at least, never mount Pega′sus or water him in Heli′con, and that he will leave Mu′seum to the more vulgar sphere and obtuser sensibilities of Barnum. Where Nature has sent genius, she has a right to expect that it shall be treated with a certain elegance of hospitality.

ARTICLES AND ESSAYS

What I Had I Gave:
Another Look at Whittier

Reading straight through the 478 crowded, double-column, small-print pages of Whittier's collected poems is an experience that I should imagine I share with very few other people today. The experience included its anticipated long stretches of boredom, but it also provided a good deal of quiet enjoyment and some moments of real excitement. On balance, it was a rewarding experience. Whittier wrote, I should say, a couple of dozen poems, several of them quite long, that are still very pleasurable to read, rewarding as poetry. Since he is today almost completely unread as a poet, perhaps we need to remind ourselves that this is more than enough to fill several of the sort of slim volumes that poets generally publish.

Whittier was of course a minor poet. He knew it and most of his more critical contemporaries knew it. (They did not catalogue his weaknesses quite as we should, but they knew it.) But *how* minor? Uniformly melodramatic, sentimental, bathetic? So poor as to be quite properly forgotten? Do James Thurber's wonderful illustrations for "Barbara Frietchie" make an adequate comment on Whittier's poetry as a whole? When Winfield Townley Scott wrote his memorable poem in praise of Whittier a decade ago, he praised chiefly the man, not the poet. "It is so much easier to forget than to have been Mr. Whittier." (Though he also wrote "It is easier to leave *Snow-Bound* and a dozen other items in or out of/The school curriculum than it is to have written them. Try it and see.") It is not that Whittier has wholly lacked admirers in the last thirty years, but that he has become almost exclusively the "bard of freedom," pronounced with no stress on "bard" and a heavy one on "freedom." Only George Arms's essay in *The Fields Were Green* significantly counters this trend. Now that it is a hundred and fifty years since Whittier's birth and sixty-five since his death, it is time to ask ourselves whether, or to what extent, Whittier survives as a *poet*.

It may prevent some misunderstandings if I get the necessary concessions out of the way first. Whittier's poetry most typically is not simply

*Reprinted from the *Essex Institute Historical Collections*, 95, No. 1 (1959), 32–40. (Copyright, 1959, by Essex Institute, Salem, Mass. 01970.)

"old-fashioned:" it is almost the exact counterpart of the kind of poetry that the modern poets have taught us to like and to think of as good. If James's idea that what is stated is not literature and what is literature is not stated is the whole truth, then most of Whittier's poetry is not literature. It states, emphatically. It aims to convey truth and to influence moral attitudes. It is relaxed, ruminative, placid, unambiguous, "thin." It is almost never dramatic even when it deals, as it so often does, with people, and irony is generally confined to the unread poems of reform. In the classroom most of the poetry is, unfortunately, useful in a way that does Whittier's memory no good: it illustrates what Eliot meant by the concept of the "dissociation of sensibility." (But so does a great deal of good poetry from other periods besides the nineteenth century.) Anthology pieces like "The Barefoot Boy" and "Barbara Frietchie" have become children's classics, but we are likely to feel that the absence in them of any sign of the critical intelligence at work is fatal.

A symptom, if not perhaps one of the causes, of what is all too evidently, from our point of view, Whittier's weakness as a poet may be seen in his own taste in poetry. He extravagantly admired, not some of the really fine poems that Longfellow wrote, but "The Psalm of Life," declaring it "worth more than all the dreams of Shelley, and Keats, and Wordsworth." He thought highly of the poetry of Lydia Maria Child, Grace Greenwood, and Alice and Phoebe Cary, who were, he thought, "richly gifted." He found in their verse the same unselfish dedication to the best causes that made *Uncle Tom's Cabin*, in his opinion, one of the noblest works of the century and that prompted his tribute to "sweet Eva" beginning, "Dry the tears for holy Eva,/With the blessed angels leave her." To say that Whittier's moral sense had a greater hand in shaping his literary judgments than his aesthetic sense is to indulge in understatement.

Nevertheless, Whittier's own self-estimate in "Proem" as an "untaught" versifier whose only claim to fame is that he put his verse, such as it was, to work in the service of Duty and offered it at Freedom's shrine, is too modest. Unless we are prepared to argue that typically contemporary taste and critical theory are the only defensible taste and theory, unless we are ready consciously to absolutize the relative, we had better admit that poetry which generally lacks distinction on the purely verbal level, as *style*, may yet have other qualities that make it memorable as poetry. Only if we can bring ourselves to grant that a lack of irony, ambiguity, and other hallmarks of the modern mind, and a fondness for plain statement, are qualities not necessarily fatal to poetry, can we attain a position from which it is possible to make even a limited claim for Whittier as a poet. If we can assume that a taste in poetry catholic enough to include the best of Whittier need not be a sign of confusion or lack of critical standards we need say no more at the moment of his failures and move on to consider what he accomplished at his best.

Whittier's contemporaries read him chiefly as a religious poet, and I think we shall have to also, if we are to continue to read him at all. He is I think one of a rather small number of religious poets in America whose work is still readable as poetry and not just as devotional exercise. The impression we are likely to get from some of the modern biographical treatments of Whittier, that his Quaker faith was a kind of side-issue, a personal foible having little to do with his dedication to progressive causes in an age of reform, could hardly be further from the truth.

One large section of the final edition of his poetry arranged by Whittier himself is labelled "Religious Poems," but most of his best poetry might very appropriately have been so labeled, and much of his best religious poetry is to be found in other sections of his book, in "Poems of Nature," for instance, and "Anti-Slavery Poems" and "Poems Subjective and Reminiscent." Paradoxically, it might be said that Whittier's poetry is most effectively religious when it is not explicitly "religious poetry," and that his poems of nature and reform are seldom memorable except when they are informed by a strongly religious feeling. The very flat songs of labor are a case in point, and the poems of nature written after the Civil War are another. Only when the objects of nature serve as "attendant angels to the house of prayer" do the nature poems generally rise much above the level of the honest and conscientious. In short, the well-known hymns like "Dear Lord and Father of Mankind" express a feeling that is almost never absent from the best poetry but seldom well expressed directly.

Whittier shared, of course—both as a devout Quaker and as a man of his time and place—the tendency of nineteenth-century Protestantism to reduce religion to a matter of feeling and action in good causes, to deny the validity of religious *thought* and create a "religion of the heart." Anti-intellectualism frequently makes the positive religious affirmations in his poetry seem sentimental. His deep piety and his detestation of "the husks of creed" often combine to produce mere emphatic exhortations to faith instead of successful communications of religious thought or experience. But when he writes not of faith as such but of what he sees as the Christian demand for justice and love, he speaks with passion, with fire, and often with a fine control. Whittier's conscience was not just sensitive, it was informed, grounded in and directed by a deep understanding of the whole Gospel that he never, despite the doubts that troubled him, ceased to hold up as the controlling image in his life. He fully anticipated the Social Gospel movement on its positive side without falling into its religious negativism. He saw formal creeds separating men and repudiated them for this and other reasons, but he felt that an untheological Biblical faith could draw men together and constituted the only unanswerable argument for reform.

Some of the finest invective poetry ever written in America resulted from his feeling of what was demanded by his faith. He was always particularly outraged by religious hypocrisy and cant, by "official piety" in consort with moral insensitiveness. He was, of course, sometimes merely provincial and sectarian in his condemnation of the churches, as when, in an early poem, he speaks of the "evil" faith of Rome, or when, more frequently, he is roused to indignation by any form of worship more "outward" than silent meditation and prayer. But he writes at his best, and his best in this area is very good, when he excoriates the "church-goers" who condone slavery and injustice, the "clerical oppressors" whose "faith" never issues in "works," or the church in whose name some of the most terrible crimes have been committed.

His authentic voice comes through to us very clearly, and without suffering by comparison with any other poet in America in the nineteenth century, in such poems as "Clerical Oppressors," "Official Piety," "The Gallows," "Lines on the Portrait of a Celebrated Publisher," "Letter: From a Missionary of the Methodist Episcopal Church South, in Kansas, to a Distinguished Politician," and "On a Prayer-book: With Its Frontispiece, Ary Scheffer's 'Christus Consolator,' Americanized by the Omission of the Black Man." The voice here is angry, even outraged, but never self-righteous or shrill or merely moralistic. Here for once Whittier is even capable of a kind of humor, as he registers the gap between word and deed and explores the characteristics of a "dead" faith. The result is a group of jeremiads that often rise to thoroughly effective satire and usually contain at least a few lines of memorable invective. When he returned to the theme in the poems written after the Civil War, it continued to inspire him to some of his best writing. Here's a sample from the Prelude to "Among the Hills:"

> Church-goers, fearful of the unseen Powers,
> But grumbling over pulpit-tax and pew-rent,
> Saving, as shrewd economists, their souls
> And winter pork with the least possible outlay
> Of salt and sanctity; in daily life
> Showing as little actual comprehension
> Of Christian charity and love and duty,
> As if the Sermon on the Mount had been
> Outdated like a last year's almanac . . . .

This, I submit, is good didactic poetry. Though it is above Whittier's average performance in its succinct wit, there is a good deal more like it. To dismiss Whittier's poems of reform as versified propaganda, as we have tended to do, is easier if we have not read them than if we have. In Whittier's best work we have an expression of the religious conscience at its purest and best. If all the reformers of the age had had Whittier's humility and his faith and vision, Hawthorne might not have been moved to satirize reformism in *The Blithedale Romance* or James in *The Bostonians*. Whittier's anti-slavery poems are not irrelevant to us because legal slavery no longer exists, nor is their relevance simply a function of the fact that the fight for justice and freedom and brotherhood is never ended. The poems themselves supply the explanation of their continuing vitality: they are not propaganda verse so much as they are visions of the great society, the city of God on earth, and denunciations of all that hinders its arrival.

Whittier was less blind to the full range and complexity of human experience, even in his poems dedicated to his great cause, than some of his modern defenders are. Over against the demands of conscience for reform, on the one hand, he felt what he called, in Hawthornesque terms, the brotherhood of guilt in "secret sin." "Guilt shapes the terror," he acknowledged, in a mood that did not often find so overt an expression but that generally qualifies the moralizing. The recognition of tragedy is seldom wholly absent for long from his best verse. At his best the optimism is not fatuous or the moralizing shallow. More than once he counselled what he once called "the lesson of endurance," that the sensitive conscience might not be blunted but be "taught by suffering."

The same Biblical faith that is ultimately responsible for keeping his poems of reform from being glib also keeps his best nature poetry from falling very often into the clichés of romantic primitivism. Whittier felt no impulse to turn and live with the animals; he did not think impulse, instinct, or whim sufficient guides. His view of nature was consistent with his view of man and man's destiny. True, he tended usually to idealize New England scenery and he had an unfailing taste for the picturesque that makes us feel how necessary the modern revolt from the picturesque to the "anti-poetic" was. But he repeatedly dissociated himself from any "cult of nature shaming man." It seems to me undeniable that his conservative Quaker faith preserved both his humanism and his sense of the urgency of the need for moral decision and commitment. Starting with the interest in and feeling for nature that was the gift of his period, he tried, with only intermittent success to be sure, to read nature as revelation, and saw, unfailingly, a vision of "our common earth a holy ground." When nature seemed most undecipherable as revelation, he turned with undiminished hope to the accomplishment of the vision.

"Sweeter than the song of birds/Is the thankful voice." Responsive to what he once called "the sacramental mystery of the woods," but with no intellectual tools to help him to interpret the sacrament except in the most general terms, he was often troubled by nature's "silence," but he never wavered in his conviction that man is "more than his abode,/The inward life than Nature's raimant more," as he says, a little awkwardly, in "Monadnock from Wachuset." Whittier's frequent withdrawals to nature were always at once means of communion with God and preparations for a return to man.

Perhaps the aspect of the thought in Whittier's poems that most dates them today is the unfailing faith in progress. When he writes of progress in the abstract, that is, of Progress, the result is usually no better than "The Psalm of Life." On this subject Whittier had no guide but what he once called the "moral steam-enginery" of his age. But these passages are easy to winnow out, and they are not a good enough reason for forgetting the rest of his work. Whittier had more Hope than we generally have in this unhopeful age, in both the strict Pauline and the Quaker sense. But though we find it difficult to respond readily to cheerful writing, we ought to recognize that Whittier is, at his best at any rate, saved from the inanities of a too easy faith by his belief that social progress and individual redemption are not unrelated and that neither is automatic or inevitable. He knew that man had to choose, and that choice was not easy or success guaranteed. His life-long devotion to "liberal" causes can only be fully understood when we realize the extent to which he was "conservative"—in the only viable sense of the term. The "eternal step of Progress" that resounds through his poetry is finally reducible to faith in God's finding willing hands to do His work. We need not share this faith to agree that it is not inane or necessarily unintelligent. As Whittier said of himself,

> He reconciled as best he could
> Old faith and fancies new.

There is a sense in which it must be said that Whittier was a poet in spite of himself, in spite of some of his most significant ideas and attitudes. With at least a part of his mind Whittier did not finally believe in poetry. His work aspires, Quaker-wise, to silence. His attitude toward poetry was as ambivalent as his attitude toward nature: could nature be trusted to lead us to God, could words be trusted to communicate? He quite evidently distrusts the symbol even while he is using it, and often explicitly undercuts it.

Fundamentally Whittier distrusted the whole symbolizing process. He wanted to see nature as sacramental and often felt that he had succeeded, but he was repeatedly disturbed by the feeling that "the hollow sky is sad with silentness." His profound distrust of the "cumberings" of form and creed in religion is parallel with and related to his distrust of the symbol in poetry. Aspiring, as he said, to the "deepest of all mysteries, silence," much of his verse *tells* us to have no confidence in the intellect or in mere forms, tells us in flat, prosaic, intellectual statements with no imaginative flesh on their abstract bones. This is one of the reasons why we should reread the anti-slavery poems today. In them Whittier's imagination was energized by moral fervor and often found the adequate symbol. On the subjects to which he responded most deeply, the strength of his feeling carried him beyond distrust of symbolization, but his ideas on the subject never wavered and were never qualified:

> The outward symbols disappear
> For him whose inward sight is clear.

Perhaps. But then I suppose we shall have no poetry, or at least none but abstractly didactic verse written in purely denotative language. Whittier could never quite rid himself of the suspicion that this would be no great loss, despite his real respect for the older poets who excelled, he felt, in ways in which he was weakest. "The world will have its idols,/ And flesh and sense their sign." Aesthetic theory and practice in Whittier's work are more obviously related to his fundamental religious convictions than they are in the work of most of his contemporaries. "Let sense be dumb, let flesh retire." It is not surprising that though it urges transcendence of the material and the formal, the bulk of his work fails to transcend univocal statement and mechanical form.

If we make all these damaging concessions, if we grant them even a partial justice, can we still honestly, and without confusion, claim that Whittier should continue to be read? Should we go on teaching him in the schools and colleges? Clearly I think the answer is *yes* or I should not be calling, as I am, for a fresh reading and re-evaluation of his poetry. There were after all two subjects on which Whittier could feel without distrusting his feelings, think without distrusting his thought, and write without distrusting his symbols—the demands of the religious conscience, and the experiences of childhood. "Snow-Bound," which is certainly his finest poem, but which has been widely enough and well enough appreciated so that it has seemed unnecessary to add any further comment of my own—"Snow-Bound" shows us what he could do with the latter subject: he could create out of it one of the most memorable poems in nineteenth century American literature. The familiar "Ichabod" or "Massachusetts to Virginia"—or, perhaps better because fresher for us, "Official Piety"—shows us what kind of poetry he could make out of moral feeling. These and others like them are distinguished works of art, for which no apology whatever is needed. Whether they are "great" poems or not is arguable, but they certainly seem to me very much alive.

Whittier's claim for himself was typical of the man, modest and just and true. "What I had I gave." I think we should decide that what he had was no major poetic talent, and the talent he had was weakened a good deal of the time by an outlook that made him distrust symbolization, but what he had was well worth the giving. Not just American life but American poetry too is richer because he lived and wrote.[1]

Note

1. The following poems seem to me to offer the best basis for a defense of Whittier's achievement as a poet. They are at any rate the ones I have had chiefly in mind in making the claim that a significant number of his poems are still rewarding to read. It seems to me that many of the least known of them are better than many of those that are most commonly anthologized. I list them in the order which Whittier gave them in his final arrangement: "Telling the Bees," "The Double-Headed Snake of Newbury," "Mabel Martin," "The Prophecy of Samuel Sewall," "Among the Hills" (the whole poem, but especially the Prelude), "The Pennsylvania Pilgrim," "The Fruit Gift," "The Old Burying-Ground," "Monadnock from Wachuset," "A Summer Pilgrimage," "Ichabod," "The Tent on the Beach," "Massachusetts to Virginia," "The Christian Slave," "Lines on the Portrait . . . ," "Official Piety," "The Haschish," "Letter: From a Missionary . . . ," "The Panorama," "On a Prayer-Book," "My Namesake," "Snow-Bound," "Laus Deo," "Trust," "Trinitas," "Our Master."

Whittier Reconsidered

Howard Mumford Jones*

No poet more cogently illustrates than Whittier does the transvaluation of values that has quietly taken place in American literary history during the last half century. When he died in 1892, there was small doubt that his was a major voice. Today it is a real question whether he is read at all except by children and students. The one-hundred-and-fiftieth anniversary of his birth finds no critic interested in him as critics are interested in Whitman, his fellow in the Quaker tradition. No literary historian is concerned to "place" Whittier in our intellectual development, and the scholars are few who work at the text of his writings, the exhumation of uncollected verse and prose, or the enrichment of his biography. The magnificent bibliography by Thomas F. Currier cannot be bettered as a piece of workmanship; it is not Mr. Currier's fault that it has the air of a mausoleum. The *Literary History of the United States* remarks with justice that *The Life and Letters of John Greenleaf Whittier* by Samuel T. Pickard, revised just fifty years ago, is still the best biography.[1]

It was not always so. The "Yard of American Poets" that used to hang in many a schoolroom included Whittier along with Lowell, Longfellow, Bryant, and Holmes. The game of Authors played by Edwardian children allotted four cards to Whittier; and my recollection is that the cards were named "Barbara Frietchie," "Snow-Bound," "Maud Muller"— and what was the fourth? The fatal capacity of the mind, noted by Holmes, when it has to remember n things, to remember $n-1$ things intervenes. Was it "Ichabod"? "The Lost Occasion"? "The Eternal Goodness"? I do not know, but the fourth item, like the other three, implied moral improvement, I am sure, in terms simpler and more direct than those in Mr. Faulkner's celebrated Nobel Prize address.

> Our fathers to their graves have gone;
> Their strife is past, their triumph won;
> But sterner trials wait the race
> Which rises in their honored place;
> A moral warfare with the crime
> And folly of an evil time.

*Reprinted from the *Essex Institute Historical Collections*, 93, No. 4 (1957), 231–46. (Copyright, 1957, by Essex Institute, Salem, Mass. 01970.)

So Whittier. Mr. Faulkner carries on his own peculiar kind of moral warfare, I do not doubt, but it is not that of "Skipper Ireson's Ride," a poem that is now just a hundred years old. The modern reader needs to be told that Skipper Ireson, for his hard heart, was tarred, feathered and carried in a cart by the women of Marblehead. One also remembers (or at least the scholar does) Whittier's handsome apology prefixed to his later printings of the poem after he had learned that his historical sources did not substantiate the story, just as one remembers the fine charity of the headnote prefixed in 1888 to "Ichabod." I wonder if any modern author is capable of this moral courtesy?

Something, it is clear, has vanished from our literary life. Christian gentlemanliness is out of key with the world of literary agents, book promotion, publishers' scouts, cocktail parties, and astringent academic quarterlies. What has vanished may be the genteel tradition. Or it may be politeness, or self-effacement, or idealism, or what you will. Anyway, it is gone, and the national life is presumably the poorer in its passing.

However one may lament the loss, lamentation does not, alas! improve either the art or the intellectual stature of this diffuse poet, now perpetually assigned to the schoolroom and the harmless introductory course in American literature. Especially have we turned our backs upon the public rhetoric of Whittier's verse; and though the Civil War annually produces its library of new books, our interest in that titanic conflict fails to revive the indignation Whittier poured into his rhymed attacks on slaveholders. Possibly the abolitionists have been so deflated by modern historians, his wrath seems hollow today, his indignation misplaced. Certainly he knew nothing of slavery from experience.

. . .

The twenty-odd volumes of verse Whittier published indicate his fatal inability to distinguish between having a poem to write and having to write a poem. The occasional verse, to which he was professionally addicted, is, for the most part, rhetoric. "The Shoemakers," for example, appears in all the college anthologies, but it is mere meter, not a meter-making argument. A poem addressed in 1851 to Kossuth, to take another example, is in the line of the anti-slavery pronouncements, sounding

the hoarse note of the bloodhound's baying,
The wolf's long howl behind the bondman's flight.

Even the rhymed address to Burns, occasioned by "receiving a sprig of heather in blossom," though full of honorable sentiments, is diffuse (it runs to 116 lines) as Burns is seldom diffuse and concludes with ten moralizing stanzas on the frailities of the author of "The Cotter's Saturday Night."

When we ask why this sort of thing interests Whittier, we confront a principal but unacknowledged difference between the uses of poetry in the nineteenth century and its uses in the twentieth. In the nineteenth century, particularly during its first fifty years, the poet fulfilled a function he has since abandoned. He wrote for the newspapers, and in writing for the newspapers he was at once, or at times, columnist, editorial writer, cartoonist, and propaganda maker. Thus it was that Coleridge rhymed for the Tory papers and Moore wrote for the Whig journals. Thus it was that Tom Hood sparkled. Moreover, the century was the period of the album and the giftbook. Explorers of the bibliographies of even highly respectable nineteenth-century bards must be puzzled by the many items first published in these ephemeral volumes or in the newspapers, but this form of publication explains in some degree the popularity of the writer. Newspaper verses were clipped by readers or republished by other members of the free and independent press, and contributions to the giftbooks turned up afterwards in all sorts of unexpected places. A specious currency was given to many names (for example, that of Felicia Hemans), including names of a more perdurable sort, and one suspects that many a poet was led to confuse poetry and journalism. One can hardly imagine a T. S. Eliot or a Wallace Stevens mistaking the art of the newspapers for the art of poetry.

Is Whittier no more than a producer of rhymed rhetoric that, however effective in its time, has lost its fire and energy? Is there no portion of his work that can still give aesthetic pleasure? If we will but remember Pater's injunction that beauty has been produced in many periods in many styles and in many forms, I think one can find even today a small but permanent portion of beauty in Whittier. That portion is not, I think, in popular and facile successes like "Maud Muller" and "Barbara Frietchie," but is rather found in three sorts of poems: those in which he writes about nature in New England; those in which (alas, too rarely!) he presents character; and those which concern—how shall I put it?—his notion of the relation of God and man.

One must distinguish between sentimentality and simplicity. Whittier, however manly in his private life, is incorrigibly given to sentimentality—far more so than is Longfellow. But there is in him likewise a vein of honest simplicity, particularly when he looks at the natural world about him, that anticipates and parallels the later effects of Robert Frost. I doubt that "The Last Walk in Autumn" is widely known, and I shall therefore quote rather more of its opening stanzas than I should otherwise do:

i

O'er the bare woods, whose outstretched hands
Plead with the leaden heavens in vain,

I see, beyond the valley lands,
    The sea's long level dim with rain.
Around me all things, stark and dumb,
    Seem praying for the snows to come,
And, for the summer bloom and greeness gone,
With winter's sunset lights and dazzling morn atone.

ii

Along the river's summer walk,
    The withered tufts of asters nod;
And trembles on its arid stalk
    The hoar plume of the golden-rod.
And on a ground of sombre fir,
    And azure-studded juniper,
The silver birch its buds of purple shows,
And scarlet berries tell where bloomed the sweet wild-rose!

iii

With mingled sound of horns and bells,
    A far-heard clang, the wild geese fly,
Storm-sent, from Arctic moors and fells,
    Like a great arrow through the sky,
Two dusky lines converged in one,
    Chasing the southward-flying sun;
While the brave snow-bird and the hardy jay
Call to them from the pines, as if to bid them stay.

. . .

It is, to be sure, descriptive poetry, it is not poetry in which the psychology of the writer interpenetrates the universe and writes a gigantic ego across the sky, but it is, somehow, "true," and we accept it with pleasure because it shows how good and simple and direct the nineteenth century at its best could be, in verses of this sort. There is more of this excellence in Whittier than readers are aware of. Alas, that it seldom concentrates in a single poem! Yet there are lovely passages scattered through the "Narrative and Legendary Poems," the "Poems of Nature" and the "Personal Poems" of the collected edition; as, "The Garrison of Cape Ann," the prelude to "Among the Hills," "Hampton Beach," "The River Path," and "In Peace" with its quiet opening:

A track of moonlight on a quiet lake,
    Whose small waves on a silver-sanded shore
    Whisper of peace.

. . .

Whittier's ballads seldom come off, but *Snow-Bound: A Winter Idyl* remains a delight to those capable of reading it. I say "capable of reading it" for the reason that Whittier, like Mendelssohn, cannot be approached as if he were Bartok or Ives. The poem overcomes its flaws. The little sketches of personalities and the reflections they occasion are admirable in their kind; and, somehow, the final address to the "Angel of the backward look," despite its obviousness, does not offend, it fits the mood of the poem, placing "these Flemish pictures of old days" in right perspective. The work *is* an idyl (we commonly overlook the sub-title) and is therefore entitled to its mood of idyllic nostalgia for something lovely and lost. The opening is properly famous; and the line-by-line heaping up of detail about the storm and about the effect of the storm upon human life has the ring of truth and simplicity. "I read the other day," writes Emerson at the opening of "Self-Reliance," some verses written by an eminent painter which were original and not conventional. The soul always hears an admonition in such lines, let the subject be what it may." The souls hears an admonition in *Snow-Bound*: an admonition not too hastily to throw away the past. In the poem the beauty of memory is made the more poignant because of the

> restless sands' incessant fall,

the importunate hours that bid

> The dreamer leave his dream midway.

We know the life of *Snow-Bound* as we know the village of Grand-Pré in *Evangeline*, the House of Seven Gables, the Old Manse, and Thoreau's cabin at Walden Pond. They are part of our inheritance, which no incessantness of teaching can wholly obliterate.

Religious verse of the first water by American writers is small in quantity, but to this small anthology of Christian utterance Whittier contributes. The instinct that breaks "The Eternal Goodness" into smaller units and uses these for singing in our Protestant churches is, I think, sound. To be sure, God is also a mighty fortress, but there are many mansions in heaven with room for gentleness and peace. In such poems Whittier is at his best unsurpassed. What writer in English can better the serenity of stanzas like these?

> And so beside the Silent Sea
> I wait the muffled oar;
> No harm from Him can come to me
> On ocean or on shore.
>
> I know not where His islands lift
> Their fronded palms in air;
> I only know I cannot drift
> Beyond His love and care.

Whittier has, I suppose, only so much of mysticism as the Quaker faith allows. His poetry expresses no dark night of the soul; yet, believing that

> God should be most where man is least,

he has his flashes of marvelous quietude:

> Where pity dwells, the peace of God is there,

he writes in one poem, and in another:

> Here let me pause, my quest forego;
> Enough for me to feel and know
> That He in whom the cause and end,
> The past and future, meet and blend,—
> Who, girt with his Immensities,
> One vast and star-hung system sees,
> Small as the clustered Pleiades,—
> Moves not alone the heavenly quires,
> But waves the spring-time's grassy spires,
> Guards not archangel feet alone,
> But deigns to guide and keep my own.

There are too many S-sounds in the antepenultimate line in this passage, but this, one of the best portions of "Questions of Life," seems to me finely fashioned. Here again, however, diffuseness is the fatal flaw. "Andrew Rykman's Prayer," which has all the potentialities of a notable religious expression, goes on and on. The present state of literary criticism is indifferent or hostile to religious poetry unless it take the form of high church Anglicanism; and so we forget that no American writer has more finely phrased a trust in the goodness of God.

In Whittier this trust is not only part of the religious tradition into which he was born, it is counterpart to the one over-riding consideration in all his verse, which is Time itself. No American writer is more conscious of transience:

> So when Time's veil shall fall asunder,
>   The soul may know
> No fearful change, nor sudden wonder,
> Nor sink the weight of mystery under,
> But with the upward rise, and with the vastness grow,

he writes in "Hampton Beach," all in the best manner of Victorian optimism, but nevertheless Time is incessant, Time takes away the loveliest and the best, Time closes the school-house by the road, and Time occasions the much quoted "moral" of "Maud Muller." There is here no originality of thought or of interpretation, but Whittier again and again avails himself of what I may call the temporal fallacy to achieve his poetical effects. Thus *Snow-Bound* is seen, as it were, down a long tunnel

of Time, its colors the clearer, its outlines the sharper by reason of the
fact that the poet is almost sixty; and Whittier most applauds those who
can look through the veil of Time and know it for illusion. Autumn
attracts him as it does Archibald MacLeish because it is the human
season; and in the Cambridge edition of the *Complete Poetical Works*
I find it of some significance that "My Triumph" succeeds *Snow-Bound,*
and opens:

> The autumn-time has come;
> On woods that dream of bloom
> And over purpling vines,
> The low sun fainter shines.
> The aster-flower is failing,
> The hazel's gold is paling;
> Yet overhead more near
> The eternal stars appear!

Contrasts of time and eternity are the commonplaces of poetry; my point
is only that in so far as he is mystic, Whittier, troubled by the "harder
task of standing still," as he somewhere says, meets the implications of
time more immediately as a part of his problem of faith and progress
than careless readers perceive. You can see him at his obvious worst on
this theme in a poem like "The New Year," but you can also find his
unexpected excellence in a poem like "The Prayer of Agassiz":

> Him, the endless, unbegun,
> The Unnamable, the One
> Light of all our Light the Source,
> Life of life, and Force of force.

But one returns, as one must always return in this category of his art,
to the marvel of stanzas like these from "Our Master":

> But warm, sweet, tender, even yet
>   A present help is He;
> And faith has still its Olivet,
>   And love its Galilee.
>
> The healing of His seamless dress
>   Is by our beds of pain;
> We touch Him in life's throng and press,
>   And we are whole again.

Not even the seventeenth century can surpass this simple perfection of
religious statement.

Note

1. Both Whitman Bennett's *Whittier: Bard of Freedom* (Chapel Hill: Univ. of North Carolina Press, 1944) and John A. Pollard's *John Greenleaf Whittier: Friend of Man* (Boston: Houghton, Mifflin, 1949) tend to concentrate upon the social reformer, not the poet as artist.

The Basis of Whittier's Critical Creed: The Beauty of the Commonplace and the Truth of Style

John B. Pickard*

Although Whittier professed to scorn "the tricks of art"[1] and evinced little interest in aesthetic theory as such, his writing does bear a definite relationship to what he thought to be the basis of beauty and art. His beliefs, contradictory and vacillating in his youth, gradually matured under the pressures of political and abolitionist work into a doctrine of the beauty of the commonplace and the truth of style, which served as the critical basis for his best genre poetry and ballads. The full extent of his search for a critical creed and its function in shaping his artistry has never been fully examined.[2] This paper will attempt to highlight the evolution of his mature critical beliefs and briefly indicate their function as a valid measure for his poetic achievement.

A brief survey of Whittier's formative years (to 1833) reveals three main influences which fashioned his critical concepts and caused the lifelong struggle between the lure of external beauty and the "inner light" of the spirit: his Quaker background, Burns' poetry, and the English and American Romantics. His Quaker training, strengthened by his Biblical knowledge, stressed the necessity of individual striving for perfection against the set rules of dogma; of putting into action the humanitarian doctrines of social equality; of trusting in the inner spirit of God; and of viewing all phases of life—cultural, political, and economic—from a spiritual aspect. Also his readings in the works of Penn, Chalkley, Barclay, and Bunyan taught him to appreciate books which were "shorn of all ornament, simple and direct . . . dead to self-gratification, careless of the world's opinion."[3] The strict ethical tone and polemical purpose of these writings strengthened his moralistic view of literature and distrust of the passions. Many of Whittier's early poems dealt with social and political issues; and already the practical aspects of Quakerism led him

*Reprinted from *Rice Institute Pamphlets*, 47, No. 3 (1960), 34–50 by permission of *Rice University Studies* and John B. Pickard.

to defend fighters for human liberty, to enlist in the temperance movement, to dedicate himself as the poet of peace, and finally to devote his
mature years to the cause of abolition.

Whittier's isolated rural background, lack of education, and his
Quaker dedication to humanitarianism strangely paralleled the career of
Robert Burns; and it seemed only fitting that his early introduction to
Burns stimulated his poetic ambitions. Whittier said about his reading
of Burns' poetry: "This was about the first poetry I had ever read . . . and
it had a lasting influence upon me. I began to make rhymes myself, . . .
In fact I lived a sort of dual life, and in a world of fancy, as well as in
the world of plain matter-of-fact about me."[4] The themes, subject matter,
and finally the style of Burns had a direct and lasting effect upon Whittier.
Burns was a poet who appealed to his own people as he wrote of their
ordinary thoughts and feelings. His themes were theirs too—the dislike
of the harsh Calvinistic church rule, belief in the innate dignity of man
and social equality, an admiration for simple rural virtue, and love of
nature. He delighted in the common things of the local community, its
social gatherings, folklore, and superstitions. These themes predominate
in Whittier's poetry and there can be no doubt that Burns first showed
him their poetic value.[5] Finally, all of Burns' better poems have an
underlying realism achieved by the use of the Scottish dialect with its
rich, native terms, by the manipulation of simple, ordinary words, and
by the presentation of ideas with visual, concrete detail. Also he draws
heavily on the familiar objects of farm and nature as source material
for his poetry. These characteristics were also to be Whittier's when he
had achieved a truth of style.

However, Burns' steadying influence was lost as Whittier succumbed
to the third influence of his immature years. The lure of the exotic, the
mysterious, and the romantic in the works of Scott and Byron captured
his imagination;[6] while their American counterparts, Mrs. Sigourney
and N. P. Willis, excited his interest in sentimental and exaggerated
love themes and led him to imitate their affected literary style.[7] Fortunately most of these attempts were only passing fads, but the presence
of so many of these poems illustrates how susceptible Whittier was to
popular taste. Their themes, lost love, desire for fame, melancholy, praise
of the imagination and poetry, are significant, for they indicate how far
Whittier had come from the strict Quaker view that art must be practical
and, above all else, moral. Again, one of the main tensions in his literary
career is put in focus, the lure of beauty in its own sphere against a
moralistic view of art. From earliest childhood Whittier had been rigor-
ously trained to believe that sensuous beauty and the fine arts drew men
away from spiritual goodness. The Quaker attitude on the arts was a
negative one, a series of do not read novels, do not attend the theatre,

do not listen to music—all of which was grounded in their belief that the human impulses of man were divorced from the Divine. Like the early Puritans they feared that a delight in sensuous beauty would replace the "inner light" of spiritual perfection. So Whittier's earliest writings stressed the beauty of "a spirit of a higher mould—A being unallied to earth"[8] and emphasized beauty's holiness and sanctity. Yet, his imitations of Byron and Willis show the conflict between his religious training and his ardent emotional spirit. In "Stanzas" he depicts the broken hearted lover who cannot escape the powerful appeal of sensuous beauty:

> For Beauty hath a charming spell,
>   Upon the human will,
> Though false the heart it veils so well,
>   It hath its homage still.[9]

Even more revealing are the pseudo-confessions of an opium eater who rhapsodizes on the witchery of his former love: "It is idle to talk of the superior attraction of intellectual beauty, when compared with mere external loveliness . . . the beauty of form and color, the grace of motion, the harmony of tone, are seen and felt and appreciated at once" (*Works*, V, 284). Of course these two pieces are imitative of the then prevailing literary modes and only imaginatively reflect the young Quaker's personal views on beauty; yet, they do highlight part of the emotional struggle that must have been taking place in his mind. Even though he avowedly condemned the sensuous, he was intrigued by it. Similarly, his early statements on art often emphasized its divine mission and the supreme creativeness of the artist. For a period he seemed to believe that the art of poetry could be an end in itself, rising above the moral issues of life and existing in its own domain of fancy and imagination.[10] He wrote glowing tributes to Chatterton, Ossian, and Byron, echoing their desire for one "high and haughty hour . . . One grasp at fleeting power."[11]

In 1833 these romantic dreams were swept completely away when Whittier joined the abolitionist party. Previous to this, along with his literary pursuits, Whittier's activities as an editor and politician had shown his sympathy for the underprivileged and he had followed Garrison's abolitionist movement with some interest.[12] But when his poetic ambitions failed to materialize, political hopes had been defeated, and ill-health plagued his body, he returned to the Haverhill farm in a receptive frame of mind for Garrison's burning letter which pleaded: "The cause is worthy of Gabriel—yea, the God of hosts places himself at its head. Whittier enlist—Your talents, zeal, influence—all are needed."[13] The appeal cut to the core of Whittier's Quaker beliefs on slavery and gave his susceptible, still uncertain, temperament a strength and directness of purpose for which it had been searching. So, the "dreamer born" left the "Muse's haunts to turn / The crank of opinion-mill" ("The Tent on the Beach") and reconciled his conflict between art and life, sense and spirit, desire and duty. "The Reformer," a poem typical of Whittier's feelings during the next twenty years, shows how far this trenchant devotion was to carry him. The reformer is the "strong one" who destroys the godless shrines of men to build a better future. Significantly, he lays waste not only the hypocritical church and the various worldly monuments to sin, but he also demolishes art with all her old treasures, ignoring the sad surprise of "young romance." Naive as the poem's belief in the efficacy of moral reform may be, it undoubtedly does reflect Whittier's attitude at this time.[14]

The beauty of ethical action and self-sacrifice became major themes in Whittier's poetry. Scores of poems praised a beauty that "Walks hand in hand with duty" (My Triumph") and repudiated the "hands that idly fold, / And lips that woo the reed's accord" ("The Summons"). He entitled his 1850 volume of poetry *Songs of Labor* rather than *Songs of Love,* since his were only simple poems of rural toil written to show "The unsung beauty hid life's common things below" ("Dedication"). He saw the aesthetic failings of the Puritan founders and, yet, excused them because "they lived a truer poetry than Homer or Virgil wrote" (*Works,* V, 363). Such a moral concept of beauty had little connection with poetic fancy and imagination, while his critical pieces put a similar emphasis on morality and especially praised those who agreed with the abolitionist position. Art in the pure sense was anathema for the militant reformer, for it "builds on sand" ("Wordsworth"). Despite these unimaginative and stifling tenets Whittier still wrote ballads and genre pieces which minimized moralistic content. But his abolitionist conscience had to justify even these and so he stated in the introduction to "Amy Wentworth" that the soft play of art, songs, and pictures have their function in soothing the reformer's "storm-stunned" mind and providing temporary relief from "the sharp strifes and sorrows of today." Art viewed as an escape from his editorial pressures and political activities was far removed from his early desire to find in it a source of pure unfading joy. After the Civil War Whittier tempered his austere denunciation of non-moralistic art and admitted that it "beguiled some heavy hours and called / Some pleasant memories up" ("The Bay of Seven Islands"), but still it seemed of secondary value and even questionable worth.

Whittier's fullest statement on the function of art in general came in *The Tent on the Beach* (1867). Here he presented his final view, a minor reconciliation between the doctrine of art for its own sake and an art which only serves moral ends. He admits that his poetry has been too moralistic and that his ethical conscience has thwarted fancy's imaginative flight; yet, when one of the speakers in the poem comments that art needs no other justification than beauty itself, Whittier responds characteristically in the person of the singer:

> Better so (to have a moral in poetry)
> Than bolder flights that know no check;
> Better to use the bit, than throw
>   The reins all loose on fancy's neck.
> The liberal range of Art should be
> The breadth of Christian liberty,
>
>   . . . .
>
> Beyond the poet's sweet dream lives
>   The eternal epic of man.

And Whittier concludes by saying that the "truth" of art, its faithfulness to the dicta of Christianity, does not need the "garnish of a lie," or that elements of beauty for their own sake are not necessary for good poetry. Confusing religion with aesthetics, Whittier's concept of the function of art remained obscured throughout his life.

Of course, Whittier's intense reform activity strengthened his devotion to literature based on Christian goodness and truth, and this conviction formed an essential part of his mature views on beauty. Once his reform interests lessened in the 1850's, his confidence in outward action and social progress changed to a reliance on inner values and individual search; and his concepts of the beautiful and its relationship to the artist deepened accordingly. The beauty of silence and peace, fundamental to his belief in the "inner light," assumed a larger and more influential role in his poetry. Perhaps the best expression of his changing views is in an essay entitled "The Beautiful." Written in 1844, the article fully indicates the transition that Whittier was making from his stringent abolitionist position to a more inclusive view of beauty. It states unequivocally that the external elements of form and shape do not constitute the beautiful, nor does a "mechanical exactness" based on classically correct rules. Rather, true beauty comes from the mind as a radiation of "holiness, of purity, of that inward grace that passeth show." The artist must understand this and discern in the "outward environment . . . a deeper and more real loveliness." Conversely, Whittier claims that ugliness or deformity occurs only when there is an absence of virtue or the presence of sin. This inner spiritual beauty transcends rules and techniques, as Whittier once remarked of John Woolman's writings: "Beauty they certainly have, but it is not that which the rules of art recognize" (*Works,* VII, 345).

Obviously this idea of beauty is intimately connected with his belief in the Quaker doctrine of the "inner light," which maintained that the indwelling of the holy spirit in each man was a personal, introspective experience, and, at times, a mystical relationship. In striving for individual perfection, no set dogma or creed is followed, only the subjective voice of the "inner light." So, when Whittier commented that "beauty, in and of itself, is good" ("To Avis Keene"), he meant something far different from Keats' similar statement. Following Emerson's organic view of art, Whittier believed that goodness, truth, and beauty were one and that the material was only a reflection of the Divine archetype. As a corollary, Whittier held that the appreciation of beauty was a personal thing which could be found anywhere and by anyone. The attraction of an external object was dependent on "an instantaneous reflection as to its history, purpose, or associations." Such a view followed the prevailing romantic belief in Alison's comments on the subjectivity of the beautiful—that the mind not only received but also created in its appreciation of the beautiful. Thus, beauty was no longer intrinsic or absolute in the Neoclassic sense, but dependent upon states of mind, resulting from associations enkindled in our imaginations by external objects. Whittier responded to this concept quite early, for in 1833 he had a fictional character explain how his physical attraction for a young lady had become blended with all the former ideas he had of "female excellency and purity and constancy" (Works, V, 284).

One other aspect of the doctrine of associations, its connection of the material and spiritual worlds, was investigated in an article, "Swedenborg" (1844). Whittier lauded the power of Swedenborg's transcendental theories in stripping bare the sense objects of the world to reveal "the types and symbols of the world of spirit." Stressing the associations that an imaginative man like Swedenborg could make between the "facts" of this world and the spiritual values of the next, Whittier also praised his realistic expression of these abstract ideas. This relation of the spiritual to the material and the importance of personal associations paralleled Emerson's 1836 doctrine of correspondence in its far-reaching effects on Whittier's artistic creed and writing. Undoubtedly it seconded in a theoretical way the practical and religious training of Quakerism and further strengthened his moral view of beauty. More importantly it led him to perceive that an accurate record of his personal experiences with their multitude of concrete impressions could reveal the implicit values hidden beneath the physical form. So, tardily, Whittier found in the ordinary things of his life—his farm background, the local Haverhill scenery, his knowledge of Quaker history, Essex county legends, boyhood memories—factual images that could be transmuted by personal associations and imaginative effort into authentic, worthwhile materials for poetry. The romance that he hoped to find in these familiar things was based on the awareness that the truth of humble experiences and simple feelings had as much wonder and beauty as his former dreams "of lands of gold and pearl, / Of loving knight and lady" ("Burns"). This theory of the beauty of the commonplace formed the cornerstone for his finest poems written in the 1850's. Now his subject matter, an old rhyme about a calloused Marblehead skipper, his birthplace in a snowstorm, a girl raking hay on a summer's day, a local tale about a Hampton witch, was based directly on the commonplace incidents of his own experience.

Associated with this final understanding of the proper material for his writing was the problem of finding the appropriate manner for expressing these feelings. From his earlier literary experiments he came to believe that style was the communication of an emotion or an idea, usually associated with some ethical or practical end, in the clearest, most direct manner. In his essay on Robert Dinsmore he praises that rural poet for calling things by their right names without any euphuisms or transcendental terms. Similarly he approves E. P. Whipple's prose, because "he wrote with conscience always at his elbow, and never sacrificed his real convictions for the sake of epigram or antithesis" (*Works*, VI, 318). Increasingly he emphasized the necessity of dressing truth in a somber guise, rather than garnishing it by ornamentation or elaborate stylistic devices. This truth of style actually meant a fidelity to personal experience, a realization of one's own powers and insights, and an attempt to present them in the clearest possible manner. Numerous critical comments stressed the intention of the author and the relationship between the emotional experiences of the man and his method of expression.[15] In theory, at least, Whittier was presenting the organic belief that form should follow function. When joined to his love of the commonplace, this truth of style enabled Whittier to see that mere surface ornamentation or tricks of rhetoric were harmful; that a writer must first be himself and then concentrate on style; that the inner emotional quality of a work rises above mere literary technique; and finally, that the subject matter must bear a direct relation to the author's own personal experience. Though this emphasis on truth often caused Whittier to overmoralize and disregard valid literary techniques, it never allowed him to equate sincerity with dullness. His best works do attempt to "throw a golden haze of poetry over the rough and thorny pathways of every-day duty" (*Works*, VI, 216) and to utilize "the extraordinary richness of language and imagery" (*Works*, VII, 287) which Whittier so admired in other writers.[16]

Practically, it is revealing to see how Whittier employed these beliefs in his own writing. He consistently uses images which have their source in the everyday experiences of farmlife, the harvest, the change of seasons, growth of crops, husking, planting, and his most effective poems abound in descriptions which are taken directly from a specific section of Essex county. The opening of "The Last Walk in Autumn" literally transcribes the scenery along the Merrimack River; while the town in "The Countess" is an accurate picture of Rocks Village, a small settlement a few miles from Whittier's house. "Snow-Bound," "Skipper

Ireson's Ride," "A Sea-Dream," and "Among the Hills" are similarly dependent on exact local description. Also his finest genre sketches rely on the careful accumulation of these realistic details. Note the series of images from the poem "In Peace":

> A track of moonlight on a quiet lake,
>   Whose small waves on a silver-sanded shore
> Whisper of peace, and with the low winds make
> Such harmonies as keep the woods awake,
> And listening all night long for their sweet sake;
>
> A green-waved slope of meadow
> . . . .
> A slumberous stretch of mountainland
> . . . .
> A vale-fringed river, winding to its rest
> . . . .
> Such are the pictures which the thought of thee,
> O   friend, awakeneth,—

These images taken from familiar Essex county scenes are expanded to connote the general theme of peace and beauty. By imaginative association Whittier links the various scenes with the feelings he had for his friend, for only that way could the hidden virtues be expressed with concrete sense appeal. Here, justifiably, external physical beauty complements and heightens the moral beauty of man's inner nature.

How successfully Whittier could apply his beliefs to poetry may be seen by an examination of "Telling the Bees." The story hinges on a local Essex county superstition that a death in the family would drive away the bees and the custom of draping the hives in black mourning colors to prevent this. The narrative itself records the delayed visit of a young man to the farmhouse of his beloved Mary. The tone of the poem is informal, almost conversational, and Whittier relates the tale as if he and the reader were rewalking the ground on which it took place. In the first lines, directly addressing this reader and insisting that he follow the scene closely, Whittier points out:

> Here is the place; right over the hill
>   Runs the path I took;
> You can see the gap in the old wall still,
>   And the stepping-stones in the shallow brook.
>
> There is the house, with the gate red-barred
>   And the poplars tall;
> And the barn's brown length, and the cattle-yard
>   And the white horns tossing above the wall.

The details are plain and unelaborated: the poplars are merely "tall" the barn just "brown," and the cattle are depicted only by "white horns." A series of "ands" connects one detail to the next in almost childlike fashion.[17] Then, as if pausing in this trip with the reader, Whittier notes that, although a year has passed, everything is still the same:

> And the same rose blows, and the same sun glows,
> And the same brook sings of a year ago.

The reiteration of the adjective "same" and the definiteness and confidence of the repeated "there is" intensify the mood of assurance as the poet recalls how carefully he had prepared for his former visit. Then excitedly, reliving that past moment, he exclaims, "I can see it all now . . . just the same"; and by repeating the description of the opening stanzas, the poet emphasizes the "sameness" of the scene. Yet, the mood shifts when the poet, coming closer to the house, almost casually notes: "Nothing changed but the hives of bees." This one small detail breaks the continuity and with increasing tension he hears the drearily singing chore girl and sees the ominous shreds of black on the hives. The warm June sun of an earlier stanza now chills like snow as the eventual discovery is foreshadowed. Still, the poet refuses to abandon his former confidence and assumes that Mary's grandfather must be dead. Suddenly, he sees the old man sitting on the porch and is now close enough to understand the song of the chore girl:

> "Stay at home, pretty bees, fly not hence!
> Mistress Mary is dead and gone!"

Whittier concludes the poem with the surprise revelation of her death and allows the reader's imagination to supply the resulting horror and shock of the loss. Only then is the reader aware of the skillful manipulation of theme, as the careful development of the attractiveness and assurance of external nature hides the inevitable destruction of human beauty and earthly love. The ironic contrast of the boy's trust and expectation with the true situation offers a psychological insight into the problem of death.[18] As a whole the poem succeeds because of the utter simplicity of its prose-like phrasing and ballad meter, and because of its firm structural unity created by the progression from assurance to fear and then surprise. The stylistic devices are few: some repetitions in the use of the adjective "same" and similar physical detail; some parallelisms, like the balance in "heave and slow," "forward and back"; some alliteration as the "s" sounds in the last stanzas; and a restatement of detail with a changed significance when the warm sun is transformed into a chilling snow and the happy song of the brook is altered into the dreary chant of death. The poem's artlessness shows Whittier's mastery of simple narration, his truth of style; while its theme employs a rural situation and local environment to emphasize an underlying problem of human existence. The beauty of the commonplace here is one of wonder and surprise that causes reflection in the reader's mind.

The best of Whittier's genre pieces and his ballads illustrate the essential truth which he had first recognized in Burns' poetry: that underneath the most commonplace objects lay beauty, rich treasures of life's tragedy and comedy. His regional works reveal the inner love of a man for the environment that moulded him, the tradition that inspired him, and the people that loved him. Acting on his belief in the beauty of the commonplace and the truth of style, Whittier worked these materials of the home and affections into artistic creations that proved the validity of his critical theories.

Notes

1. *The Complete Poetical Works of John Greenleaf Whittier*, ed. Horace E. Scudder, Cambridge Edition (Boston: Houghton, Mifflin, 1894), p. 189. All poems cited and all quotations of poetry will be from this book, unless otherwise stated.

2. The notes on Whittier in Harry Hayden Clark's *Major American Poets* (New York: American Book Co., 1936), pp. 802–16, contain the most complete account of Whittier's poetic theories and indicate a three-fold maturing in the poet from romanticism to political liberalism to "religious humanism." The best introduction to Whittier's critical approach is found in Edwin H. Cady and Harry Hayden Clark's *Whittier on Writers and Writing* (Syracuse: Syracuse Univ. Press, 1950). They note the wide variety of Whittier's critical interests and indicate his developing an "individual sort of realism" (p. 9). Frances Mary Pray, *A Study of Whittier's Appenticeship as a Poet* (Bristol, N. H.: Musgrove Printing House, 1930), pp. 1–110, has a detailed investigation of the early influences on Whittier's poetry, but goes no further than 1835. Clarence Arthur Brown in his *The Achievement of American Criticism* (New York: Ronald Press Co., 1954) places Whittier in a definite historical perspective and concludes that Whittier was not insensitive to literary technique but that "he always subordinated it to the moral and humanitarian values of art" (p. 171).

Biographers of Whittier since George Rice Carpenter's *John Greenleaf Whittier* (Boston: Houghton, Mifflin, 1903) have almost completely ignored this important aspect. The most recent biography, John A. Pollard, *John Greenleaf Whittier: Friend of Man* (Boston: Houghton, Mifflin, 1949), eliminates the poet for a detailed consideration of the humanitarian.

3. *The Works of John Greenleaf Whittier*, Standard Library Edition, 7 Vols. (Boston: Houghton, Mifflin, 1892), II, 10. Hereafter cited as *Works*.

4. Carpenter, p. 299.

5. The poem, "Burns," written in 1854, when Whittier had finally found his true métier, indicates this debt by commenting that Burns had taught him to see "through all familiar things/The romance underlying."

6. Poems like "Moll Pitcher" and "Mogg Megone" imitate the narrative type of historical romance which Scott had made so popular. In his critical works Whittier refers to Byron more than anyone else and for over ten years (1824–1834) the poetry of the unsophisticated Quaker mirrored the disillusioned, anti-social attitudes of the Byronic hero. "The Exile's Departure" expresses the *Weltschmerz* of

an outcast warrior as he leaves his country; "The Fratricide" shows the downfall of a rebel against the moral code; "Life's Pleasures" reflects the disillusionment of a young man; and "Lines," written after reading Byron's account of a tempest in the Alps, glory in the storm and grandeur of the landscape. These last three poems are found in Pray, which contains many other examples.

7. In Pray, poems like "Night," "Lyre," "Ocean," follow the loose poetical phrasing and rhetorical exaggerations of Mrs. Sigourney; while there are over a dozen poems (like "The Declaration") which attempt the sophisticated, lightly romantic tone of Willis' love poetry.

8. Pray, p. 239.

9. Pray, p. 242.

10. In a letter quoted by Carpenter, pp. 96–97, Whittier says: "I am haunted by an immedicable ambition—perhaps a very foolish desire of distinction, of applause, of fame, of what the world calls immortality."

11. Pray, p. 193.

12. In 1831 he published "To William Lloyd Garrison," praising him for his "steadfast strength of truth" and "martyr's zeal."

13. Carpenter, p. 118.

14. The fervid moralistic tone of this poem is typical of over two-thirds of Whittier's poetry written from 1833–1850. Titles like "The Slave-ships," "The Hunters of Men," "Clerical Oppressors," and "The Moral Warfare" indicate how engrossed Whittier had become in his abolitionist work.

15. See Works, VI, 201, 218–19, 221–22, 225–56; VII, 344–45.

16. Whittier's taste is far wider than one might imagine and his appreciation of different styles is more catholic. He admired four main types of writing and tried to emulate them: the poetic, sentimental school which abounded in vague, romantic descriptions, as seen in Grace Greenwood and John Neal; the dramatic, often theatrical, appeal of writers like Charles Brockden Brown and Harriet B. Stowe; the forceful, balanced style found in Milton and Burke; and the plain, simple style of Bunyan or Woolman.

17. The scene described here is an exact duplication of the path the boy Whittier often took from Job's Hill, west of the birthplace, through a break in the cemetery wall, continuing on down by the brook to his home.

18. Typically the fact that there was no moral or religious consolation attached bothered Whittier. And he wrote to Lowell about it: "I send thee a bit of rhyme which pleases me, and yet I am not quite sure about it. What I call simplicity may be only silliness. . . . But I like it and hope better things of it." Houghton, Mifflin, 1907), p. 414.
Quoted in Samuel T. Pickard's Life and Letters of John Greenleaf Whittier (Boston:

John Greenleaf Whittier

Gay Wilson Allen*

Though Whittier was born only four years after Emerson and began writing about the same time Emerson did, the versification of the two poets is from fifty years to a century apart. Indeed, Whittier's technique has more in common with that of the Colonial poets than even Freneau's. It is not so easy, however, to place it with respect to the chronological development of English poetry, since it certainly possesses none of the strait-laced, polished perfection of typically eighteenth-century English versification, nor the naturalness and freedom which we find in the 1798 *Lyrical Ballads*, though in other respects Wordsworth and Whittier do have much in common. But it is impossible to ignore Whittier's metrical practices or to dismiss his poetry as no longer important. The astounding popularity, for example, of *Snow-Bound* (on which, it is said, the poet made a profit of $10,000) shows how representative of its age Whittier's poetry was.

The circumstances under which Whittier wrote and the particular poems with which he first achieved recognition are highly significant in understanding his versification. His first published poem, *The Exile's Departure*, was printed in a small newspaper, the Newburyport *Free Press*, which also published other juvenile poems of Whittier's. This was only the beginning of the young poet's connection with newspapers, for he learned his art, such as it was, by contributing verse to what we today call "country newspapers." It is not surprising, therefore, that he should have become a journalistic poet.

We must not forget that Whittier's education was extremely meager, and part of his metrical limitations are no doubt the result of insufficient education. Miss Pray, whose thorough study of Whittier's apprenticeship as a poet makes her opinions authoritative, says, "In regard to young Whittier's early literary models we know that his main source for work of contemporary writers was the weekly newspaper. This contained scattered examples of Scott, Moore, Hemans, Byron, Willis, 'L. E. L.,' Sigourney, Brainard, Percival, and others of less importance . . . Whittier

*Reprinted from *American Prosody* New York: American Book Co., 1935 by permission of Gay Wilson Allen.

had read at least some of 'Ossian' at an early age . . . when about four-teen or fifteen, he bought a copy of Shakespeare when on a trip to Boston, . . . Burns and Dinsmore were also early poetic acquaintances. These, with the Bible, were probably about all the poetic inspiration he received until his three terms at Haverhill Academy broadened his acquaintance with literature."[1]

At Haverhill Whittier no doubt studied the English "classics," but he began his metrical experiments at an early age, and it is safe to say that his poetic style had already begun to crystallize before his knowl-edge of literature was wide enough for extensive influence. The poetry of Burns, the Bible, and the few contemporary poets mentioned by Miss Pray must not be minimized as sources of Whittier's versification, yet the journalistic influence was surely very great, both in bringing the young poet into contact with poems printed in newspapers and in pro-viding a means of presenting his own poems to the public. Of course Whittier's own native abilities directed to a large extent his choice of rhythms, measures, and stanzas, but the forms which the Quaker poet used all of his life were those which we might expect as a result of his contact with newspaper verse: namely, ballad measure, octosyllabics, and pentameter—in other words, the simplest and most conventional forms. About a third of all of Whittier's poems are four-stress, about a fourth are ballad meter, and somewhat over a tenth are iambic pen-tameter.[2]

Whether the Quaker poet adopted the style and the technique of the journalist in order to be heard, or whether he was unconsciously influenced by the newspapers to which he contributed in early life, it is difficult to say precisely, and relatively unimportant, though both ex-planations are probably true.

But it is of considerable importance to the present discussion that we have no evidence that at any time Whittier groped for a technique to express the poetry he felt and thought. "It is doubtful," said the late Professor Cairns, "that he ever fully appreciated the value of form in poetry."[3] He lived until 1892, writing almost to the very end, but Emer-son, Poe, Whitman, Tennyson (who was born a year later and died the same year as Whittier), and other poets of his lifetime had hardly the slightest evident influence on his poetic technique.

Though Whittier did write some literary criticism, there is scarcely a word on prosody. About as near as he ever came to expressing a theory on verse technique is the remark he made to Lucy Hooper that a long poem "unless consecrated to the sacred interests of religion and humanity would be a criminal waste of life."[4] Yet this really does not even imply a theory of prosody, though it may indicate preferences. About the *Psalm of Life,* which he had just read in the *Knickerbocker,* he says: "It is seldom that we find an article of poetry so full of excellent philosophy and *common sense* as the following. We know not who the author may be, but he or she is no common man or woman. These nine simple verses are worth more than all the dreams of Shelley, and Keats, and Wordsworth. They are alive and vigorous with the spirit of the day in which we live—the moral steam enginery of an age of action."[5]

This emphasis on "the spirit of the day in which we live" is an expression of that typical American idealism of the times, which we find in Emerson's *American Scholar* (and in the national aspect of his theory of poetry), as well as in Walt Whitman's whole poetic theory; but the "moral steam" is typical of no one, not even Longfellow, so much as Whittier himself. And it indicates, if not an antagonism, at least an obtuseness toward artistic form and technique. Emerson can theorize about natural ruggedness and Walt Whitman can "chant his barbaric yawp over the roofs of the world," but Whittier can write as "rugged" or as "barbaric" as either and apparently never give the question much thought one way or the other, notwithstanding the fact that he occasionally remembers to justify himself by expressing a preference for the heart rather than the head:

> To paint, forgetful of the tricks of art,
>   With pencil dipped alone in colors of the heart.
> *In Peace*

Of course Whittier did write to the editor of *The Atlantic Monthly* regarding *Snow-Bound:* "I hope I have corrected a little of the bad grammar and rhythmical blunders which have so long annoyed Harvard graduates." Some of the grammatical changes were most urgently necessary, but the final versification of the poem is not greatly different from many other poems which do not seem to have been revised.

Whittier's indifference to prosody, however, does not make his versification uninteresting to examine; and though we have emphasized his reversion to older forms and techniques rather than the progressiveness of his metrical practices, there are, nevertheless, some aspects of his style and diction which point to the future rather than the past. Kreymborg, for instance, finds Whittier's conversational tones of Yankee speech "anticipating the poetic methods of Robert Frost."[6] And if this is true, then certainly Whittier has an important place in the historical development of American versification.

. . .

Whittier's rhythms are almost never spontaneously lyrical, overflowing the bounds of rules because the poet feels more emotion than he can express by "the tricks of art." His prodigious output and his journalistic style suggest that he composed easily, but his rhythms impress us as being simple and his cadences few and awkward because his own poetic abilities were meager. This deduction is borne out by the poet's inability to write good iambic pentameter, the failure being greatest in blank verse. The octosyllabic line and the simple ballad measure are the only metrical forms that Whittier could use with anything like repeated success. Even within these restricted rhythms, the phrase and the half-line appear to have been his rhythmical units. Whether or not he really composed by half-lines is immaterial; the final effect is what we might expect if he had. It is obvious, therefore, why he never wrote a sonnet, or any poem in a form that demanded perfect control over technique.

Most critics deride Whittier for his inferior rimes, a subject to which too much importance is usually attached. If bad rimes do not prevent John Milton's poetry from attaining immortal grandeur, then, we might say, they are not worth discussing. But Milton's versification is so superb in almost every other respect that it is an impertinence to criticize his rimes. Whittier's prosodic violin has too few strings anyway, and his bad rimes certainly do not help, even if they do not hinder a great deal. However, they are probably fewer than most of his adverse critics realize.

Some of the offending rimes are simply due to dialect pronunciation, as in "foot"—"root," possibly in "wrongs"—"tongues" and "mows"—"cows," and certainly in that famous couplet from *Maud Muller:*

> For of all sad words of tongue or pen,
> The saddest are these: "It might have been!"

In *St. John,* "Estienne" is three times rimed with "again" and once with "seen." Either way may be questionable, but certainly both are not right.

A more serious fault is bad grammar. In *Knight of St. John,* we find, "Closed o'er my steed and I." Despite Whittier's assurance to the editor of *The Atlantic Monthly* that he had corrected *Snow-Bound* to please Harvard graduates, there is an awkward shift of tense in the second paragraph. And the past tense is used in every other clause in the passage except in one line: "The cattle *shake* their walnut bows."

This same poem contains other awkward and puzzling passages, such as:

> The bridle-post an old man sat
> With loose-flung coat and high cocked hat;

wherein the adverb *like* was apparently omitted to preserve the count of eight syllables. Again we find in the same poem:

> Our uncle, innocent of books,
> Was rich in lore of fields and brooks,
> The ancient teachers never dumb
> Of Nature's unhoused lyceum.

But while we know that "ancient teachers" must be in apposition to "fields and brooks" and not "uncle," the passage is none the less awkward. (We can shrug our shoulders over "dumb"—"lyceum.")

A characteristic of Whittier's style which has not so far been mentioned is his wealth of biblical allusions and paraphrases. Allusions are not ordinarily a trait of versification, yet Whittier's poems contain so many that they color his style, and raise an interesting question regarding his rhythms. Why, since Whittier was so steeped in biblical phraseology, was he not influenced by the cadences of the King James Version? We find them in Walt Whitman, who used much fewer allusions, but not in Whittier's strained inversions and monotonous octosyllabic couplets. The answer is obvious: Whittier did not have the ear to catch the marvelous music of the biblical cadences. He was a reporter of rustic life, a newspaper versifier, and a ballad singer of some ability. But despite his heavy-fingered rhythms, Whittier's poetic diction is idiomatic, with a Yankee resonance that may well remind Kreymborg of our contemporary Yankee, Frost. *Snow-Bound* even contains three images prophetic of Emily Dickinson, far-fetched as that comparison may seem!

> The shrieking of the mindless wind,
> The moaning tree-boughs swaying blind,
> And on the glass the unmeaning beat
> Of ghostly finger-tips of sleet.

. . .

Notes

1. Frances Mary Pray, *A Study of Whittier's Apprenticeship as a Poet* (Bristol, N. H.: Musgrove Printing House, 1930), pp. 107–08.
2. This estimate does not include the juvenile poems printed by Miss Pray, but the fractions would probably be about the same even if these poems were counted.
3. William B. Cairns, *History of American Literature* (New York: Oxford Univ. Press, 1912), p. 263.
4. Bliss Perry, *Whittier, A Sketch of His Life* (Boston: Houghton, Mifflin, 1897), p. 12.
5. Perry, p. 13.
6. Alfred Kreymborg, "A Rustic Quaker Goes to War," in his *Our Singing Strength* (New York: Coward-McCann, Inc., 1929), p. 89.

"The Light That Is Light Indeed"

Edward Wagenknecht*

"I am a Quaker," said Whittier, "because my family before me—those whom I loved—were Quakers." But he was no sectarian, and he admitted that Friends' ways would not satisfy all temperaments. He was patient with Elizabeth Lloyd when she left the Society, and in *Margaret Smith's Journal* he allowed his heroine to state her decision against Friends quite without rancor:

> My Uncle Rawson need not fear my joining with them: for, although I judge them to be a worthy and pious people, I like not their manner of worship, and their great gravity and soberness so little accord with my natural temper and spirits.

For Whittier himself, however, no other religious affiliation was conceivable. In "The Pennsylvania Pilgrim," "The Meeting," "First-Day Thoughts," and elsewhere, he tried to describe what Quaker worship means.

> "So sometimes comes to soul and sense
> The feeling which is evidence
> That very near about us lies
> The realm of spiritual mysteries.
> The sphere of the supernal powers
> Impinges on this world of ours.
> The low and dark horizon shifts;
> The breath of a diviner air
> Blows down the answer of a prayer:
> That all our sorrow, pain, and doubt
> A great compassion clasps about,
> And law and goodness, love and force,
> Are wedded fast beyond divorce."
>
> [From "The Meeting."]

When Lucy Larcom joined Trinity Church, he said, "Well, if I was

*From *John Greenleaf Whittier: A Portrait in Paradox* by Edward Wagenknecht. Copyright © 1967 by Edward Wagenknecht. Reprinted by permission of Oxford University Press, Inc.

going to join any church myself, I would join Phillips Brooks's church." But he added, "I am mighty glad I haven't got to join any church."

The point has already been made elsewhere that Whittier was an old-fashioned Quaker with no sympathy for the evangelical tendencies that came into the Society with Joseph Gurney and others. He wanted no music in meeting, and he did not care much for speaking either. What he wanted was "to get into the silence," which, in view of his own statement that meditation was very difficult for him,[1] may seem somewhat surprising. He criticized Friends for their slowness to take a stand, their "narrowness and coldness and inactivity, the overestimate of external observances, the neglect of our own proper work while acting as a conscience-keeper for others." He complained of "uncouthness of apparel" and of "nasal *tone* and conventicle cant." He lamented their neglect of education and scholarship and thought their "plain speaking" sometimes deteriorated into rude speaking. He did not allow Bunyan's dislike of the "vile and abominable things fomented by the Quakers" to prejudice him against Bunyan, and though he was indignant over Macaulay's charges against William Penn, he realized that no reply could serve unless based on a scholarship equal to Macaulay's own. "The truth is what we want. If the character of William Penn will not abide the test of investigation, let it fall."[2] Though he tends to play down Quaker extremism and fanaticism in colonial days, he does not wholly deny it, and the picture of Margaret Brewster in the poem "In the 'Old South'" is considerably less favorable than the one in *Margaret Smith's Journal*.

Whittier's Quakerism was bred in the bone; he could not tear himself up by the roots, and he could no more have avoided being a Quaker than Gandhi could have prevented himself from being a Hindu or Martin Luther King, a Negro. But he never made a fetter of his Quakerism; within the bounds imposed upon him by his nature and his background, he was free. When he was in the legislature he would not take an oath or wear crape on his arm for a fellow member who had died; he refused to attend Angelina Grimké's wedding (though he sent greetings) because she was marrying "out of society"; he thought it too ostentatious to permit a silver cake-basket to be used in his house though it had been sent to him as a gift, and he clung to the Quaker "thee" even in his intercourse with non-Friends. But these were matters of sentiment rather than principle; as he once expressed it to Mary Claflin with reference to the last point named: "It has been the manner of speech of my people for two hundred years; it was my mother's language, and it is good enough for me; I shall not change my grammar." But where principle was concerned, he followed his own Inner Light, regardless of whether or not it coincided with that of his fellow Quakers, and this is just what, as a good Friend, he ought to have done. Some Quakers disapproved even of *Uncle Tom's Cabin* because it was a work of fiction, but this did not keep Whittier either from writing *Margaret Smith's Journal* or devouring other writers' novels by the bushel-basketful. At the Whittier centenary in 1907 a Quaker writer observed:

> Glad as we are now to recognize his place among us, we should not forget that, especially during his more strenuous years, he was rarely regarded by our forefathers with complacency. He was radical and uncompromising in his religious as well as in his political attitude, and he expressed himself in ways which gave occasion for much heart-burning to the elders of his Church. The only orthodoxy to which he could subscribe was that of the Master who lived the life of love in the presence of God.

Though Quakerism has no formal creed, Whitier's own categorical statement of his religious beliefs is sufficient to establish his fundamental Christian orthodoxy:

> God is One; just, holy, merciful, eternal, and almighty Creator, Father of all things; Christ, the same eternal One, manifested in our Humanity, and in Time; and the Holy Spirit, the same Christ, manifested within us, the Divine Teacher, the Living Word, the Light that lighteth every man that cometh into the world.

Though he often found the Hicksite or Unitarian Friends more in sympathy with his anti-slavery ideas than his more orthodox brethren there is no justification for the attempt which has sometimes been made to represent him as Unitarian in his own religious views. He honored William Ellery Channing deeply but the prefatory note to his poetic tribute carefully disclaims sympathy with his "peculiar religious opinions." He sympathized with the anti-Calvinist bias of the Unitarians, and he defended them against those who sought to exclude them from the Christian fellowship, but that was all.[3]

Chauncey J. Hawkins lists the following terms applied by Whittier to Christ: Christ of God; The Holy One; Suffering Son of God; The Lowly and Just; Humanity Clothed in the Brightness of God; Loved of the Father; Christ the Rock of Ages; Elder Brother; the World's Overcomer; Immortal Love; Light Divine; and Healer. Though he would have been—and was—horrified by the jaunty intimacy with Christ which some Evangelicals assume, his religion was Christocentric if any man's ever was.

> "So, to the calmly gathered thought
> The innermost of truth is taught,
> The mystery dimly understood,
> That love of God is love of good,
> And, chiefly, its divinest trace
> In Him of Nazareth's holy face."
> [From "The Meeting."]

And, at greater length, in one of his most famous devotional passages:

> But warm, sweet, tender, even yet
>   A present help is He;
> And faith has still its Olivet,
>   And love its Galilee.
>
> The healing of His seamless dress
>   Is by our beds of pain;
> We touch Him in life's throng and press,
>   And we are whole again.
>
> Through Him the first fond prayers are said
>   Our lips of childhood frame,
> The last low whispers of our dead
>   Are burdened with His name.
>   [From "Our Master."]

He had always believed (as Browning teaches in "Saul") that the creature cannot surpass the Creator, that God reveals Himself supremely in human life, and that the best in humanity is a key to the character of God, and it has always been the heart of Christian belief that in Christ God made the supreme revelation of Himself in terms which human beings could understand. After reading Gail Hamilton's book, *What Think Ye of Christ?* Whittier wrote the author:

> My own mind had, from the same evidence which thee ad-
> duce, become convinced of the *Divinity* of Christ; but I cannot
> look upon him as other than a man like ourselves, through
> whom the Divine was made miraculously manifest. Jesus of
> Nazareth was a man, the *Christ* was a God—a new revelation
> of the Eternal in Time. Thy book seems to me written with
> wonderful clearness and ability, and will command the respect
> and attention of the best thinkers.

For all his love for Jesus, Whittier did not *confine* the Christ-manifestation to him, though it is clear that he found there its supreme expression. He liked Alexander V. G. Allen's book *The Continuity of Christian Thought* (1884) for "its resuscitation of the doctrine of the Divine Immanence as taught by the Greek Church in the early Christian centuries." Harking back to Justin and Clement of Alexandria, he believed in an Eternal Christ, immanent in every race and clime, the manifestation of a God who has never left Himself without witnesses, the Light that lighteth every man coming into the world, and he reminds us that William Penn thought Socrates as good a Christian as Richard Baxter. Consequently he had no sympathy with religious exclusivism in any form, and nothing could have been more foreign to his spirit than to attempt to set bounds to the Father's redemptive love.

> All souls that struggle and aspire,
>   All hearts of prayer by Thee are lit;
> And, dim or clear, Thy tongues of fire
> On dusky tribes and twilight centuries sit.
>   [From "The Shadow and the Light."]

Theories of the Atonement did not greatly concern Whittier, for he had never believed that God was estranged from men. "Man turns from God, not God from him," and the barrier that must be surmounted if harmony is to be re-established is in the heart of man; there is nothing in the nature of God that needs to be propitiated.

> . . . to be saved is only this,—
> Salvation from our selfishness,
> From more than elemental fire,
> The soul's unsanctified desire,
> From sin itself, and not the pain
> That warns us of its chafing chain.
>   [From "The Meeting."]

Obviously, such salvation cannot be achieved by believing something in the sense of yielding intellectual assent to it, and neither can it be lost by intellectual error. The most orthodox believer may be damned if he lacks charity, and the most blatant heretic may find union with Christ in the spirit of love. In prose and verse alike, Whittier says many harsh things of creeds, speaking of those who rest "in bondage to the letter still" and even of the salvation achieved "in spite of all the lies of creeds."

> From the death of the old the new proceeds,
> And the life of truth from the rot of creeds.
>   [From "The Preacher."]

And again:

> Hatred of cant and doubt of human creeds
> May well be felt; the unpardonable sin
> Is to deny the word of God within![4]

But, as Rufus Jones points out, none of this indicates any "weakness of faith" or "blurring of truth" in the poet's mind. "It only meant that he looked upon religious truth, as all mystics do, primarily as personal experience and not as dogma, and as therefore being too rich, complex, and many-sided to be forced into inelastic phrases." Actually, he did not have much interest in theology, formal theology at any rate; he shows this very clearly in his essay on Richard Baxter. He loved those persons whose lives showed their kinship with the spirit of love and whose faith expressed itself in works of charity and love. As he himself puts it:

Of course I object to creeds which virtually compel people to profess to believe them, when they really do not. In speaking of religious matters I have ventured only to speak of my own experience and conscientious belief. . . . Some of the worst forms of blasphemy are embodied in creeds which good men try to persuade themselves that they believe in.

Whittier believed in prayer as a necessity of our human nature: "we cannot live without it: and that we do pray is itself evidence that Our Father is near us." But it seemed to him presumptuous for any man to believe that he had such control over the Divine Will as to be sure that he would get everything he prayed for, and he once modestly expressed doubt that his own prayers accomplished much.

He was in line with the traditional Quaker position in regarding the Bible as "*a* rule, not *the* rule of faith and practice." Of "The Pennsylvania Pilgrim" he records that

> Within himself he found the law of right,
> He walked by faith and not the letter's light,
> And read his Bible by the Inward Light.

Not so interpreted, it became a stumbling-block and was used to justify monstrous established evils like war and slavery. "We can do without Bible or church," he says: "we cannot do without God." It is not surprising, then, that he scornfully rejected the prooftext method upon which Fundamentalists have always relied nor that such of his religious poems as he devoted to Biblical paraphrase should be bad while those which rest upon his own first-hand religious experience are good. If the Bible sanctions evil, then the Bible itself must be rejected; the only alternative would be to deny God's witness in the worshipper's own heart, close the book of revelation, and make a vital religious life thereafter impossible.

> If the light given *immediately* by the Holy Spirit is *dim* [so Whittier once wrote Lyman Abbott], what must that be which comes to us through the medium of human writers in an obsolete tongue? Is the bible more and better than the Spirit which inspired it? Shall the stream deny the fountain?

Whittier himself was steeped in the Bible, but his Bible references, though numerous, are not pietistic. Indeed, he draws upon the Bible for inspiration and illustration much as he draws upon other books. But when he seems to denigrate it, it is only because he will not allow even the Bible to replace God.

> He went to it [writes Rufus Jones], he lived upon it, he loved it, because it found him and searched his heart and spoke to his condition and revealed life to him and made him confident that in all ages God, who was speaking here, spoke His thoughts, and made known His will in the shekinah within men's souls.

Because Whittier's religious assurance rested finally upon the witness within himself and not upon any material witness in the world outside, he escaped the whole dismal (and terribly misnamed) "conflict between religion and science" which was such a live issue in his time. "We must never be afraid of truth; truth can never contradict itself." He was aware that something was going on both in natural science and in the application of scholarly or scientific principles to the study of the Bible. He could call Mrs. Humphry Ward's novel, *Robert Elsmere*, which deals with a clergyman's departure from Christian orthodoxy through the Higher Criticism, "unsettling" and tell Celia Thaxter that "to think of one's venerable ancestor, like Coleridge's devil clad in

> breeches of blue
> With a hole behind where his tail came through!

isn't agreeable at all." But he was never seriously troubled.

These and other controversial matters are bravely faced and clearly considered in "Our Master," but the lyricism of the poem so outweighs its controversial quality that the latter is often missed.

> We may not climb the heavenly steeps
>   To bring the Lord Christ down:
> In vain we search the lowest deeps,
>   For Him no depths can drown.
>
> Not holy bread, nor blood of grape,
>   The lineaments restore
> Of Him we know in outward shape
>   And in the flesh no more.

Here is the Quaker rejection of the sacraments, and specifically of the Eucharist, as an outward observance, along with the doctrine of transubstantiation or any other doctrine which may replace it, and, by implication, of the whole sacramental conception of religion. The days of Christ's flesh are past and cannot be restored. Now He can only be known spiritually, and to identify Him with anything material is to degrade Him.

> He cometh not a king to reign;
>   The world's long hope is dim;
> The weary centuries watch in vain
>   The clouds of heaven for Him.

The Jews are still waiting for the Messiah to come; Christians are waiting for Christ to come again. Both will be disappointed. Whittier here voices an out-and-out rejection, again on the ground of unspirituality, of millenarian belief or the doctrine of the Second Advent, about which many people were seriously disturbed in his time, partly because

of the activities of the notorious William Miller and his "Millerite" followers, who not only preached the Second Advent, but actually set
dates for it.[5]

> The letter fails, the systems fall,
>   And every symbol wanes;
> The Spirit over-brooding all
>   Eternal Love remains.
>
> And not for signs in heaven above
>   Or earth below they look,
> Who know with John his smile of love,
>   With Peter his rebuke.

The "signs" are the circumstances which seem to indicate the immi-
nence of the Second Advent; the "systems" are creeds and ecclesiastical
organizations; the "symbols" are whatever means the churches may have
used as a means of expressing religious truth. But what can the "letter"
be except the Bible itself, toward which the Higher Criticism was
forcing believers to take up a fresh attitude?

> In joy of inward peace, or sense
>   Of sorrow over sin,
> He is His own best evidence,
>   His witness is within.
>
> No fable old, nor mythic lore,
>   Nor dream of bards and seers,
> No dead fact stranded on the shore
>   Of the oblivious years:—

(nothing, in other words, that depends upon historical evidence, or is
recorded in the Bible or any other book)

> But warm, sweet, tender, even yet
>   A present help is He;
> And faith has still its Olivet,
>   And love its Galilee.

Here is the heart of the Quaker—as of all mystical conceptions—of
religion, not as belief but as experience. The final reliance is not upon
what any book records or any church teaches, but upon what the believer has felt within himself. Sources external to himself have not given
him his faith, and therefore they cannot take it away from him. To quote
from Rufus Jones again, but now in a wholly different connection:

> The most the mystic can say in the last resort is that something
> in the very structure of the soul seems to be linked up with
> that higher world with which he feels himself in contact. He is
> committed to the faith that we can trust this highest verdict

of the soul as surely as one can trust the testimony of mathematics or of beauty. It feels to him like the surest and safest cosmic investment. But to the non-beholders he can only cry in the wilderness: "I have seen and here are my tokens."[6]

Whittier is quite in harmony with all this when he writes in "Miriam":

> Why mourn above some hopeless flaw
> In the stone tables of the law,
> When scripture every day afresh
> Is traced on tablets of the flesh?

He spells it out in prose also:

. . . Christianity is not simply historical and traditional, but present and permanent, with its roots in the infinite past and its branches in the infinite future, the eternal spring and growth of Divine love; not the dying echo of words uttered centuries ago, never to be repeated, but God's good tidings spoken afresh in every soul,—the perennial fountain and unstinted outflow of wisdom and goodness, forever old and forever new.

They fail to read clearly the signs of the times who do not see that the hour is coming when, under the searching eye of philosophy and the terrible analysis of science, the letter and the outward evidence will not altogether avail us; when the surest dependence must be upon the Light of Christ within, disclosing the law and the prophets in our own souls, and confirming the truth of outward Scripture by inward experience. . . .

And in 1884 he wrote President Thomas Chase, of Haverford College:

It was Thomas Story, a minister of the Society of Friends, and member of Penn's Council of State, who, while on a religious visit to England, wrote to James Logan that he had read on the stratified rocks of Scarborough, as from the finger of God, proofs of the immeasurable age of our planet, and that the "days" of the letter of Scripture could only mean vast spaces of time.

May Haverford emulate the example of these brave but reverent men, who, in investigating nature, never lost sight of the Divine Ideal, and who, to use the words of Fénelon, "Silenced themselves to hear in the stillness of their souls the inexpressible voice of Christ." Holding fast the mighty truth of the Divine Immanence, the Inward Light and Word, a Quaker college can have no occasion to renew the disastrous quarrel of religion and science. Against the sublime faith which shall yet dominate the world, skepticism has no power.

No possible investigation of natural facts; no searching criticism of letter and tradition can disturb it, for it has its witness in all human hearts.

. . .

Notes

1. He wrote Harriet Pitman, Jan. 24, 1885: "The lack of concentration of thought, which thee complain of, is the result of nervous debility. I have for years suffered from it: and it is only by a painful effort that I can hold my thought steadily before me. But, after all I think, it may be quite as well. To have *fixed* ideas is insanity: and it is safest to let the mind wander a little at its own sweet will. Some one has said that 'thinking is an idle waste of thought.'"

2. See the *Bulletin of the Friends' Historical Association,* 37 (1948), 23–35.

3. See George W. Cutter, "Whittier," *Unitarian,* 6 (1891), 526–28, which reports a conversation with Whittier, and Edward D. Snyder, "Whittier and the Unitarians," *Bulletin of the Friends' Historical Association,* 49 (1960), 111–16. Miss Sparhawk says Whittier told her he had asked Emerson whether he did not believe that Christ was divine and Emerson had said yes. "If thee does," said Whittier, "thee ought to confess it in thy writings." See also Mary B. Clafin, *Personal Recollections of John Greenleaf Whittier* (New York: Thomas Y. Crowell & Co., 1893), pp. 26–27.

4. From "The Word." See also "The Bridal of Pennacook," "The Chapel of the Hermits," "The Book," "Requirement," and the Prelude to "Among the Hills."

5. "The New Year" (1839) is the only poem of Whittier's in which I can find even a suggestion that he ever believed in the Second Advent, and this reference is too vague to build upon. Generally he treats it as a species of madness: see the papers "Fanaticism," "The World's End," and "James Nayler." In the last named, seventeenth-century millenarians are considered. It should be remembered that millenarian beliefs were a very important element in the eccentricity of Harriet Livermore, the "not unfeared, half-welcome guest" of *Snow-Bound;* see Samuel T. Pickard, *John Greenleaf Whittier,* I, 35–36, and *Whittier-Land* (Boston: Houghton, Mifflin, 1904), p. 39.

6. *New Eyes for Invisibles* (New York: Macmillan, 1943).

Whittier the Religious Man

Frederick M. Meek°

Rufus Jones has said that John Greenleaf Whittier was the finest expression of Quaker beliefs and principles in American life and English life between the years 1830 and 1880. What Jones was really saying is that Whittier was the outstanding Quaker in the nineteenth-century English-speaking world. If we would understand John Greenleaf Whittier the man, and if we would grasp the measure of his achievements and influence, and understand his motivating direction in the fields of human social concern that absorbed the first fifty-odd years of his life, and understand his personal victory over his own handicapping adversities, it is necessary that we come to an awareness of the fact that the roots of his life were deeply and definitely religious.

The theologians have never openly acknowledged, nor have they really been concerned with, the significance of Whittier's poetry in transmitting important religious ideas and experiences to the common people. But he made this contribution to American religious life in a way that was far more creative and lasting than was the work of many an eminent theologian directed to the same end. In his poetry Whittier frequently expressed religious ideas that were on the frontier of the religious thinking in his day, and he helped to break the hold of the rigid, outmoded New England theology upon the religious life of this part of the United States.

I have a particular personal interest at this point, because one of my predecessors, the Scotch immigrant, George A. Gordon, one of the most influential religious figures in nineteenth-century American life, was a devoted admirer of John Greenleaf Whittier. This minister of Old South Church and the Quaker poet had much in common in their thought and in their outreach. And when toward the latter part of his life, George A. Gordon gave three addresses on "What is Christianity?," in the third address he chose to speak of an outstanding Christian person as an example of what he meant. And of all the people available to him from whom to choose his prime example, he chose John Greenleaf Whittier.

°Reprinted from the *Emerson Society Quarterly*, 50, (1968), 86–92 by permission of Kenneth Walter Cameron.

Evidence is offered by Rufus Jones that Whittier was profoundly influenced by Horace Bushnell of Hartford, that creative figure in New England religious life in the period from 1830–1865. Bushnell believed profoundly in Christian nurture and in the goodness that is innate in the human person coming from the hand of God. There are, as Rufus Jones indicates, attention-compelling parallels between Whittier's poetry and Bushnell's revolutionary religious writing.

In his earlier days the fires of personal ambition burned fiercely within Whittier, and he desired public recognition for himself and his work, but that ambition was harnessed and sublimated for the cause of anti-slavery, for the well-being of his fellow men, and for the God whom he served, and the by-product was a later fulfillment of his ambition for fame. In the 1840's, however, he came to a distinct and decisive religious crisis. The background of his Quaker home life had always been profoundly religious, particularly as provided by his mother and his aunt. Always he had attended the Quaker Meetings; a succession of leading Quakers had been visitors in their home. The seed had been planted in the boy's life, and after lying fallow in his late teens and twenties, it was to begin to find its fruition when he was in his thirties. I have not read the correspondence which seems to indicate that Whittier "had a distinct religious awakening and a deepening of his spiritual life at Newport in 1840." But Rufus Jones indicates that after having read the correspondence, it is his judgment that there was such an awakening.

John A. Pollard in his biography of Whittier gives evidence, taken from Whittier's writings, of this religious change in Whittier's life during the 1840's. In 1840 Whittier wrote, "I feel that there are too many things of the world between me and the realization of a quiet communion with the pure and Holy Spirit." In a published letter in the *National Era* in 1847, he said, "I am constrained to believe, with him (Milton), that that truth which alone can cure the ills of humanity is 'bred up between two grave and holy nurses, the doctrine and the practice of the Gospel of Christ.' "

In 1848 in the *National Era* there appeared a poem, "The Wish of Today," in which he expressed the desire for "a will resign'd, O Father, to Thine Own." It would seem that in that poem he had come at last to a decision, an all-important decision, the results of which were with him for the rest of his life. The humility and the far reaches of that decision are set out in these lines:

"And now my spirit sighs for home,
And longs for light whereby to see,
And like a weary child would come,
O Father, unto Thee."

For Whittier there had been a turn in the road, and thereafter he tried first to do what he believed was God's Will. His assurance of God and His leading came not in institutions and churches and phrases and creeds, but from the Inner Light objectified in service to man. He had chosen what in his earlier years he would have regarded as being the lesser portion. But as he lost himself in service to man and God, he came upon the fulfillment of his life.

Thus, Whittier, the Quaker, was critical of form and institution in religion. For him creed, ritual, and even church were unnecessary. Indeed he prophesied the time when "the world will become uneasy and disgusted with shams and shadows . . . love will take the place of fast, penance, long prayers, and heathenish sacrifices; altar, church, priest and ritual will pass away; but the human heart will be the Holy of Holies where worship will still be performed, not in set forms and on particular occasions, but daily and hourly, a worship, meet and acceptable to Him Who is not deceived by the pomp of outward cere-monial and Who loves mercy better than sacrifice."

John Greenleaf Whittier was profoundly disturbed as he watched Christian people and the bulk of the Christian churches, either indif-ferent to the tragedy of slavery or else actually giving their support to it, and even claiming Biblical sanction for that support. Some of the most scathing lines ever written by a poet are found in Whittier's poem "Clerical Oppressors."

Whittier believed profoundly in the Inner Light, in the inner voice, in the immanence of God within the human soul. For him "the unpar-donable sin is to deny the word of God within" (The Word). This inner voice, this indwelling spirit, in many instances took precedence over Scripture itself for Whittier. Although no first-rate American literary figure has known the Bible as Whittier knew it, the basis of religion for him was the communion of the human spirit with the Divine Spirit. And he believed that this Divine Spirit was constantly seeking to make itself known to all men. For him worship was not to be found in outward form or in the observances of liturgy; rather it was to be found in this communion with the Eternal Spirit. And it was inevitable that this profound truth should have been stated many times in his writings, for it was sound Quaker doctrine.

Whittier believed in following this Inner Light when it came. We cannot tell how many of the important critical decisions in his life were made as the result of the leading of the Inner Light. But he believed in it, even to the point of saying that it often led men in strange ways. His dependence upon this Inner Light is set out in the beginning of "The Eternal Goodness":

> "I trace your lines of argument;
> Your logic linked and strong

I weigh as one who dreads dissent,
And fears a doubt as wrong.

"But still my human hands are weak
To hold your iron creeds:
Against the words ye bid me speak
My heart within me pleads.

"Who fathoms the Eternal thought?
Who talks of scheme and plan?
The Lord is God! He needeth not
The poor device of man."

Reverend George A. Gordon (to whom I have already referred) gives an account of the origin of "The Eternal Goodness," an account which I believe has never been noted by any of Whittier's biographers. Gordon said:

"There were two sisters, one an invalid, the other a toiler supporting herself and the invalid sister. The fight was desperate; the invalid grew worse and worse in health, the toiler worked harder and harder, sacrificed more and more for the benefit of the beloved sister, defeat stared them in the face, but still they went bravely onward. By and by the invalid lost courage, lost hope, and in despair died by her own hand. The day of the funeral came, and a high Calvinist minister conducted the service. He preached the customary sermon on the sovereignty of God and the predestination of the order of the world. This poor life ran in the channel marked out for it by the Eternal decree; all that had happened was an evolution from God's purpose for that poor afflicted woman, and she went to her eternal doom for the manifestation of the glory of God. The half-crazed surviving sister went to her friend Whittier, whom she knew slightly, for relief from the horror and for comfort to her bleeding heart. Whittier gave her both abundantly, and as the interview closed he said to her, 'It is time that I told my fellow-citizens what I believe.' Out of that experience came 'The Eternal Goodness.'"

In 1878 Oliver Wendell Holmes wrote to Whittier: "Who has preached the Gospel of love to such a mighty congregation as you have preached it? Who has done so much to sweeten the soul of Calvinistic New England? You have your reward here in the affection with which all our people, who are capable of loving anybody, regard you." Three years later Holmes, writing in the *North American Review* about Whittier's poem "The Minister's Daughter," said of Burns that his "songs have done more to humanize the hard theology of Scotland than all the rationalistic sermons that were ever preached." Then he added, "Our own Whittier has done and is doing the same thing, in a far holier spirit than Burns, for the inherited beliefs of New England and the country to which New England belongs."

John Bright, the English statesman, wrote in 1884 when Whittier's portrait was being presented to the Friends' School in Providence: "The Eternal Goodness is another poem which is worth a crowd of sermons which are spoken from the pulpits of our sects and churches. . . . It is a great gift to mankind when a poet is raised up among us who devotes his great powers to the sublime purpose of spreading among men principles of mercy and justice and freedom. This our friend Whittier has done in a degree unsurpassed by any other poet who has spoken to the world in our noble tongue."

Whittier believed in the essential goodness of God. Much of the contemporary thought of his day seemed to emphasize God's wrath, God's vengeance, but for Whittier, God was essentially good; and He was a God of love. Behind all, as the one single reality, is God:

> "I know not where His islands lift
> Their fronded palms in air;
> I only know I cannot drift
> Beyond His love and care."
>   [From "The Eternal Goodness."]

In 1884 Whittier wrote to Lydia Maria Child, "What is there for us but to hold faster and firmer our faith in the goodness of God? That all which He allots to us or our friends is for the best!—best for them, for us, for all. Let theology, and hate, and bigotry talk as they will, I for one will hold fast to this, God *is* our Father. He knows what love is, what our hearts, sore and bereaved, long for, and He will not leave us comfortless. Is He not love?" For Whittier, God is not the God Who *was*, He is the God Who *is now*. He puts it in these words:

> "I reverence old-time faith of men,
> But God is near us now as then."
>   [From "The Meeting."]

Whittier was unwilling to attribute to God what he himself would not attribute to a good parent. He refused to believe that suffering came as punishment, or that it came as the direct result of God's anger. He could not equate this then current belief about God's harshness with God's goodness and God's love. And always, whatever came, he believed he and those who trusted in God's goodness were in God's hands, even though reason had failed, even though the mystery of life could not be understood.

The recognition of the Presence of God in the Inner Light was a source of strength for Whittier in his despairing hours. It gave him a sense of assurance and a sense of stability. This was particularly true among the many convulsive changes through which he himself lived. The sense of this assurance he put into these words:

> "Have ye not still my witness
> Within yourselves always?"
> [From "The Vision of Echard."]

As he saw the necessity of living by the best we know in spite of the turmoil, he wrote about "calmly wait[ing] the births of Providence." Whittier saw in events the Hand of God, even though man himself is perplexed. In the same poem he writes:

> "No gain is lost; the clear-eyed saints look down
> Untroubled on the wreck of schemes and creeds;
> Love yet remains . . . the Inward Word survives,
> And day by day its revelation brings;
> Faith, hope and charity, whatsoever things
> Which cannot be shaken, stand."

In spite of the strength of his trust and hope and faith, Whittier himself constantly felt the pressure of unanswered questions:

> "The same old baffling questions!
> O my friend, I cannot answer them."
> [From "Trust."]

He felt that reason by itself can never give the final answer, and only faith can bring the person through:

> "For he is merciful as just;
> And so, by faith correcting sight,
> I bow before his will, and trust
> Howe'er they seem, he doeth all things right."
> [From "The Shadow and the Light."]

Whittier stood midway between Unitarian belief and the contemporary orthodoxy of the day with regard to his belief in Jesus and who He was. In a very real sense Whittier believed in the divinity of Christ, but he believed so profoundly in His humanity that there were many in orthodox circles who could not follow him and go along with his beliefs. He spoke of Jesus:

> "Most human and yet most divine,
> The flower of man and God . . .
> We know in Thee the fatherhood
> And heart of God revealed."
> [From "Our Master."]

In 1877 he wrote to Gail Hamilton, who had just written a book about belief in Christ, in these words: "My own mind had, from the same evidence that thee had used, become convinced of the Divinity of Christ; but I cannot look upon Him as other than a man like ourselves, through whom the Divine was made miraculously manifest." And John Greenleaf Whittier was in line with a great deal of the most devout religious thinking of our own time.

Whittier found in Jesus the greatest example for conduct that we have. In Him was the ultimate standard. His example and standard are with us as a continuing presence. And so he lived very near to his Master. Whittier believed that we cannot and that we do not reach our best apart from Jesus and His life. Whittier felt that man was not a prisoner of impersonal law by which he was surrounded, but that by the guidance of the Inner Light and by the sustaining power of God he could free himself for a better life than he had known. And in man's experience Whittier believed that God's was the final victory:

> "Truth is stronger than a lie,
> And righteousness than wrong."
> [From "The Emancipation Group."]

While Whittier believed profoundly in a man's personal relation with God, for him that personal relation always brought a man into avenues of service on behalf of his fellow human beings. Whittier himself was one of the finest examples of this belief.

After Charles Sumner's death, Whittier wrote a memorial poem to be read at the Boston Memorial Service. And the lines that he wrote as a description of Sumner were unwittingly a description of Whittier himself:

> "No trumpet sounded in his ear,
> He saw not Sinai's cloud and flame,
> But never yet to Hebrew seer
> A clearer voice of duty came.

> "God said: 'Break thou these yokes;
> Undo these heavy burdens, I ordain
> Work to last thy whole life through
> A ministry of strife and pain.

> "'Forego thy dreams of lettered ease,
> Put thou the scholar's promise by,
> The rights of men are more than these.'
> He heard, and answered, 'Here am I.'"

Nature spoke intimately and compellingly to Whittier, but it spoke to him plainly of God and of the things of the Spirit. He found in nature an interpretation of life, and that interpretation of life helped him find God and love and immortality. It brought to him a vivid awareness of

God's greatness, and he saw in its beauty and in its power the hand of God. In his poem "Sunset on the Bearcamp," Whittier writes:

> "Touched by a light that hath no name,
> A glory never sung,
> Aloft on sky and mountain wall
> Are God's great pictures hung."

Perhaps the poem which above all others gives Whittier's own confession of faith is the poem "Requirement":

> "We live by Faith; but Faith is not the slave
> Of text and legend. Reason's voice and God's,
> Nature's and Duty's, never are at odds.
> What asks our Father of His children save
> Justice and mercy and humility,
> A reasonable service of good deeds,
> Pure living, tenderness to human needs,
> Reverence and trust, and prayer for light to see
> The Master's footprints in our daily ways?
> No knotted scourge nor sacrificial knife,
> But the calm beauty of an ordered life
> Whose very breathing is unworded praise! —
> A life that stands as all true lives have stood,
> Firm-rooted in the faith that God is Good."

Constantly present was Whittier's concern about the mystery of the final ending of life. We have had no poet in American literature who can so aptly be called "the poet of immortality" as John Greenleaf Whittier. He wrote, "The little circumstance of death will make no difference to me." And at another time he wrote, "I shall have the same loves and aspirations and occupations (after death). If it were not so, I should not be myself, and surely I should lose my identity." His faith in immortality resided ultimately in his belief in God. He could not believe that a just god would permit a life of love and trust to be finally lost. In his faith Whittier could not comprehend the idea of the annihilation of a personal life. And so he found himself at wide divergence from many of the contemporary ideas about life after death. He believed that death itself did not close man off from the opportunity to turn toward God. So many of his contemporaries, believing in an eternal hell, held that what man did in these few years of his existence would determine for him an eternity spent in the punishment of the fires of hell. And this Whittier could not believe. Whittier believed that what we do here and now has a profound influence upon us, so that we carry the results of it into the next life:

"The tissue of the life to be
We weave with colors of our own."
[From "Raphael."]

Whittier's religious poems represent a unique contribution in American literature. And from them have come our largest single body of hymns. It is strange that Whittier, the Quaker, who himself had no basic appreciation of music, and who belonged to a sect that did not use music in its services, should have become perhaps the foremost hymnist in the last hundred and fifty years of American life. Whittier never imagined himself to be a hymn writer. His whole religious background was without music. He speaks of the Quaker Meeting, "where never hymn is sung, nor deep-toned organ blown."

Henry Wilder Foote, in his definitive study on *Three Centuries of American Hymnody*, suggests that the first "hymnic use" of Whittier's poetry specifically as "a hymn" occurred when Samuel Longfellow and Samuel Johnson, students at Harvard Divinity School, issued "A Book of Hymns" in 1846. There is a record of Whittier's poetry printed in a book as a hymn, and labeled "A Hymn," at least three years earlier. In 1843, Jarius Lincoln issued a book of "Anti-Slavery Melodies" printed in Hingham. The first section of that book is labeled, without apology, "Hymns," and in that section appears the poem, "O Thou Whose Presence went before our fathers in their weary way," a hymn first sung in Haverhill ten years before, on July 4, 1833, at a church school celebration.

Whenever he turned his hand definitely to the writing of a hymn, he was only tolerably successful. His best hymns are segments that are taken out of his longer poems. And with the passing years, segments of his poetry have been used more widely as hymns, and they have found a deeper response in the experience of the English-speaking peoples than the religious writings of any other American poet. Henry Wilder Foote speaks of these as Whittier's "unintended hymns." In the same book Foote describes Whittier's poem "At Last" as being the American equivalent of "Crossing the Bar." . . .

His hymns appeal to people because of their confidence in God. They are affirmative; they are not denunciatory; they are free from self-consciousness, even when they express the most profound religious beliefs and experiences.

The influence of John Greenleaf Whittier has gone deep into American life. He had a share in shaping some of the most creative events in our nation's history. At the end of the nineteenth century and the beginning of the twentieth century, he was the most widely quoted of all American poets. But since then, with changing literary tastes, his recognized (not his real) influence has grown temporarily less. But over the years the influence that he had in the fields of race, of labor relations, of opposition to capital punishment, of war and peace, and of foundational political affairs, are all built into America as a nation; and he has continued to speak (even though less widely heard) his message of hope and trust, of faith and confidence, and of profound religious experience, to the minds and hearts of the people of the whole English-speaking world.

John G. Whittier: Puritan Quaker

Vernon Lewis Parrington*

If Garrison was the flintiest character amongst the militant Abolitionists, Whittier was certainly the gentlest. Among many lovable men he was perhaps the most lovable. Bred in a faith that had never been dominant in New England, he escaped the induration that was the price the New England conscience paid for its hard dogma. No thick shell of Calvinism incrusted for him the soul of humanitarian religion. In the Society of Friends righteousness was not daily twisted into unloveliness, nor the beauty of holiness forgotten; and in consequence, it was easier for him than for his Calvinist neighbors to fashion his life upon the principles of the New Testament, and set Christ above the Prophets.

Whittier's family escaped many temptations by following quiet paths to their own ends. Prosperity had never wooed the Massachusetts Quakers away from the simple life, as it had done with so many Philadelphia Friends, but a narrow domestic economy and social nonconformity had nourished their religion of peace and good will. Long before Channing discovered the religion of love in the teachings of French humanitarianism, the early Quakers had found that primitive gospel in the byways of Carolinian England, and had brought it to the new world. There they had borne testimony in their daily lives to the excellence of Christian fellowship, and there they had suffered the reproaches and the blows of bigoted conformists. Their faith had been tried in the fires of persecution, and the Society of Friends had justified its use of that most excellent of sectarian names. In the sincerity of their equalitarian fellowship the Quakers were the friends of humanity, of the poor and the outcast of this world. Their religion was of the week-day as well as the Sabbath. With its mystical doctrine of the inner light—of the Holy Spirit that speaks directly to the soul without the intermediation of priest or church—it unconsciously spread the doc-

*Reprinted from *Main Currents in American Thought*, Volume II by Vernon L. Parrington, copyright 1927 by Harcourt Brace Jovanovich, Inc.; renewed 1955 by Vernon L. Parrington, Jr., Louise P. Tucker, and Elizabeth P. Thomas. Reprinted by permission of the publisher.

trine of democracy in an autocratic world. It interpreted literally the principle that members of the Christian fellowship are equals in the sight of God and in each other's eyes—that on earth there is neither high nor low but a common brotherhood in Christ. It quietly set aside the pretentions of priestly hierarchies, and substituted the principle that religion is a matter that lies with the individual and God. Naturally a "hireling ministry" could not look with favor on such doctrine, and the sharp hostility it aroused in theocratic New England, sprang from the realization that the ideals of the Quaker fellowship were dangerous to the ideals of a priestly theocracy. The autocratic rulers of Massachusetts Bay could see little good in the democracy of the Friends.

As became a Quietist, the master passion of Whittier's life was ethical. He was neither a transcendental nor a Utopian visionary, but a primitive Christian, an apostle of good will and a friend of justice. Sprung from a long line of New England yeomen, wholly of the soil, simple in wants, quietly independent, he was the last lineal expression in our literature of the primitive faith, the last authentic echo of the spiritual democracy of the seventeenth century. A thorough Yankee in character, the Yankee never dominated him. As a young man, to be sure, he temporized with his Quakerism and dreamed fond dreams of worldly ambition. The stirrings of youthful romance awakened the desire to be a Byronic poet, and a Yankee knack with politics led him to meddle with the hope of representing his district in Congress. He was hand-in-glove with the time-serving Caleb Cushing, and the temptations of political intrigue almost led to his backsliding; but he soon put the devil behind him and gave security for his better behavior by coming out for the cause of Abolitionism. That was the end of his hopes of political preferment, and the more surely to burn his bridges he published in 1833, at his own cost, a little Abolition tract entitled *Justice and Expediency*, which was re-issued by Lewis Tappan in a great edition and scattered broadcast. The same year he attended as delegate the National Anti-Slavery Convention at Philadelphia, and subscribed his name to its pronouncement. Thenceforth for over thirty years he gave his best strength to the cause, writing abundantly in prose and verse, serving as editor of Abolition publications, and suffering the unpleasant experiences common to the group, at one time being hunted by a mob and stoned.

This deliberate alignment with an unpopular cause, this calm response to the summons of conscience, was the fruit of his Quaker training. It was no new experience for the Quaker to dissent. The Whittier family had been Come-outers for generations, sacrificing material well-being for their faith, and he had grown up in dissent. The long struggle for democratic freedom in Massachusetts was a familiar story to him. The record had come down by word of mouth and stories of early persecutions were fireside tales in the Whittier household. His ancestors had lived in the hard old Puritan theocracy, and yet detached from it; and this detachment had rendered them shrewdly critical and sensitive to injustice. With their quiet dissent from what the Quaker conscience regarded as unrighteous, and their practical nullification of unjust authority, Whittier was in full sympathy. His intimate knowledge of early Massachusetts history had taught him certain things which official historians had overlooked, the chief of which was that dissent had been the ally and friend of freedom in New England. From his youth up he had been a loving student of the old annals, of those intimate narratives that preserve the voice and manner of the past; and as he discovered how often persecution had left its stain on the record, he was drawn to consider the superstitious aberrations of a people supposedly devout. In middle life he gathered up in *Leaves from Margaret Smith's Journal of Massachusetts Bay, 1678–79*, materials that he had long been collecting, and which, interpreted by a sympathetic imagination, provides a surprisingly vivid account of life in New England in the second generation.

All in all, it is Whittier's most notable achievement in prose. Pieced together out of old records, it is authentic as the yellow documents from which it was drawn. The soft light of romance lies upon its pages, sobered by historical fact and tempered by creative sympathy. Loving yet critical, quite devastating at times in its implications, it is an amazingly intimate narrative. The mind of Puritan New England is uncovered in these unpretentious pages, and it does not show to advantage. There was many a knot and seam in the old Puritan life, much that was mean and ugly woven into the honest web. The Puritan proneness to Quaker-baiting—aggravated to be sure by the ill manners of the Ranters; their vulgar credulity that encouraged witch-hunting; their callous treatment of the Indian and negro; their hardness of nature that made them grasping and censorious: such knots and seams in the Puritan character did not escape Whittier's eye, but they appear in the sketches of avaricious deacons, sour women, intolerant magistrates—the Deacon Doles and Goody Lakes and Roger Endicotts, whose bigotry tyrannized over the better natures of the community. Whittier sifted his materials carefully to gather up what good wheat there might be, yet the showing it must be confessed is but paltry. Honest Robert Pine who will have none unjustly treated, good Mr. Russ who counsels moderation in dealing with the unhappy victims of mob suspicion, Captain Samuel Sewall who speaks up bravely for the outcast—these are the remnant in Israel, the generous minority that cannot leaven the dour and credulous mass. Yet even they are not heroic figures to Whittier. His heroes are the Come-outers, and in particular Peggy Brewster—reminiscent evidently of his great-grandmother, the Quakeress Mary Peaslee, who married

Robert Whittier in 1694—who is the good Samaritan of the Puritan neighborhood, and whose loving-kindness wins a reluctant good will that stops short of toleration of her non-conformity.

Such intimate studies in the psychology of persecution were a liberal education, and Whittier would have been no Quaker had he not learned his lesson. He was justified in not thinking well of the social conscience of respectable New England. Religious conformity, he had come to understand, had not kept alive the torch of freedom in Massachusetts, nor had Puritan righteousness befriended justice. Not the great of earth but the simple may be counted on to do God's work. So taking his lesson to heart he quietly put aside ambition, and like Peggy Brewster numbered himself among the remnant. Like her he would be a Come-outer and bear his testimony against the uncleanness of the American people in this matter of negro slavery. Not with musket and ball would he fight, like old John Brown; but with the sword of the spirit. The solution must lie with the conscience of the American people. As a Friend, a man of peace, he would not deal harshly with the supporters of slavery; he would not counsel violence. But as a Yankee with a gift for politics, he would use political means to jog a slothful conscience and marshal its forces. And so Whittier became the politician amongst the Abolitionists. He proved himself a skillful lobbyist. He was active in getting up petitions to Congress. He supported John Quincy Adams and put pressure on the slippery Caleb Cushing. He advocated the policy of boring from within the old parties, but when such methods proved futile he became an active leader in the third party movement. He was an early supporter of the Liberal party—that in 1844 drew enough votes from Clay in New York to defeat him for the Presidency—of the Free-Soil party, and later of the Republican party.

It was this insistence upon the use of political methods that brought about the unhappy break with Garrison. Immediately it was no more than a difference over tactics, but it was embittered by a wide cleavage of political theory. With Garrison's conversion to spiritual anarchism the Abolition movement was sundered by a division between the perfectionists and the political actionists. The principle of non-voting and of refusing allegiance to the Constitution aroused strong opposition, and Whittier went with Birney and Gerrit Smith, with Jonathan Sewall, John Pierpont and the Tappans in rejecting the perfectionist policy. His political common sense turned naturally to political agencies to accomplish his ends. "Moral action apart from political" seemed to him an "absurdity." But when he applied the Quaker principle of Come-outism, and advocated separate party alignment, Garrison attacked him with his habitual intolerance. The latter feared a third party movement as certain to provide a rallying cry for the commercial interest to muster the mob to its support, and overwhelm the minority with the unthinking and selfish mass. "All political minorities," he argued, "are more or less liberal," and by throwing the Abolition strength to such organized minorities, the movement would be "feared and respected by all political parties" (Wendell Phillips Garrison, *William Lloyd Garrison, 1805–1879: The Story of His Life Told by His Children* [Boston: Houghton, Mifflin, 1889], II, 310–11). The wisest strategy, he believed, was to seek to hold the balance of power between the old parties—rewarding friends and punishing enemies—while laboring to arouse the conscience of America, for ballots without conscience were the enemies of justice.

Whittier was no such root-and-branch spirit as Garrison, and in the political field he was a practical, somewhat prosaic Yankee, little given to abstract speculation, skillful in minor strategical skirmishes, inclined to opportunism. He belonged to no school of political thought. His equalitarianism came as a heritage from his Quaker religion rather than from political theory. To prepare himself for his work he read Milton and Burke. The pamphlets of the great Puritan appealed to him as the voice of the moral fervor of a heroic age, but Milton's aristocratic republicanism he seems to have examined no more critically than Burke's Whiggish legalism. Neither held anything in common with Quaker equalitarianism. Rousseau and Tom Paine and Jefferson, with whom he certainly would have sympathized, he seems not to have been acquainted with. In Whittier's New England they were in ill repute, and the young Whittier was as naïvely provincial in his political partisanship as was Garrison. Economics had no part in his thought, and the economic interests that divided Federalism and Anti-Federalism he seems never to have understood. Though sprung from six generations of farmers who tilled the same acres, he reveals no sympathy with agrarianism. He swallowed Clay and the American System without a qualm, and as a young editor he wrote with pride of the developing industrialism of Massachusetts. Neither in politics nor in economics was he a rebellious soul. He was conscience rather than intellect. He felt rather than thought. Only a moral issue could draw him into strife, and even in such contests he was ill equipped to lead the prosaic debates. His moral indignation found its natural expression in verse, and he early took his place as the poet of the Abolition movement, distilling into ready lyrics the emotion of the moment.

A great, even a noteworthy poet, Whittier certainly was not. Compared with Whitman he is only a minor figure. Among the better known American poets Bryant alone is so narrow in range and barren in suggestion. His austere and meager life bred too little sensuousness of nature and too few intellectual passions. An over-frugal watering of the wine of paganism had left the New England character thin. The sap of humor that ran so boisterously through the veins of the West, exuding

a rough wit from Davy Crockett to Mark Twain, was quite gone out
of the Yankee blood. His homely imagination was unquickened by a
hearty village life as was the case with the English Bunyan and the
Scotch Burns. He had become a bundle of Yankee nerves, responding
only to moral stimuli. The comment of Whitman sums up the Quaker
poet adequately:

> Whittier's poetry stands for morality . . . as filtered through
> the positive Puritanical and Quaker filters; is very valuable
> as a genuine utterance. . . . Whittier is rather a grand figure
> —pretty lean and ascetic—no Greek—also not composite and
> universal enough (doesn't wish to be, doesn't try to be) for
> ideal Americanism. (Carpenter, *Life of Whitman* [New York:
> Macmillan, 1909], p. 293.)

Never a great artist, rarely a competent craftsman, he wrote for the
most part impassioned commonplace, with occasional flashes that are
not commonplace.

The high-water mark of lyric indignation was reached in the lines
to Webster. Written at white heat, they have the passionate directness
of Thoreau's prose. Like other Abolitionists, Whittier had clung to his
hopes of Webster in spite of frequent signs of the latter's backsliding.
He did not sufficiently appreciate the economic alliances that tied
Webster to State Street, and he underrated his presidential ambitions.
But when the blow came with the Seventh of March Speech, it staggered
him—not alone the defection of Webster, but the demonstrative approval
of his wealthy constituents. For having "convinced the understanding
and touched the conscience of a nation," Webster was formally thanked
by some seven hundred addressers from the most respectable circles of
Massachusetts—great men like Rufus Choate, George Ticknor, W. H.
Prescott, President Jared Sparks and Professor Felton of Harvard, Moses
Stuart and Leonard Woods of Andover Theological Seminary. It was an
hour of profound discouragement that laid bare what colossal difficulties stood in the way of Abolitionism. "The scandalous treachery of
Webster and the *backing* he has received from Andover and Harvard,"
wrote Whittier to Garrison, "show that we have nothing to hope for
from the great political parties and religious sects" (William Sloane
Kennedy, *John G. Whittier* [New York: Funk and Wagnalls Co., 1892],
p. 113).

The scathing lines of *Ichabod* were read throughout the North,
and they must have rankled in Webster's heart. Even Whittier was
troubled by their severity and thirty years later he wrote a second
Webster poem which he set beside *Ichabod* in his collected works.
The Lost Occasion is a testimony to the kindliness of Whittier's Quaker

heart that did not love to offend; but no kindliness of memory could change or soften the just verdict of the lines:

Of all we loved and honored, naught
    Save power remains;
A fallen angel's pride of thought,
    Still strong in chains.

All else is gone; from those great eyes
    The soul is fled:
When faith is lost, when honor dies,
    The man is dead!

Then, pay the reverence of old days
    To his dead fame;
Walk backward, with averted gaze,
    And hide the shame!

If Whittier was ill acquainted with the Boston of State Street and the Back Bay, and the Cambridge of Harvard culture, he knew intimately the Massachusetts of the village and the farm, and the overwhelming repudiation of Webster and the Whig party, following the Seventh of March Speech, would seem to have justified his lyric confidence expressed in the vigorous heptameters of *Massachusetts to Virginia.* For those who lived in the social world of Commissioner Loring—professor of law at Harvard—and Rufus Choate, it was hard not to think that Massachusetts had come to degenerate days. The fine old-school Federalist, Josiah Quincy, commenting on the Boston that watched Sims return to slavery, wrote:

When the [Fugitive Slave] law passed, I did think the moral sense of the community would not enforce it; I said that it never would be. But now I find that my fellow-citizens are not only *submissive* to, but that they are earnestly active for, its enforcement. The Boston of 1851 is not the Boston of 1775. Boston has now become a mere shop—a place for buying and selling goods; and I suppose, also, of *buying and selling men.* (Garrison, *William Lloyd Garrison,* Vol. III, p. 328.)

And Lowell, living in the same mean atmosphere, wrote:

Massachusetts, God forgive her,
    She's akneelin' with the rest,
She, thet ough' to ha' clung ferever
    In her grand old eagle-nest.
                                        (*Biglow Papers* I, i.)

But Whittier professed to think better of the conscience of New England. A strong pride of the commonwealth runs through the lines that name over the towns of Massachusetts, from "free, broad Middle-sex," westward and northward to the hills of Hampshire:

And sandy Barnstable rose up, wet with the salt sea spray;
And Bristol sent her answering shout down Narragansett Bay!
Along the broad Connecticut old Hampden felt the thrill,
And the cheer of Hampshire's woodmen swept down from Holyoke Hill.

The voice of Massachusetts! Of her free sons and daughters,
Deep calling unto deep aloud, the sound of many waters!
Against the burden of that voice what tyrant power shall stand?
No fetters in the Bay State! No slave upon her land!

When at last the long controversy was over and release from the struggle came to Whittier, his poetry grew richer and mellower. He was not made to be a fighter, and it was with a sigh of relief that he turned to the Elysian fields he had dreamed of, while he was turning with his plow the rough stubble of a cause. Looking back upon those arduous days, he sketched half whimsically his own portrait in *The Tent on the Beach.*

And one there was, a dreamer born,
    Who, with a mission to fulfill,
Had left the Muses' haunts to turn
    The crank of an opinion-mill,
Making his rustic reed of song
    A weapon in the war with wrong,
Yoking his fancy to the breaking-plough
That beam-deep turned the soil for truth to spring and grow.

Too quiet seemed the man to ride
    The wingéd Hippogriff Reform;
Was his a voice from side to side
    To pierce the tumult of the storm?
A silent, shy, peace-loving man,
    He seemed no fiery partisan
To hold his way against the public frown,
The ban of Church and State, the fierce Mob's hounding down.

For while he wrought with strenuous will
    The work his hands had found to do,
He heard the fitful music still
    Of winds that out of dream-land blew.
The din about him could not drown
    What the strange voices whispered down;
Along his task-field weird processions swept,
The visionary pomp of stately phantoms stepped.

The common air was thick with dreams,—
    He told them to the toiling crowd;

Such music as the woods and streams
    Sang in his ear he sang aloud;
In still, shut bays, on windy capes,
He heard the call of beckoning shapes,
And, as the gray old shadows prompted him,
To homely moulds of rhyme he shaped their legends grim.

Many excellent things he did in those quiet years; old time pictures like *Snowbound*, with its homely fireside economy long since buried under the snows of forgotten winters; vigorous tales like *Abraham Davenport*; ballads like *Skipper Ireson's Ride*, that have something of the spirit of the primitive. He had given thirty years of his life to the cause of social justice, and surely none would grudge him in old age his rambles in pleasanter fields. It was well that he could turn to the past, for the America of the new exploitative age, the New England of Lowell and Lawrence, he never understood. Black slavery he understood, but wage slavery he comprehended no more than did Garrison. To the end he remained a primitive soul, ill equipped to understand a materialistic philosophy of society. There is something pathetic in his *Songs of Labor*. His economics, like his democracy, was of a bygone time, having no kinship with a scrambling free-soilism or a rapacious capitalism. There is scant room in this world for the Friend with his unmilitant dream of the fellowship. With his passion for freedom, established in the gospel of righteousness, the Quaker Whittier was fast becoming an anachronism in industrial New England that was concerned about very different things. How old-fashioned he had become is suggested by certain lines that phrase his greetings to later times. Spare, somewhat halting in rhythm, yet transparently sincere, they constitute an apologia that New England need feel no shame for.

Yet here at least an earnest sense
Of human right and weal is shown;
    A hate of tyranny intense,
    And hearty in its vehemence,
As if my brother's pain and sorrow were my own.

O Freedom! if to me belong
Nor mighty Milton's gift divine,
    Nor Marvell's wit and graceful song,
    Still with a love as deep and strong
As theirs, I lay, like them, my best gifts on thy shrine!
                                        [From "Proem."]

Whittier's Abolitionist Poetry

John B . Pickard[*]

Whittier's abolitionist poetry has always attracted more attention from the biographer and historian than from the critic. Still, Whittier regarded them as a significant area in his writings, for his collected works include ninety-three poems under the title "Anti-Slavery." In addition forty or more poems listed in different categories are directly concerned with abolitionism and scores of other poems comment on slavery. "Ego," for example, a "Subjective and Reminiscent" poem, analyzes the moral compulsion that made Whittier "pour the fiery breath of storm / Through the harsh trumpet of Reform," when his poetic heart yearned for "young Romance, and gentle Thought."[1] Similar statements and comments appear in his Legendary, Occasional, and Religious poems; even "Snow-Bound" contains three distinct slavery references. Perhaps a third of Whittier's collected poems deal with slavery in some way. A critical examination of their artistic merits seems long overdue and this paper will suggest some lines of approach.[2]

Whittier recognized the shortcomings of his abolitionist poetry and succinctly stated the problem in the introduction to his collected works: "They were written with no expectation that they would survive the occasions which called them forth: they were protests, alarm signals, trumpet-calls to action, words wrung from the writer's heart, forged at white heat, and of course lacking the finish and careful word-selection which reflection and patient brooding over them might have given."[3] Ambivalently Whittier both apologizes for and defends them. Knowing their deficiencies, he retains a pride in their significance as a part of the antislavery movement. In their defense Whittier argued that a studied wit and polished phrase were best suited for thought, but that a poet needs feeling and speaks from his heart with words that arouse an emotional response. The uneasy alliance between the humanitarian and the poet is significantly highlighted in "The Tent on the Beach" where Whittier characterizes himself as a "dreamer born" whose delight in graceful lays and rustic pastorals has been put aside to turn

[*]Reprinted from the *Emerson Society Quarterly*, 50 (1968), 105–13 by permission of Kenneth Walter Cameron.

the "crank of an opinion mill." This harsh split between moral obligation and the inner love of the beautiful underscores the tensions of the
propagandist and the poet which caused the artistic failure of so many
abolitionist poems.

A typical verse from "The Slave-Ships" illustrates the poetic difficulty Whittier had in transforming his emotional and moral indignation
at slavery's barbarism into poetry. An early stanza reads:

> Hark! from the ship's dark bosom,
>   The very sounds of hell!
> The ringing clank of iron,
>   The maniac's short, sharp yell!
> The hoarse, low curse, throat-stifled;
>   The starving infant's moan,
> The horror of a breaking heart
>   Poured through a mother's groan.

This brief survey of the slaves imprisoned on the ship maintains them
as abstractions without any real characterization and consequently
unfelt as human beings. Types, not individuals, are presented: a maniac,
a starving child, a heartbroken mother. The threadbare, unimaginative
phrasing fails to provide the concrete dramatization necessary to
embody the bare idea with an emotional life. The imagery, rife with
cliché and hampered by the rhetorical pattern, forces the emotion into
bathos. Whittier editorializes, telling the reader that the scene is a
"hell" and filled with "horror," since there has been no tangible development of these emotions. Basically the appeal remains on a crude level of
propaganda where the issue is starkly presented in terms of good
and evil and where stereotyped images elicit desired emotional responses.

Over a thirty year period Whittier's most successful contemporary
abolitionist poems depended on these propaganda elements and utilized
all the available media for disseminating their message. They were
printed in northern newspapers, circulated in broadsides throughout
the country, declaimed by orators and school children, set to music,
and even presented as memorials to the state legislatures. Because of
their topical interest, broad emotional appeal, and moral intensity, they
affected thousands of common readers who were rarely touched by
sermons or newspaper editorials. "Our Countrymen in Chains"[4] typifies
Whittier's standard approach and in turn reveals another underlying
conflict in Whittier's nature, the tension of the Quaker pacifist and the
radical abolitionist. Originally printed in the *Liberator* in 1834, this
poem was reissued as an antislavery best seller broadside for the next
six years. The top half of the broadside contained a cut of a kneeling
negro who raised his manacled hands with the cry "Am I not a man and
a Brother?" Below was Whittier's poem, consisting of a long series of

rhetorical questions contrasting America and Europe which climaxed in the demand for slavery's destruction. The poem opens with an incredulous tone, as Whittier contrasts the present sordid reality of slave-dominated America with the bright dreams of her revolution. Stock phrases ask for the conventional emotional responses as the familiar "falling lash, the fetter's clank" lead into a depiction of the negro mother whipped and driven from her child. Whittier employs sensational details for their own sake to increase the sense of horror, luridly contrasting the soil once red with patriot's blood to that "reddening with the stains / Caught from her scourging, warm and fresh!"

The long central section ironically contrasts America's hypocritical posture as the champion of freedom with Europe's actual liberation of her slaves. As a practised orator, Whittier goads his audience on with a series of rhetorical questions, rising to an emotional climax: "Shall our own brethren drag the chain / Which not even Russia's menials wear?" Assured of a thunderous "no" answer to this question, Whittier exhorts his audience in the name of liberty to "break the chain . . . and smite to earth Oppression's rod." Although Whittier's condemnation of war and plea "not in strife" qualify this call to action, his hopes for peace sound hollow and within the context of the poem they remain unconvincing. His emotional and moral outrage and the controlling images of bloodshed and war force the conclusion that slavery must be immediately destroyed.

Similarly "A Sabbath Scene," "Le Marais Du Cygne," "The Rendition," and "The Sentence of John L. Brown" demand that its readers "Speak out in acts. The time for words / Has passed, and deeds suffice alone."[5] Whittier may affirm that his words are not threatening or "Sedition's trumpet-blast,"[6] but their emotional sense impells an opposite conclusion. The contradictory attitudes of the Quaker pacifist and the abolitionist caused serious artistic problems as well. The structure of these poems depended heavily on a similar question-answer technique or a cataloguing of melodramatic incidents. Narration as such was interrupted by Whittier's editorializing and extensive moral commentary. The incidents chosen were usually topical and developed in a sensational manner which demanded an excessive emotional response. As a result the imagery was derivative and repetitious, extraneous rather than organically related to the theme of the poem. Phrases and figures were repeated from one poem to the next,[7] while similar Biblical allusions provided little enrichment to the theme. In these poems the propagandist dwarfs the poet and they remain prime source material for the biographer and historian.

Rarely does propaganda serve the ends of art or can conflicting attitudes be harmonized, but such a poetic fusing occurs in "Massachusetts to Virginia." Again a topical incident generated the poem, the arrest of a fugitive slave, George Latimer, in Boston and his forced return to his Virginia owner. Whittier's abolitionist outrage was deepened by his shock as a citizen of Massachusetts whose rights had been abused. Primarily the poem warns the south, especially Virginia, that its violations of freedom would not be tolerated by an aroused, united Massachusetts (and by implication the whole north). Behind this surface assurance, however, lay the bitter knowledge that northern businessmen and politicians willingly acquiesced to Virginia's demands. They wanted no change in the existing situation and resented the abolitionist's attempts to raise a moral issue. Only a small minority opposed Latimer's arrest, hardly the one hundred thousand that Whittier dramatically portrays in the poem. While the poem offers some hope for a peaceful solution, its heaviest stress falls on the north's determination to resist any renewed assaults on its basic freedoms.

The opening lines exemplify this contrast as a warlike defiance breathes through the surface posture of peace and reconciliation:

> The blast from Freedom's Northern hills, upon its Southern way,
> Bears greetings to Virginia from Massachusetts Bay:
> No word of haughty challenging, nor battle bugle's peal,
> Nor steady tread of marching files, nor clank of horseman's steel.
> No train of deep-mouthed cannon along our highways go;
> Around our silent arsenals untrodden lies the snow.

Whittier's greeting, a "blast" of icy northern resolution, is hardly a message of peace and the following images all stress challenge, battle, soldiers, steel, and guns. The very term "blast" connotes destruction and annihilation, while its later associations with nature's storms, "wintry blasts," and God's just anger, "blasting of Almighty wrath," imply both a physical and moral sanction for the north's attitude. Although Whittier asserts the north's unwillingness to employ such force, the bleak picture of the "deep mouthed-cannon" and the silent arsenals in the frozen snow emphasize the industrial might of the north and its military potential. The next three stanzas develop these ideas by a definition of northern manhood and a survey of its occupations. Significantly the first images are of a worker's "brown, hard hand" and of a lumberman's swinging his axe against mountain oaks, associating manhood with primitive natural forces. The "brown, hard hand" aptly conveys the strength of northern free labor, while suggesting the darker brown hand of the southern slave whose forced labor supported the south, but whose potential freedom terrified. Coupled with this looms the image of the man with the axe, demolishing giant oaks. Continuing his portrayal, Whittier emphasizes the northern man's daily struggle with the natural forces around him, the wind, ice, fog, cold, storm, which toughen his character, develop an inner self reliance and foster an independent attitude that "laugh[s] to scorn the slaver's threat against their rocky home." The underlying imagistic pattern in these five introductory stanzas present a strong defiant posture of natural strength which can well destroy any southern opposition.

Unlike many other abolitionist poems "Massachusetts to Virginia" has a definite, carefully controlled structure, balancing defiance with reconciliation. The opening five stanzas categorize the northern man and briefly survey his individual occupations, while the next nine stanzas plead with Virginia to recollect her revolutionary heritage of freedom. The concluding ten stanzas return to the imagery and tone of the opening. Here Whittier's presentation of northern power expands from individuals to a vast panoramic survey of the united strength of all Massachusetts' communities—an overwhelming northern "blast" to Virginia.

The second section of the poem contains a more conventional appeal to Virginia to recover her former great leadership and, like Massachusetts, remain loyal to her democratic legacy. As the section develops, Whittier's confident assertion of northern allegiance to freedom's principles deteriorates and he notes bitterly:

> We hunt your bondmen, flying from Slavery's hateful hell;
> Our voices, at your bidding, take up the bloodhound's yell;
> We gather, at your summons, above our father's graves,
> From Freedom's holy altar-horns to tear your wretched slaves!

As the final Biblical allusion connotes, what particularly galled Whittier was Massachusetts' willing desecration of its own sacred liberties. Few cared about Latimer as a slave and even fewer understood that his arrest threatened their most basic democratic rights. As if such realism were unbearable, Whittier immediately asserts that Massachusetts will not endure such degradation, pleading with his northern readers to make this assertion a fact. Perhaps to cover the weakness of the north's position, Whittier attacks the depravity of slavery. Familiar clichés, "woman's shriek beneath the lash, and manhood's wild despair" climax in crude melodrama where, separated from her children, the "maddened mother" cries out in woe. The Biblical allusion in "We wash our hands forever of your sin" reflects the hollowness of Whittier's stance, for at its best Massachusetts can only repeat Pilate's evasive attempts to ignore the issue. On the propaganda level, however, these stanzas probably served as an emotional climax for many readers, arousing the desired response of disgust and loathing.

The concluding section returns to the exhortation and assurance of the opening stanzas. The movement from individuals to whole communities signifies what Whittier hoped the poem and the abolitionist appeal would do, to unify a divided north. Appropriately the images return to the previous martial pattern, Whittier sanctions the Revolution as a holy war and pictures one of its main memorials, the shaft of Bunker Hill, as threatening the prowling southern man thief who hunts his human prey beneath its very shadow. The implication that the north must now wage a similar battle for freedom and that its man with the axe might well become the minute man of today is re-enforced by the later depiction of "The shaft of Bunker calling to that of Lexington." In the climax of the poem Whittier enlarges the lone brown hand of his opening to "a hundred thousand right arms . . . lifted up on high." No pun was intended on the word "arms," but in the context of the belligerent tone and warlike images, it suggests the willingness of freedom's lovers to lift military arms in her defense. The poem now sweeps along with its catalogue of specific Massachusetts' communities, Essex with its looms and mills, Barnstable rising up "wet with the salt sea spray," and rural Worcester stung by "wintry blasts," to re-emphasize Massachusetts' elemental toughness and industrial resources. Even in the last stanza where Whittier seems to qualify his defiance, "We wage no war, we lift no arm, we fling no torch within / The fire-damps of the quaking mine beneath your soil of sin," the underlying tone implies that, although we do not lift arms, we can. The image of the fire-damp ready to be exploded by a northern torch underscores exactly what this poem urged and ultimately obtained; it ignited and coalesced a divided north into a vigorous force which would defy and finally destroy slavery. Perhaps some of these effects were unconscious, but the pattern of images and the emotional movement of the poem lead to this conclusion. The incongruous mixture of poet, abolitionist, and Quaker, for once, produced poetry as well as powerful propaganda.

In Whittier's most successful abolitionist poems an openly religious tone and sense of moral indignation help purge their topical and journalistic nature. At times extensive Biblical allusions and a prophetical manner fuse with structure and imagery to develop wider spiritual dimensions. The successive assaults on the basic principles of free speech, press, and assembly occurring throughout the pre-civil war period inspired Whittier's utterances as Israel's national crises had moved her ancient prophets. Repeatedly Whittier describes his abolitionist poems as a "voice and vision" passing before his soul, a "lip of fire," a "burdened prophet's" cry, "living coals of Truth."[8] Hyatt Waggoner has well expressed it: "The poems themselves . . . are not propaganda verse so much as they are visions of the great society, the city of God on earth, and denunciations of all that hinders its arrival."[9]

Poems like "Clerical Oppressors," "The Crisis," "The Sentence of John L. Brown," "The Pastoral Letter," "Moloch in State Street," "The Summons," and "What of the Day?" amply demonstrate Whittier's prophetic approach. In the classical manner of Amos or Isaiah Whittier interprets the north-south slavery conflict in terms of Israel's apostasy from God's law, uttering his vision of God's coming judgment and doom. As he surveys both north (Israel) and south (Judah), Whittier curses them together and specifies the advent of God's wrathful anger on his chosen people. In the traditional prophetic manner he extends the hope that a response to the word of God might avert destruction. Such future salvation, reserved for a small "remnant," will come only after a "long night silence"[10] and a purging holocaust. On the ruins of the old will arise a new Jerusalem, heralding an era of paradisiacal glory.

In "Clerical Oppressors" Whittier condemns the southern clergy for their pro-slavery sentiments and describes their acts as a desecration of "Israel's Ark of light." He rails at them as "paid hypocrites" whose hire is the price of blood, a priesthood who barter truths away. In scathing lines, drawn from Isaiah's ironic advice to his backsliding people, Whittier encourages the ministers to further their own damnation:

> Feed fat, ye locusts, feed!
> And, in your tasselled pulpits, thank the Lord
> That, from the toiling bondman's utter need,
> Ye pile your own full board.

With muted bitterness in "The Pastoral Letter" Whittier mocks the futile attempts of northern clergy to prevent a discussion of slavery in their churches. He taunts the ineffectiveness of these "parish popes" by contrasting their weak war of words with the brandings and scourgings of their Puritan forebears. The latter half of the poem leaves invective for open prophecy. The "earthquake voice" that spoke to Moses and Elijah and God's "right arm of power" that smote Israel's enemies will crush those ministers as "stubble and hay" are consumed. In a stanza clustered with Biblical allusions Whittier envisions the "glorious remnant"

> Whose lips are wet at Freedom's fountains
> The coming of whose welcome feet
> Is beautiful upon our mountains!
>   .   .   .
> Whose joy is an abiding spring,
> Whose peace is as a gentle river!

For these shall witness the "brightness of His coming" and participate in the glorious hour when freedom will be universal. This vision of the Prince of Peace and the arrival of the New Jerusalem as portrayed in Revelation is most explicitly stated in "The Curse of the Charter Breakers." Here Whittier presents his ideal priest who reforms the world and interprets God's vision for his people. The lines unconsciously characterize Whittier's own verse:

> Catching gleams of temple spires,
> Hearing notes of angel choirs,

Where, as yet unseen of them,
Comes the New Jerusalem!

Like the seer of Patmos gazing
On the glory downward blazing;
Till upon the Earth's grateful sod
Rests the City of our God!

Whittier's most apocalyptic poem "What of the Day?" has its own curious history. Whittier wrote the poem in 1854, long before the Civil War broke out. He was hoeing in his garden when the inspiration for the poem came and he rushed inside to write it at his desk. After finishing the poem, he read it over several times without knowing what it meant and then put it in a drawer where it remained for two years before publication. Openly called "the burden of the prophet's vision," the poem depicts the final cataclysmic struggle between good and evil on "Armageddon's plain." This day is one of darkness, whirlwinds, thunders, and garish red glares; foes tread with challenge while eagles wheel above, heralding the "turn and o'erturn" which will destroy established order. Dismayed and frightened, Whittier doubts whether he can read these signs correctly for the vast dimness and chaos allow no sure vision or easy religious affirmation. Only a humble "Thy will be done" is possible and Whittier accepts the holocaust of violence and war if that alone will destroy slavery. In the light of his own doubts and uncertain vision, the image of the new Jerusalem arising from this carnage assumes an added significance. Finally, through the clouds of dust Whittier perceives the "chaffless grain" heaped gloriously on the earth's threshing floor, having been flailed by God's thunder. What Whittier sensed in 1854 was the coming Civil War which brought not only the destruction of slavery, but the terrible end to his hopes for peace. The prophetic manner provided an adequate artistic framework for presenting the tensions of the abolitionist and Quaker.

"Ichabod," Whittier's most famous abolitionist poem, can also be examined in this Biblical prophetic category. Although the poem has been extensively analyzed, no critic has fully explored the relationship of the "Ichabod" allusion to the meaning of the poem.[11] Taken from I Samuel 4:21, the title is intimately associated with one of Israel's great national crises, just prior to the establishment of the monarchy. The dominant figure of these chapters is Eli who functions not only as high priest, but as a national and political leader as well. Age, familiarity with power, and a variety of personal weaknesses have dulled his once clear moral vision and caused him to confuse personal desires with God's sacred duty. He refuses to punish his sons' open profanation of the temple and then allows them to desecrate the Ark, Israel's holiest symbol, by carrying it into battle against the Philistines. Disaster results: the ark is captured, the sons killed in battle, and a pathetic Eli, stunned with the realization of his failure and the national disgrace, falls dead. Hearing the news, his daughter-in-law, just before her own death in childbirth, cries out that the new born should be called Ichabod as a sign that the glory has departed from Israel.

In Whittier's eyes the parallels with Webster's actions were striking. Webster clearly represents the aging high priest, long having served God and his people in his senatorial role and especially honored for defending the sacred constitutional guarantees of freedom—America's holy ark. Webster's own personal desire for the presidency, his long years of compromise, and his age have blurred his moral vision also. His vote for the Fugitive Slave Law in 1850 permitted America's sacred ark to fall into the hands of its southern enemies and perilled his country's basic integrity. This sense of shame and betrayal guides the entire poem and is symbolized by the mother's despair at the moment of childbirth. Joy becomes sorrow and death is preferable to life. A tone of sadness and muted sorrow convey the extent of the national disgrace and the depth of the betrayal. By paralleling Eli and Webster, Whittier suggests the vast, eternal moral dimensions of Webster's act and then goes one step further. Shamed with the knowledge of his responsibility, Eli dies, but Webster continued to live. The contrast implies that Webster's spiritual nature has so atrophied that he remains unaware of his inner death. So Whittier and the entire nation perform the rites of burial for a living corpse, a formal ceremony that transcends personal rancor or individual vilification. Only a new high priest can restore the glory to Israel and America.

Such a brief survey of Whittier's abolitionist verse merely suggests the varied mixture of abolitionist, prophet, Quaker, propagandist, and poet that created them. At best, their earnest sincerity and religious intensity redeemed their topical nature, simplified their digressive tendency, and toughened their derivative phrasing. Few of them succeed as well as "Massachusetts to Virginia," "What of the Day?" or "Ichabod" in expressing Whittier's moral feelings with restraint and artistry. But all attempt the following:

> O Freedom! if to me belong
> Nor mighty Milton's gift divine,
>   Nor Marvell's wit and graceful song,
>   Still with a love as deep and strong
> As theirs, I lay, like them, my best gifts on her shrine![12]

Notes

1. All poetry quotations are taken from *The Complete Poetical Works of John Greenleaf Whittier*, ed. Horace E. Scudder, Cambridge Edition (Boston: Houghton, Mifflin, 1894).

2. Other abolitionist groupings like Whittier's humorous satires of slavery or his personal portraits of abolitionists and other political figures are not considered in this paper, although they too would repay critical scrutiny.

3. "Introduction," *Complete Poetical Works*, xxi–xxii.

4. Originally entitled "Stanzas," the poem was finally printed as "Expostulation" in the *Complete Poetical Works*.

5. From "The Sentence of John L. Brown."

6. From "In the Evil Days."

7. Compare, for example, the similar images and phrases in "Stanzas for the Times" (1835) and "The Moral Warfare" (1838) or the following two verses; one from "Clerical Oppressors" (1836) and the second from "The Christian Slave" (1843):

> How long, O Lord! how long
> Shall such a priesthood barter truth away,
> And in Thy name, for robbery and wrong
> At Thy own altars pray?

> God of all right! how long
> Shall priestly robbers at Thine altar stand,
> Lifting in prayer to Thee the bloody hand
> And haughty brow of wrong?

8. These quotations are from the following poems: "The Panorama," "Lines from a Letter to a Young Clerical Friend," "The Sentence of John L. Brown," and "Our Countrymen in Chains."

9. Hyatt H. Waggoner, "What I Had I Gave: Another Look at Whittier," *EIHC*, 95 (1959), 38–39.

10. From "At Washington."

11. See especially Notley S. Maddox, "Whittier's 'Ichabod' 33–36," *Explicator*, 18 (1960), Item 38; Lewis Leary, *John Greenleaf Whittier* (New York: Twayne, 1961), pp. 105–09; and John B. Pickard, *John Greenleaf Whittier: An Introduction and Interpretation* (New York: Holt, Rinehart and Winston, 1961), pp. 106–07.

12. From "Proem."

Whittier

Robert Penn Warren*

When Whittier, at the age of twenty-six, came to knock "Pegasus on the head,"[1] the creature he laid low was, indeed, not much better than the tanner's superannuated donkey. In giving up his poetry he gave up very little. Looking back on the work he had done up to that time, we can see little achievement and less promise of growth. He had the knack, as he put it in "The Nervous Man," for making rhymes "as mechanically as a mason piles one brick above another," but nothing that he wrote had the inwardness, the organic quality, of poetry. The stuff, in brief, lacked content, and it lacked style. Even when he was able to strike out poetic phrases, images, or effects, he was not able to organize a poem; his poems usually began anywhere and ended when the author got tired. If occasionally we see a poem begin with a real sense of poetry the poetry gets quickly lost in some abstract idea. Even a poem as late as "The Last Walk in Autumn" (1857) suffers in this way. It opens with a fine stanza like this:

> O'er the bare woods, whose outstretched hands
> Plead with the leaden heavens in vain,
> I see beyond the valley lands,
> The sea's long level dim with rain,
> Around me, all things, stark and dumb,
> Seem praying for the snows to come,
> And for the summer bloom and greenness, gone,
> With winter's sunset lights and dazzling morn atone.

But after five stanzas, the poem dies and the abstractions take over for some score of stanzas.

For a poet of natural sensibility, subtlety, and depth to dedicate his work to propaganda would probably result in a coarsening of style and a blunting of effects, for the essence of propaganda is to refuse qualifications and complexity. But Whittier had, by 1833, shown little

*John Greenleaf Whittier's Poetry: An Appraisal and a Selection by Robert Penn Warren. © Copyright 1971 by the University of Minnesota. University of Minnesota Press, Minneapolis.

sensibility, subtlety, or depth, and his style was coarse to a degree. He had nothing to lose, and stood to gain certain things. To be effective, propaganda, if it is to be more than random vituperation, has to make a point, and the point has to be held in view from the start; the piece has to show some sense of organization and control, the very thing Whittier's poems had lacked. But his prose had not lacked this quality, nor, in fact, a sense of the biting phrase; now his verse could absorb the virtues of his prose. It could learn, in addition to a sense of point, something of the poetic pungency of phrase and image, and the precision that sometimes marked the prose. He had referred to his poems as "fancies," and that is what they were, no more. Now he began to relate poetry, though blunderingly enough, to reality. The process was slow. It was ten years—1843—before Whittier was able to write a piece as good as "Massachusetts to Virginia." This was effective propaganda; it had content and was organized to make a point.

Whittier had to wait seven more years before, at the age of forty-three, he could write his first really fine poem. This piece, the famous "Ichabod," came more directly, and personally, out of his political commitment than any previous work. On March 7, 1850, Daniel Webster, senator from Massachusetts, spoke on behalf of the more stringent Fugitive Slave Bill that had just been introduced by Whittier's ex-idol Henry Clay; and the poem, which appeared in March in the *Washington National Era*,[2] a paper of the "political" wing of the Abolition movement, deals with the loss of the more recent and significant idol. "This poem," Whittier wrote years later, "was the outcome of the surprise and grief and forecast of evil consequences which I felt on reading the Seventh of March Speech by Daniel Webster. . . ." But here the poet remembers his poem, which does dramatically exploit surprise and grief, better than he remembers the facts of its origin; he could scarcely have felt surprise at Webster's speech, for as early as 1847, in a letter to Sumner, Whittier had called Webster a "colossal coward" because of his attitude toward the annexation of Texas and the Mexican War.

Here is the poem:

> So fallen! so lost! the light withdrawn
>   Which once he wore!
> The glory from his gray hairs gone
>   Forevermore!
>
> Revile him not, the Tempter hath
>   A snare for all;
> And pitying tears, not scorn and wrath,
>   Befit his fall!
>
> Oh, dumb be passion's stormy rage,
>   When he who might

Have lighted up and led his age,
  Falls back in night.

Scorn! would the angels laugh, to mark
  A bright soul driven,
Fiend-goaded, down the endless dark,
  From hope and heaven!

Let not the land once proud of him
  Insult him now,
Nor brand with deeper shame his dim,
  Dishonored brow.

But let its humbled sons, instead,
  From sea to lake,
A long lament, as for the dead,
  In sadness make.

Of all we loved and honored, naught
  Save power remains;
A fallen angel's pride of thought,
  Still strong in chains.

All else is gone; from those great eyes
  The soul has fled;
When faith is lost, when honor dies,
  The man is dead!

Then, pay the reverence of old days
  To his dead fame;
Walk backward, with averted gaze,
  And hide the shame!

The effectiveness of "Ichabod," certainly one of the most telling
poems of personal attack in English, is largely due to the dramatization
of the situation. At the center of the dramatization lies a division of
feeling on the part of the poet: the poem is not a simple piece of
vituperation, but represents a tension between old trust and new disappointment, old admiration and new rejection, the past and the present.
The Biblical allusion in the title sets this up: "And she named the child
Ichabod, saying, the glory is departed from Israel" (*I Samuel* 4:21).
The glory has departed, but grief rather than rage, respect for the man
who was once the vessel of glory rather than contempt, pity for his
frailty rather than condemnation—these are the emotions recommended
as appropriate. We may note that they are appropriate not only as a
generosity of attitude; they are also the emotions that are basically
condescending, that put the holder of the emotions above the object of
them, and that make the most destructive assault on the ego of the
object. If Webster had been motivated by ambition, then pity is the
one attitude unforgivable by his pride.

The Biblical allusion at the end offers a brilliant and concrete summary of the complexity of feeling in the poem. As Notley Sinclair Maddox has pointed out (*Explicator*, April, 1960), the last stanza is based on *Genesis* 9:20-25. Noah, in his old age, plants a vineyard, drinks the wine, and is found drunk and naked in his tent by his youngest son, Ham, who merely reports the fact to his brothers Shem and Japheth. Out of filial piety, they go to cover Noah's shame, but "their faces were backward, and they saw not their father's nakedness." Ham, for having looked upon Noah's nakedness, is cursed as a "servant to servants" to his "brethren."

The allusion works as a complex and precise metaphor: The great Webster of the past, who, in the time of the debate with Robert Young Hayne (1830), had opposed the slave power and thus established his reputation, has now become obsessed with ambition (drunk with wine) and has exposed the nakedness of human pride and frailty. The conduct of Shem and Japheth sums up, of course, the attitude recommended by the poet. We may remember as an ironical adjunct that the Biblical episode was used from many a pulpit as a theological defense of slavery; Ham, accursed as a "servant to servants," being, presumably, the forefather of the black race.

We may look back at the first stanza to see another complex and effective metaphor, suggested rather than presented. The light is withdrawn, and the light is identified, by the appositive construction, with the "glory" of Webster's gray hair—the glory being the achievement of age and the respect due to honorable age, but also the image of a literal light, an aureole about the head coming like a glow from the literal gray hair. This image fuses with that of the "fallen angel" of line 27 and the dimness of the "dim,/Dishonored brow" in lines 19 and 20. In other words, by suggestion, one of the things that holds the poem together (as contrasted with the logical sequence of the statement) is the image of the angel Lucifer, the light-bearer, fallen by excess of pride. Then in lines 29 and 30, the light image, introduced in the first stanza with the aureole about the gray hair, appears as an inward light shed outward, the "soul" that had once shone from Webster's eyes (he had remarkably large and lustrous dark eyes). But the soul is now dead, the light "withdrawn," and we have by suggestion a death's-head with the eyes hollow and blank. How subtly the abstract ideas of "faith" and "honor" are drawn into this image, and how subtly the image itself is related to the continuing play of variations of the idea of light and dark.

From the point of view of technique this poem is, next to "Telling the Bees," Whittier's most perfectly controlled and subtle composition. This is true not only of the dramatic ordering and interplay of imagery, but also of the handling of rhythm as related to meter and stanza, and to the verbal texture. For Whittier, in those rare moments when he could shut out the inane gabble of the sweet singers like Lydia Sigourney, and of his own incorrigible meter-machine, could hear the true voice of feeling. But how rarely he heard—or trusted—the voice of feeling. He was, we may hazard, afraid of feeling. Unless, of course, a feeling had been properly disinfected.

In the "war with wrong," Whittier wrote a number of poems that were, in their moment, effectively composed, but only two (aside from "Ichabod") that survive to us as poetry. To one, "Song of Slaves in the Desert," we shall return; but the other, "Letter from a Missionary of the Methodist Episcopal Church South, in Kansas, to a Distinguished Politician," not only marks a high point in Whittier's poetic education but may enlighten us as to the relation of that education to his activity as a journalist and propagandist.

The "Letter," as the full title indicates, grew out of the struggle between the pro-slavery and the free-state forces for the control of "Bleeding Kansas." Though the poem appeared in 1854, four years after "Ichabod," it shows us more clearly than the earlier piece how the realism, wit, and irony of Whittier's prose could be absorbed into a composition that is both polemic and poetry. The polemical element is converted into poetry by the force of its dramatization—as in the case of "Ichabod": but here specifically by an ironic ventriloquism, the device of having the "Letter" come from the pen of the godly missionary:

> Last week—the Lord be praised for all His mercies
> To His unworthy servant!—I arrived
> Safe at the Mission, *via* Westport; where
> I tarried over night, to aid in forming
> A Vigilance Committee, to send back,
> In shirts of tar, and feather-doublets quilted
> With forty stripes save one, all Yankee comers,
> Uncircumcised and Gentile, aliens from
> The Commonwealth of Israel, who despise
> The prize of the high calling of the saints,
> Who plant amidst this heathen wilderness
> Pure gospel institutions, sanctified
> By patriarchal use· The meeting opened
> With prayer, as was most fitting. Half an hour,
> Or thereaway, I groaned, and strove, and wrestled,
> As Jacob did at Penuel, till the power
> Fell on the people, and they cried "Amen!"
> "Glory to God!" and stamped and clapped their hands;
> And the rough river boatmen wiped their eyes;
> "Go it, old hoss!" they cried, and cursed the niggers—
> Fulfilling thus the word of prophecy,
> "Cursed be Canaan."

By the ventriloquism the poem achieves a control of style, a fluctuating tension between the requirements of verse and those of "speech," a basis for the variations of tone that set up the sudden poetic, and ironic, effect at the end:

> P.S. All's lost. Even while I write these lines,
> The Yankee abolitionists are coming
> Upon us like a flood—grim, stalwart men,
> Each face set like a flint of Plymouth Rock
> Against our institutions—staking out
> Their farm lots on the wooded Wakarusa,
> Or squatting by the mellow-bottomed Kansas;
> The pioneers of mightier multitudes,
> The small rain-patter, ere the thunder shower
> Drowns the dry prairies. Hope from man is not.
> Oh, for a quiet berth at Washington,
> Snug naval chaplaincy, or clerkship, where
> These rumors of free labor and free soil
> Might never meet me more. Better to be
> Door-keeper in the White House, than to dwell
> Amidst these Yankee tents, that, whitening, show
> On the green prairie like a fleet becalmed.
> Methinks I hear a voice come up the river
> From those far bayous, where the alligators
> Mount guard around the camping filibusters:
> "Shake off the dust of Kansas. Turn to Cuba—
> (That golden orange just about to fall,
> O'er-ripe, into the Democratic lap;)
> Keep pace with Providence, or, as we say,
> Manifest destiny. Go forth and follow
> The message of our gospel, thither borne
> Upon the point of Quitman's bowie-knife,
> And the persuasive lips of Colt's revolvers.
> There may'st thou, underneath thy vine and fig-tree,
> Watch thy increase of sugar cane and negroes,
> Calm as a patriarch in his eastern tent!"
> Amen: So mote it be. So prays your friend.

Here quite obviously the ventriloquism is what gives the poem a "voice," and the fact instructs us as to how Whittier, less obviously, develops through dramatization a voice in "Ichabod." The voice of a poem is effective—is resonant—insofar as it bespeaks a life behind that voice, implies a dramatic issue by which that life is defined. We have spoken of the complexity of feeling behind the voice of "Ichabod," and in the present case we find such a complexity in the character of the missionary himself. At first glance, we have the simple irony of the evil man cloaking himself in the language of the good. But another irony, and deeper, is implicit in the poem: the missionary may not be evil, after all; he may even be, in a sense, "good"—that is, be speaking in perfect sincerity, a man good but misguided; and thus we have the fundamental irony of the relation of evil and good in human character, action, and history. Whittier was a polemicist, and a very astute one, as the "Letter" in its primary irony exemplifies. But he was also a devout Quaker, and by fits and starts a poet, and his creed, like his art, would necessarily give a grounding for the secondary, and deeper, irony, an irony that implies humility and forgiveness.

What we have been saying is that by repudiating poetry Whittier became a poet. His image of knocking Pegasus on the head tells a deeper truth than he knew; by getting rid of the "poetical" notion of poetry, he was able, eventually, to ground his poetry on experience. In the years of his crusade and of the Civil War, he was, bit by bit, learning this, and the process was, as we have said, slow. It was a process that seems to have been by fits and starts, trial and error, by floundering, rather than by rational understanding. Whittier was without much natural taste and almost totally devoid of critical judgment, and he seems to have had only a flickering awareness of what he was doing—though he did have a deep awareness, it would seem, of his personal situation.

. . .

As for the relation to the poet's personal life, *Snow-Bound* came after another manifestation of the old inhibition that forbade his seeking solace from Elizabeth Lloyd's healing hands (and this as he neared the age of sixty, when the repudiation of the solace must have seemed more nearly and catastrophically final). It came after the death of the sister had deprived him of the motive of his life. And it came, too, toward the end of the Civil War, when he could foresee the victory of the cause to which he had given his energies for more than thirty years and which had, in a sense, served as his justification for life, and as a substitute for other aspects of life. Now the joy of victory would, necessarily, carry with it a sense of emptiness. Furthermore, the victory itself was in terms sadly different, as Whittier recognized, from those that he had dreamed.

Snow-Bound is, then, a summarizing poem for Whittier; but it came, also, at a summarizing moment for the country. It came when the country—at least all the country that counted, the North—was poised on the threshold of a new life, the world of technology, big industry, big business, finance capitalism, and urban values. At that moment, caught up in the promises of the future, the new breed of American could afford to look back on his innocent beginnings; and the new breed could afford to pay for the indulgence of nostalgia—in fact, in the new affluence, paid quite well for it. Whittier's book appeared on February 17, 1866,[3] and the success was immediate. For instance, in April, J. T. Fields, the publisher, wrote to Whittier: "We can't keep the plaguey thing quiet. It goes and goes, and now, today, we are bankrupt again, not a one being in crib." The first edition earned Whittier ten thousand dollars—a sum to be multiplied many times over if translated into present values. The poor man was, overnight, modestly rich.

The scene of the poem, the "Flemish picture," as Whittier calls it, the modest genre piece, is rendered with precise and loving care, and this scene had its simple nostalgic appeal for the generation who had come to town and made it, and a somewhat different appeal, compensatory and comforting no doubt, for the generation that had stayed in the country and had not made it. But the poem is not simple, and it is likely that the appeals would have been far less strong and permanent if Whittier had not set the "idyl" in certain "perspectives" or deeper interpretations. In other words, it can be said of this poem, as of most poetry, that the effect does not depend so much on the thing looked at as on the way of the looking. True, if there is nothing to look at, there can be no looking, but the way of the looking determines the kind of feeling that fuses with the object looked at.

Before we speak of the particular "perspectives" in which the poem is set, we may say that there is a preliminary and general one. This general perspective, specified in Whittier's dedicatory note to his "Winter Idyl,"[4] denies that the poem is a mere "poem." The poem, that is, is offered as autobiography with all the validation of fact. In other words, the impulse that had appeared in "The Vanishers" as fanciful is here given a grounding in the real world, and in presenting that world the poem explores a complex idea—how different from the vague emotion of "The Vanishers"—concerning the human relation to Time.

The literalness of that world is most obviously certified by the lovingly and precisely observed details: the faces sharpened by cold, the "clashing horn on horn" of the restless cattle in the barn, the "grizzled squirrel" dropping his shell, the "board nails snapping in the frost" at night. The general base of the style is low, depending on precision of rendering rather than on the shock and brilliance of language or image; but from this base certain positive poetic effects emerge as accents and point of focus. For instance:

> A chill no coat, however stout,
> Of homespun stuff could quite shut out,
> A hard, dull bitterness of cold,
> That checked, mid-vein, the circling race
> Of life-blood in the sharpened face,
> The coming of the snow-storm told.

> The wind blew east; we heard the roar
> Of Ocean on his wintry shore,
> And felt the strong pulse throbbing there
> Beat with low rhythm our inland air.

Associated with this background realism of the style of the poem we find a firm realism in the drawing of character. Three of the portraits are sharp and memorable, accented against the other members of the group and at the same time bearing thematic relations to them: the spinster aunt, the schoolmaster, and Harriet Livermore.

The aunt, who had had a tragic love affair but who, as the poem states, has found reconciliation with life, bears a thematic relation to both Elizabeth Whittier and Whittier himself. The schoolmaster, whose name Whittier could not remember until near the end of his life, was a George Haskell, who later became a doctor, practiced in New Jersey and Illinois, and died in 1876 without even knowing, presumably, of his rôle in the poem; but as we have pointed out, there are echoes here, too, of Joshua Coffin. As for Harriet Livermore, Whittier's note identifies her. The fact that the "warm, dark languish of her eyes" might change to rage is amply documented by the fact that at one time, before the scene of *Snow-Bound*, she had been converted to Quakerism, but during an argument with another Quaker on a point of doctrine she asserted her theological view by laying out with a length of stove wood the man who was her antagonist. This action, of course, got her out of the sect. In her restless search for a satisfying religion, she represents one strain of thought in nineteenth-century America, and has specific resemblances to the characters Nathan and Nehemiah in Melville's *Clarel*. As a "woman tropical, intense," and at the same time concerned with ideas and beliefs, she is of the type of Margaret Fuller, the model for Zenobia in the *Blithedale Romance* of Hawthorne.

To return to the structure of the poem, there are three particular "perspectives"—ways in which the material is to be viewed—that can be localized in the body of the work. These perspectives operate as inserts that indicate the stages of the dialectic of this poem. The first appears in lines 175 to 211, the second in lines 400 to 437, and the third in lines 715 to the end.

The first section of the poem (up to the first perspective) presents a generalized setting: the coming of the storm, the first night, the first day, and the second night. Here the outside world is given full value in contrast to the interior, especially in the following passage, which is set between two close-ups of the hearthside, that Edenic spot surrounded by the dark world:

> The moon above the eastern wood
> Shone at its full; the hill-range stood

Transfigured in the silver flood,
Its blown snows flashing cold and keen,
Dead white, save where some sharp ravine
Took shadow, or the sombre green
Of hemlocks turned to pitchy black
Against the whiteness at their back.
For such a world and such a night
Most fitting that unwarming light,
Which only seemed where'er it fell
To make the coldness visible.

The setting, as we have said, is generalized; the individual characters have not yet emerged, the father having appeared in only one
line of description and as a voice ordering the boys (John and his only
brother, Matthew) to dig a path, with the group at the fireside only
an undifferentiated "we." This section ends with the very sharp focus
on the mug of cider simmering between the feet of the andirons and
the apples sputtering—the literal fire, the literal comfort against the
threat of literal darkness and cold outside.

Now the first perspective is introduced:

What matter how the night behaved?
What matter how the north-wind raved?
Blow high, blow low, not all its snow
Could quench our hearth-fire's ruddy glow.

But immediately, even as he affirms the inviolability of the fireside
world, the poet cries out:

O Time and Change!—with hair as gray
As was my sire's that winter day,
How strange it seems, with so much gone
Of life and love, to still live on!

From this remembered scene by the fireside only two of the partici-
pants survive, the poet and his brother, who are now as gray as the
father at that snowfall of long ago; for all are caught in Time, in this
less beneficent snowfall that whitens every head, as the implied image
seems to say. Given this process of the repetition of the pattern of Time
and Change, what, the poet asks, can survive? The answer is that "love
can never lose its own."

After the first perspective has thus grafted a new meaning on the
scene of simple nostalgia by the fire, the poem becomes a gallery of
individual portraits, the father, the mother, the uncle, the aunt, the
elder sister (Mary), and the younger (Elizabeth), the schoolmaster, and
Harriet Livermore. That is, each individual brings into the poem a
specific dramatization of the problem of Time. In the simplest dimen-
sion, they offer continuity and repetition: they, the old, were once young,

and now, sitting by the fire with the young, tell of youth remembered against the background of age. More specifically, each of the old has had to try to come to terms with Time, and their portraits concern this past.

When the family portraits have been completed, the second perspective is introduced; this is concerned primarily with the recent bereavement, with the absent Elizabeth, and with the poet's personal future as he walks toward the night and sees (as an echo from "The Vanishers") Elizabeth's beckoning hand. Thus out from the theme of Time and Change emerges the theme of the Future, which is to be developed in the portraits of Haskell and Harriet Livermore.

The first will make his peace in Time, by identifying himself with progressive social good (which, as a matter of fact, George Haskell had done by 1866). Harriet Livermore, though seeking, by her theological questioning, a peace out of Time, has found no peace in Time, presumably because she cannot seek in the right spirit; with the "love within her mute," she cannot identify herself with the real needs of the world about her (as Aunt Mercy can and George Haskell will); she is caught in the "tangled skein of will and fate," and can only hope for a peace in divine forgiveness, out of Time. After the portrait of Harriet Livermore, we find the contrast in the mother's attitude at the goodnight scene: unlike Harriet she finds peace in the here-and-now, "food and shelter, warmth and health" and love, with no "vain prayers" but with a willingness to act practically in the world—an idea that echoes the theme of "My Soul and I," which we have already mentioned. And this is followed with the peace of night and the "reconciled" dream of summer in the middle of the winter.

With dawn, the present—not the past, not the future—appears, with its obligations, joys, and promises. Here there is a lag in the structure of the poem. When the snow-bound ones awake to the sound of "merry voices high and clear," the poem should, logically move toward its fulfilment. But instead, after the gay and active intrusion of the world and the present, we have the section beginning "So days went on," and then the dead "filler" for some twenty lines. Whittier's literalism, his fidelity to irrelevant fact rather than to relevant meaning and appropriate structure of the whole, here almost destroys both the emotional and the thematic thrust, and it is due only to the power of the last movement that the poem is not irretrievably damaged.

The third "perspective" (lines 715–759), which ends the poem, is introduced by the eloquence of these lines:

> Clasp, Angel of the backward look
> And folded wings of ashen gray
> And voice of echoes far away,
> The brazen covers of thy book . . .

Then follow certain new considerations. What is the relation between the dream of the past and the obligations and actions of the future? The answer is, of course, in the sense of continuity of human experience, found when one stretches the "hands of memory" to the "wood-fire's blaze" of the past; it is thus that one may discover the meaningfulness of obligation and action in Time, even as he discovers in the specific memories of the past an image for the values out of Time. The "idyl" is more than a "Flemish picture"; it is an image, and a dialectic, of one of life's most fundamental questions that is summed up in the haunting simplicity of the end:

> Sit with me by the homestead hearth,
> And stretch the hands of memory forth
>   To warm them at the wood-fire's blaze!
> And thanks untraced to lips unknown
> Shall greet me like the odors blown
> From unseen meadows newly mown,
> Or lilies floating in some pond,
> Wood-fringed, the wayside gaze beyond;
> The traveller owns the grateful sense
> Of sweetness near, he knows not whence,
> And, pausing, takes with forehead bare
> The benediction of the air.

As a corollary to the third "perspective" generally considered, Whittier has, however, ventured a specific application. He refers not merely to the action in the future, in general, in relation to the past, but also, quite clearly, to the Civil War and the new order with its "larger hopes and graver fears"—the new order of "throngful city ways" as contrasted with the old agrarian way of life and thought. He invites the "worlding"—the man who, irreligiously, would see no meaning in the shared experience of human history, which to Whittier would have been a form of revelation—to seek in the past not only a sense of personal renewal and continuity, but also a sense of the continuity of the new order with the American past. This idea is clearly related to Whittier's conviction, which we have already mentioned, that the course of development for America should be the fulfilling of the "implied intent" of the Constitution in particular, of the American revelation in general, and of God's will. And we may add that Whittier, by this, also gives another "perspective" in which his poem is to be read.

If we leave *Snow-Bound*, the poem, and go back again to its springs in Whittier's personal story, we may find that it recapitulates in a new form an old issue. The story of his youth is one of entrapments—and of his failure to break out into the world of mature action. In love, politics, and poetry, he was constantly being involved in a deep, inner struggle, with the self-pity, the outrage, the headaches, the breakdowns. He was, to no avail, trying to break out of the "past" of childhood into the "future" of manhood—to achieve, in other words, a self.

The mad ambition that drove him to try to break out of the entrapments, became in itself, paradoxically, another entrapment—another dead hand of the past laid on him. He cried out, "Now, now!"—not even knowing what he cried out for, from what need, for what reality. But nothing worked out, not love, nor politics, nor even poetry, that common substitute for success of a more immediate order. In poetry, in fact, he could only pile up words as a mason piles up bricks; he could only repeat, compulsively, the dreary clichés; his meter-making machine ground on, and nothing that came out was, he knew, real: his poems were only "fancies," as he called them, only an echo of the past, not his own present. And if he set out with the declared intention of being the poet of New England, his sense of its history was mere antiquarianism, mere quaintness—no sense of an abiding human reality. Again he was trapped in the past. All his passions strove, as he put it, "in chains." He found release from what he called "the pain of disappointment and the temptation to envy" only in repudiating the self, and all the self stood for, in order to save the self. He could find a cause that, because it had absorbed (shall we hazard?) all the inner forces of the "past" that thwarted his desires, could free him into some "future" of action.

· · ·

Notes

1. In a letter to his Hartford friend Jonathan Law, Whittier remarked: "As to your suggestion about poetry, I must decline attending to it. I have knocked Pegasus on the head, as a tanner does his bark-mill donkey, when he is past service. I am fixed at Haverhill, as Pope says,—
  'Fixed as a plant to one peculiar spot,
  To draw nutrition, propagate and rot.'" [Ed. note.]

2. In which Whittier's only novel—or near-novel—*Margaret Smith's Journal*, had appeared the previous year, and in which *Uncle Tom's Cabin* was to appear.

3. Melville's book of poems on the Civil War, *Battle-Pieces*, appeared almost simultaneously, and was a crashing failure. As *Snow-Bound* seemed to dwell merely on the simplicity of the past, *Battle-Pieces* analyzed some of the painful complexities of the War and the present, and recognized some of the painful paradoxes in the glowing promises of the future: not what the public wanted to hear.

4. Here is the beginning of the prefatory note: "The inmates of the family at the Whittier homestead who are referred to in the poem were my father, mother, my brother and two sisters, and my uncle and aunt, both unmarried. In addition, there was the district schoolmaster, who boarded with us. The 'not unfeared, half-welcome guest' was Harriet Livermore, daughter of Judge Livermore, of New Hampshire, a young woman of fine natural ability, enthusiastic, eccentric, with slight control over her violent temper, which sometimes made her religious profession doubtful. She was equally ready to exhort in school-house prayer-

meetings and dance in a Washington ball-room, while her father was a member of Congress. She early embraced the doctrine of the Second Advent, and felt it her duty to proclaim the Lord's speedy coming. With this message she crossed the Atlantic and spent the greater part of a long life in traveling over Europe and Asia. She lived some time with Lady Hester Stanhope, a woman as fantastic and mentally strained as herself, on the slope of Mt. Lebanon, but finally quarrelled with her in regard to two white horses with red marks on their backs which suggested the idea of saddles, on which her titled hostess expected to ride into Jerusalem with the Lord. A friend of mine found her, when quite an old woman, wandering in Syria with a tribe of Arabs, who, with the Oriental notion that madness is inspiration, accepted her as their prophetess and leader. At the time referred to in *Snow-Bound* she was boarding at the Rocks Village, about two miles from us."

Elsewhere in a prefatory note to another poem, "The Countess," Whittier identifies the "wise old doctor" of *Snow-Bound* as Dr. Elias Weld of Haverhill, "the one cultivated man in the neighborhood," who had given the boy the use of his library.

Imagistic and Structural Unity in "Snow-Bound"

Relying on Whittier's comment that "Snow-Bound" portrays "Flemish pictures of old days," most critics have examined it as a loosely connected montage which quaintly evokes the atmosphere of rural New England in the 1800s.[1] Such comment accords value to Whittier's graphic rendering of physical details, to his authentic delineation of family figures, and to his fidelity to actual experience. But the poem, "old, rude-furnished" like the house, does burst "flower-like, into rosy bloom" and this artistic fruition is not a chance occurrence. The imagistic development of the poem, use of appropriate symbols, and closely organized structure provide a satisfying artistic framework for these rustic scenes. An examination of these aspects indicates a genuine literary value far beyond local or historical interest.

The theme turns on the nostalgic recall of the love and protection which the Whittier family once gave the poet, emphasizing his painful sense of present loss and hope for spiritual content. These emotions are primarily developed by a series of contrasts: of fire and snow, past and present, people and elements—which combine to form the larger theme of love and immortality struggling against pain and death. Perhaps the touchstone for interpreting the poem is the symbolic development of the wood fire. The poem is headed by a quotation from Agrippa's *Occult Philosophy*: "As the Spirits of Darkness be stronger in the dark, so Good Spirits, which be Angels of Light, are augmented not only by the Divine light of the Sun, but also by our common Wood Fire: and as the Celestial Fire drives away dark spirits, so also this our Fire of Wood doth the same." Also a second epigraph from Emerson's "The Snow-Storm" re-emphasizes the importance of the "radiant" fire. In the poem, fire is associated not only with brightness, relaxation, and physical comfort, but with the emotional and spiritual warmth of family love, with "the genial glow" of community brotherhood, and with divine pro-

*Copyright © 1960 by the National Council of Teachers of English. Reprinted by permission of the publisher and the author.

tection against the evil spirits of nature and time. Artistically delayed by the description of the "unwarming" storm, the initial lighting of the fire introduces the Whittier household, and its blaze symbolizes the reality of family love. Throughout the central section, particularly, Whittier associates the vigor and happiness of family talk, games, and interests with the color and sparkle of the glowing logs; and unites the close bond of family love with the red heat of the fire. For example, the uncle's simple tales are "warming" and cause the listeners to forget "the outside cold, / The bitter wind." Also Whittier weaves into the fire pattern the sunny richness, ripe crops, blooming hillsides, and full greenness associated with summer. Finally, the dying fire indicates the end of the evening's activities, while also symbolizing the eventual crumbling of the security and protection of the family group.

By contrast, the storm evokes sensations of fear and awe and illustrates the terrible anonymity of nature and death. It dominates the entire first section of the poem, transforming its principal antagonist, the sun, into a cheerless, dark, snowblown wanderer; and enforcing on the family a "savage" isolation which obtains no comfort from "social smoke." The storm's assault on the house is likened to the later attack of death on its individual members as Whittier recalls "the chill weight of the winter snow" on Elizabeth's grave. Conversely, the storm's magical power changes a dull, commonplace farm into a white fairyland of beauty and wonder.

A second major contrast deals with the past versus present. In "Snow-Bound" Whittier imaginatively re-creates the past, while echoing his present-day feelings of loneliness. Four main interpolations deal with this problem of time and change, contrasting past happiness with present pain and concluding with the hope for future social progress and spiritual consolation. For example, the first interpolation appropriately comes when the fire is lighted and the storm's force seems abated. As if lost in the scene he has recalled Whittier cries: "What matter how the night behaved? / What matter how the north-wind raved?" Immediately, the knowledge of "Time and Change" stop him, for what the elements failed to do that night death has since accomplished. The answering consolation of spiritual life being "lord of death" and love never losing its own contains the theme of the poem. These major contrasts are further expanded by an increasing depth of images and a movement from concrete physical description to an investigation of personality and emotions with a final return to realistic depiction. All these aspects are blended into the total theme—the strength and bond of family love.

Yet the underlying unity of the poem is developed by a time cycle. The two day's snowfall; the third day's activity and a description of the family that night; the fourth day's visit of the teamsters and doctor; until a week has passed and the isolation is completely broken. However, within this framework is a more ordered three-fold division which pits the forces of nature against the family group. The first section of the poem (to line 178) presents the physical domination of the storm and concludes with a view of the inner house and the lighting of the fire. The emphasis throughout is on exact physical detail and on the primitive forces of nature. After the first interpolation, the storm is forgotten, for human love and companionship have exorcised the raging spirits of the night. The images become more demanding and introspective as loneliness and nostalgia overwhelm the poet. The dying embers of the fire and dreams of summer open the third section (line 629) with a return to the outside physical world; correspondingly, the images also become more concrete. Here the theme of family strength is widened to the larger bond of community union. The ending interpolation emphasizes the "larger hopes and graver fears" of social responsibility that can finally unite all mankind as the bond of personal love and Quaker "inner light" had once securely linked the Whittier family. This section closes with a hope that art will also preserve some of the more valued aspects of the family group.

A closer analysis of each section reveals the skillful interweaving of the theme with structure and its artistic expansion from major imagistic contrasts. The poem opens with a description of the approaching storm and its complete domination over the "Divine light of the Sun," which is darkly circled, barely able to diffuse a sad "light." Still, as a portent, the sun briefly foreshadows the coming fire of the hearth which does temporarily defeat the storm. A sense of unusual expectation grips the early lines and the cold checks the "circling race/Of life-blood"—suggesting the eventual triumph of death over the family life. A following description of nightly chores deepens this mood by emphasizing the helplessness of all animate beings before the elements. Then the full fury of the storm breaks to create a chaos of whirling, blinding snow which destroys man's order and intelligent control. On the second morning:

> The old familiar sights of ours
> Took marvelous shapes; strange domes and towers
> Rose up where sty or corn-crib stood,
>
> . . . .
>
> The bridle post an old man sat
> With loose-flung coat and high cocked hat;
> The well-curb had a Chinese roof;
> And even the long sweep, high aloof,
> In its slant splendor, seemed to tell
> Of Pisa's leaning miracle.

The condensed details of pure fancy, clever allusion, and purposeful exaggeration evoke a childlike wonder and convey a panoramic view of the transforming power of the storm. Once more human activity intrudes as the father and boys cut through "the solid whiteness" to reach the barn, but now even labor is a delight, for their finished tunnel resembles the dazzling crystal of Aladdin's cave. These pleasing aspects of the storm are immediately counter-balanced by a piercing wind which creates a "savage" world of terror and sunlessness, eliminates "social smoke," and deadens Christian sounds.

When the snowblown and still helpless sun sets that afternoon, loving hands gather the wood and brush necessary to kindle the fire. The "curious art" displayed in these simple tasks suggests a ritual-like significance in their performance. The first red blaze metamorphosizes the kitchen into "rosy bloom," but an even greater miracle occurs as the snowdrifts outside reflect the inner fire with their own mimic flame. For the first time the fire controls and the snow receives its burning imprint. Yet, the outer elements are not so easily conquered and the moon that night reveals an eerie half-world of "dead white" snows and "pitchy black" hemlocks suffused by an "unwarming" light. Once more the fire's "tropic heat" asserts its power and the glowing light reveals a mug of simmering cider, rows of apples, and a basket of nuts—objects closely associated with the inner world of personality and life.

Though the second section of the poem opens with an emphatic defiance of the elements, this confidence is soon undercut by the painful realization that time has finally conquered. For the faces "lighted" by love and the warmth of the fire are no longer alive ("in the sun they cast no shade"). Ironically, these reflections occur just as the fire does finally dominate the outside elements. Still, forcing these melancholy thoughts from mind by utilizing the fire-snow contrast, Whittier insists that the light of breaking day will play across the mournful marbles of the tomb—that love and faith will find spiritual happiness. This consolation provides an uneasy truce which allows the poet to describe the personalities of the family. The father, mother, and uncle are fittingly characterized by warm summer days, outdoor fishing and haying, ripening corn, steaming clambakes, and sunny hillsides. Also their plain childlike natures and interests are perfectly echoed by the quaint sounding couplet rhythm, the rough unpolished inversions, and the vernacular "Yankee" rhymes. To follow these three innocent characters, Whittier introduces another group of three, the aunt and two sisters, whose more complex natures reflect some measure of life's pain, sacrifice, and loneliness. Similarly, the tone becomes more introspective and the images more expansive and thoughtful. The aunt's still youthful charm and virgin freshness are expressed in a delicate summer figure of clouds and dew:

Before her still a cloud-land lay,
The mirage loomed across her way;
The morning dew, that dries so soon
With others, glistened at her noon.

The elder sister's death is described as an entrance "beneath the low
green tent / Whose curtain never outward swings." Significantly her
death is not snow-filled or chilling; rather it is the casual drifting of a
tent-flap with the later discovery that this light opening has now been
closed with the heavy weight of "low green" sod. A following passage
on Elizabeth, "Our youngest and our dearest," introduces the second
interpolation. Once again Whittier's faith struggles with the harsh reality
of death as the chilling snows of the grave cover the summer charm and
violet beauty of Elizabeth's nature. Finally the poet asks:

Am I not richer than of old?
Safe in thy immortality,
What change can reach the wealth I hold?

At first glance the figure appears paradoxical, for how can Elizabeth's
death make the poet richer and "safe"? On one level her beauty and
purity, freed from time's inexorable destruction, are now "safe" in his
memory; but also her "immortality" secures him, since it illuminates
his final spiritual goal and provides him with a standard for judging all
his future acts.

The following two characterizations portray the visiting schoolmaster and the "not unfeared, half-welcome guest," while also introducing the third interpolation. The realistic sketch of the schoolmaster's
entertaining knowledge of the classics and rural games, his boyish
humor, and self-reliant, yet humble, nature is a fine genre portrait that
matches the earlier ones of the father and uncle. Indeed the schoolmaster's close intimacy with the family is underscored by the lines that
introduce him as one who "Held at the fire his favored place, / Its
warm glow lit a laughing face." His further delineation as one of "Freedom's young apostles" completes Whittier's portrait of the fearless
young leader whose moral strength will destroy social injustice like
slavery and open a new era of peace and progress. At the same time
the expansion of these optimistic ideas on the power of education and
reform in the third interpolation displays the thinness of Whittier's social
thought; while its abstract hackneyed imagery ("war's bloody trail,"
"treason's monstrous growth") contrasts unfavorably with the concrete
detail of other sections. The final figure, Harriet Livermore, presents an
interesting variation of the fire imagery as she combines characteristics
of both the spirits of light and blackness. Her warm and lustrous eyes
flash light, but also hold "dark languish" and wrath; while her brows

are "black with night" and shoot out a "dangerous light." This tortured nature warps and twists the "celestial fire," for she enters the family group without sharing its close affection or receiving the warm benefits of love from the wood fire. Her complex characterization is appropriately climaxed by the uneasy observation that in some natures the line between "will and fate" is undistinguishable. Structurally these two outsiders represent the various "fire-cold" aspects of a forgotten external world. The schoolmaster offers the warmth of companionship, the balance of learning, and eventual hope for social responsibility; while Harriet Livermore reveals the chill of fanaticism and the failure of personal, emotional efforts to correct injustice. Also their intrusion foreshadows the unavoidable demands that society is soon to make upon the secure family group. Appropriately, the second section concludes when the family disbands for bed and the now dull fire is extinguished. As the family falls asleep, the snow sifts through the loosened clapboards and the storm re-enters the poem (though significantly the snow no longer has the power to disturb their dreams of summer). The ending of the night's activities carefully reworks the fire image:

> At last the great logs, crumbling low,
> Sent out a dull and duller glow,
> The bull's-eye watch that hung in view,
> Ticking its weary circuit through,
> Pointed with mutely warning sign
> Its black hand to the hour of nine.
> That sign the pleasant circle broke:
> My uncle ceased his pipe to smoke,
> Knocked from its bowl the refuse gray,
> And laid it tenderly away;
> Then roused himself to safely cover
> The dull red bands with ashes over·

The crumbling of the once great logs hints of nature's eventual triumph over the family unit; while the ominous black watch, like a living spirit of darkness, also specifies that time has run out. When the uncle knocks the ashes from his pipe, he deepens the suggestion of the burned-out logs and echoes the clock's warning. Even the halting verse pattern with its awkward inversions reflects the fumbling slowness and plodding, careful manner of the uncle.

The ending section briefly returns to the physical world of the opening stanzas, as the teamsters and plows now control the effects of the storm; while the children find sport, instead of terror, in its whiteness. Finally, the local newspaper arrives and the family broadens its interests to other communities and "warmer" zones. Signalizing the larger social union which radiates from the smaller family bond, the visiting doctor utilizes the mother's skill in nursing to aid a sick neighbor.

So, love joins his "mail of Calvin's creed" with her Quaker "inner light." Now the storm's isolation is completely broken and the section ends with the joyful cry "Now all the world was ours once more."

While this appears to be the logical finish for the poem, it disregards the troubling theme of time's ultimate victory. So, in a final interpolation Whittier asks the "Angel of the backward look" to close the volume in which he has been writing. With difficulty he shakes off this mood of regret and nostalgia to respond to present day demands (much as he had pictured the young schoolmaster doing) and utilizes the image of the century-blooming aloe to dramatically portray the successful flowering of the abolitionist's aim to abolish slavery. The ending lines further console Whittier with the hope that his "Flemish" artistry has truly recreated "pictures of old days" and that others might gather a similar spiritual and emotional comfort from them by stretching the "hands of memory forth / To warm them at the wood-fire's blaze." A final summer image completes the poem as the thought of future readers enjoying his efforts refreshes him as odors blown from unseen meadows or the sight of lilies in some half-hidden pond. These lines reflect the inner serenity and imperturbable peace which offers final solace. So the poem moves in artistic transitions from the physical level of storm and fire to the psychological world of death and love, utilizing the wood fire as the dominant symbol. The dread of time and change is assuaged by the confidence that social reform will improve the future, by the knowledge that art often outlasts time's ravages, and by the certainty that spiritual immortality does conquer it completely. For this successful fusing of form and theme, Whittier well deserves that future readers would send him "benediction of the air."

Note

1. *The Complete Poetical Works of John Greenleaf Whittier*, ed. Horace E. Scudder, Cambridge Edition (Boston: Houghton, Mifflin, 1894), p. 406. One notable exception is George Arms's excellent essay on Whittier in *The Fields Were Green* (Stanford, CA: Stanford Univ. Press, 1953). My study has utilized Arms's comments on the fire symbol, the antislavery theme, and the meaning of the "century's aloe" and has been further improved by his personal criticism.

"John Greenleaf Whittier"

Barrett Wendell[*]

In this constant strength of his instinctive fidelity to Nature, Whittier distinguishes himself from almost all other American men of letters. In most of our literature there is a quality of consciousness. Sometimes this takes the form of aggressive cleverness; sometimes it deliberately assumes the traditional dignity of culture; often—and perhaps most characteristically—it half-consciously, half-unwittingly follows or revives tradition. As somebody has extravagantly said, American verse swarms with nightingales—a bird unknown on this continent. For this state of things there is a reason which these perhaps imaginary nightingales typify. An American would not be a true son of the fathers if he did not instinctively love tradition. The emigrants brought from the Old World fireside tales of things and folks, of pomps and grandeurs, of comedies and tragedies which their children could never know in the flesh. And history has moved fast with us, and society has been overturned more than once. And Western children to-day are listening to such stories of New England as Yankee children of the early days heard about Old England itself. This love of tradition, which shows itself perhaps most markedly in the passion for genealogy which permeates New England, is a prime trait of the true Yankee. Whittier was as true a Yankee as ever lived. His first published volume, we remember, was a volume of "New England Legends." New England legends he continued to write almost all his life; and, as his reading extended, he wrote many other legends, too, of regions and races that he had never known in the flesh.

Of the latter little need be said. They are not profoundly characteristic. He got them from books, and he put them into other books, where their simple ballad-form makes them pleasantly readable. He generally managed to infuse into them a certain amount of blameless moralizing which does not enhance their stimulating quality. On the whole, we may class them with that great body of innocuous American verse which is permeated with the innocent unreality of conscious culture.

[*]Reprinted from *Stelligeri and Other Essays Concerning America* (New York: Scribner's, 1893).

The New England legends are of firmer stuff. In his prose works one finds some of the material that goes to make them. "Charms and Fairy Faith," and "Magicians and Witch Folk"[1] tell of such actual traditions as were kept alive at the snow-bound fireside. "Margaret Smith's Journal,"[2] while no permanent contribution to historical fiction, is so true a picture of the Seventeenth Century in New England as to prove beyond peradventure the solidity of Whittier's study in local history. And verses like these[3] show how well he knew the ancestral Puritans:

> "With the memory of that morning by the summer sea I
> blend
> A wild and wondrous story, by the younger Mather
> penned,
> In that quaint *Magnalia Christi*, with all strange and
> marvellous things,
> Heaped up huge and undigested, like the chaos Ovid
> sings.
>
> "Dear to me these far, faint glimpses of the dual life of
> old,
> Inward, grand with awe and reverence; outward, mean
> and coarse and cold;
> Gleams of mystic beauty playing over dull and vulgar
> clay,
> Golden-threaded fancies weaving in a web of hodden
> gray."

His romantic and legendary narratives of New England, then, have much of the true flavour of the soil. He seems to have been haunted, however, by a lurking Yankee conscience which constantly suggested doubts as to whether it is quite right to tell a good story just for its own sake. His introduction to the "Tent on the Beach,"[4] the volume which contained, on the whole, his most effective narrative poems, is distinctly apologetic. Here, at fifty-nine, he writes:

> "I would not sin in this half-playful strain,—
>   Too light perhaps for serious years, though born
> Of the enforced leisure of slow pain,—
>   Against the pure ideal which has drawn
> My feet to follow its far-shining gleam."

As a result of this state of things, his narratives of New England tradition generally deal with such phases of it as have perceptible didactic significance. Naturally, he represents the Quakers heroically. A typical stanza is this from the "King's Missive," written at seventy-two:[5]

> " 'Off with the knave's hat!' An angry hand
>   Smote down the offence; but the wearer said,
> With a quiet smile, 'By the king's command

I bear his message and stand in his stead.'
In the Governor's hand a missive he laid
With the royal arms on its seal displayed,
And the proud man spake as he glanced thereat,
Uncovering, 'Give Mr. Shattuck his hat.' "

Indubitably didactic in motive, too, are those two narrative poems
of his which are apparently most familiar: "Maud Muller,"[6] written at
forty-six; and "Skipper Ireson's Ride,"[7] written at forty-nine. The merits
and the limits of his work in this kind are patent in "Maud Muller." The
little poem is very simple, and in its conventional sentimentality is very
acceptable to the great American public. In its presentation of a Yankee
judge in the character of a knightly hero of romance, it is artlessly con-
sonant with the social ideals of the Yankee country; so, too, in its tacit
assumption that the good looks of a barefoot country beauty would really
have been more congenial life-companions in an eminent legal career
than the rich dower and the fashionable tendencies of the lady whom the
Judge ultimately married in deference to

"his sisters proud and cold,
And his mother, vain of her rank and gold."

If this sort of thing were canting, it would be abominable. What saves it
is that it rings true. The man meant it seriously. We may smile at his
simplicity, if we like; but we can hardly help loving him for it. Indeed,
it is almost enough to make us forgive that insidiously dreadful rhyme—

"For of all sad words of tongue or pen,
The saddest are these: 'It might have been!' "

"Skipper Ireson's Ride," on the other hand, has much of the true
ballad quality:

"Body of turkey, head of owl,
Wings a-droop like a rained-on fowl,
Feathered and ruffled in every part,
Skipper Ireson stood in the cart.
Scores of women, old and young,
Strong of muscle and glib of tongue,
Pushed and pulled up the rocky lane,
Shouting and singing the shrill refrain:
'Here's Flud Oirson, fur his horrd horrt,
Torr'd an' futherr'd an' corr'd in a corrt
By the women o' Morble'ead!' "

Such a subject as this stirred the Yankee Quaker to the depths. A human
being, deaf to the still small voice, had acted devilishly. The weakest
creatures of his seaside home had risen up against him; and, not over-
stepping the bounds of due punishment, had held him up lastingly to

public scorn and detestation. It is perhaps instructive, in connection with such reforming enthusiasm as pervades this spirited ballad, to learn from a note in the final edition[8] that, twenty-two years after the original publication, Whittier was credibly informed that Ireson had really been innocent. Against the skipper's will, it appeared, his refractory crew had compelled him to desert his sinking townsfolk; and then, to screen themselves, they had falsely accused him, with the direful result commemorated by the poet. His answer to his informant[9] is characteristic:

> "I have no doubt that thy version of Skipper Ireson's ride is the correct one. My verse was founded solely on a fragment of rhyme which I heard from one of my early schoolmates, a native of Marblehead.
>
> "I supposed the story to which it referred dated back at least a century. I knew nothing of the participators, and the narrative of the ballad was pı e fancy. I am glad for the sake of truth and justice that the real facts are given in thy book. I certainly would not knowingly do injustice to any one, dead or living."

And having thus, introductorily, done full justice to the memory of poor Floyd Ireson, he proceeds to reprint his ballad.

In touching these narrative and legendary poems of Whittier, I have perhaps allowed myself to lay undue emphasis on phases of them that are not their best. One and all of them we may certainly call simple, earnest, artless, and beautifully true to the native traditions and temper of New England. In the last fact, however, which I have tried to emphasize, lies their weakness as literature. The temper of New England is essentially serious, always uncomfortable if it cannot defend itself on firm ethical grounds. Thoroughly good narrative, on the other hand, ought to be as free from obvious ethical admixture as are the exquisitely pure descriptions of New England landscape, which seem to me Whittier's most lasting work. At times these narratives of his blend almost inextricably with his poems of Nature; from the narratives may be selected extracts which, in simple descriptive power, are as beautiful as anything Whittier ever did. In general, however, the impression that these narratives make is one of saturation with the traditional ethical ideals of New England, curiously combined with that constant reliance on inner inspiration toward the Right which is the fundamental tenet of the Quaker faith. All men are really equal, he assumes throughout, all ought to be really free; let them be free, and all they have to do is to follow the inner light. And here these narrative poems touch close, on the other hand, the works which Whittier deemed his best—his works for reform. A passage like this, which closes the "King's Missive,"[10] might have belonged to either class:

"The Puritan spirit perishing not,
    To Concord's yeomen the signal sent,
And spake in the voice of the cannon-shot
    That severed the chains of a continent.

With its gentler message of peace and good-will
The thought of the Quaker is living still,
And the freedom of soul he prophesied
Is gospel and law where the martyrs died."

.   .   .

NOTES

1. *Prose Works*, I, 385, 399.

2. *Prose Works*, I, 9.

3. "The Garrison of Cape Ann," *Poetical Works*, I, 166.

4. *Poetical Works*, IV, 227.

5. *Poetical Works*, I, 383. We must remember that Quaker principles forbade salutation by uncovering the head.

6. *Poetical Works*, I, 148.

7. *Poetical Works*, I, 174.

8. *Poetical Works*, I, 174.

9. Samuel Roads, Jr., author of *History and Traditions of Marblehead*. [Ed. note.]

10. *Poetical Works*, I, 386.

Whittier's Ballads:
The Maturing of an Artist

John B. Pickard*

Whittier's ballads probably represent his finest poetic achievement, since they alone adequately express his lifelong interest in New England history and deep love for local legends.[1] Still, the creation of these ballads was a halting, tortuous process which reveals how slowly Whittier's artistry matured and how tardily he recognized his own abilities. Only when dealing with material that was intimately associated with his Quaker beliefs, rural background, humanitarian interests, and own Essex region could Whittier produce poetry of artistic quality and enduring value. And an awareness of these formative influences is necessary for an understanding of his artistic growth in balladry.

As a Quaker, Whittier's earliest readings and instructions had been from the journals and histories of the Friends, which contained accounts of the persecutions endured by the original Quaker settlers. Whittier grew up revering Quakers, like Margaret Brewster, who suffered for their beliefs and admiring those who resisted intolerance, such as Thomas Macy and Cassandra Southwick; while his later researches in colonial history gave him a sympathetic insight into the nature of the Puritan theocracy and the reasons for the persecutions. Then his isolated rural upbringing made him completely dependent on his family and the surrounding district for intellectual growth and emotional maturity; and the close ties formed by years of permanent association with one place instilled in him a love of locality and all the traditions connected with it. His imaginative, responsive mind never forgot the tales told around the Whittier fireplace about Essex county witches, popular superstitions, or local personages like Hugh Tallant, Floyd Ireson, Cobbler Keezar, and Mary Ingalls. It was from these sources that Whittier obtained the material for some of his best ballads. Also these local ties were the staples upon which Whittier based his particular kind of nationalism. An immature Whittier trumpeted his own and his age's confidence in the ability of America to produce worthwhile literature: "It has often been

*Reprinted from the *Essex Institute Historical Collections*, 96, No. 1 (1960), 56–72. (Copyright, 1960, by Essex Institute, Salem, Mass. 01970.)

said that the New World is deficient in poetry and romance. . . . On the contrary New England is full of romance . . . we have mountains pillaring a sky as blue as that which bends over classic Olympus: streams as bright and beautiful as those of Greece and Italy—and forests richer and nobler than those which of old were haunted by Sylph and Dryad."[2] Enflamed by the spirit of intense patriotism after the War of 1812, Whittier devoted his first book (1831) to the legends of New England, planned to write a history of Haverhill, and imitated the heroic border romances of Sir Walter Scott.

However, his entrance into the abolitionist movement in 1833 turned him from an aspiring poet of America's greatness to a dedicated reformer. The moralistic and practical nature of his abolitionist writings limited his presentation of non-didactic poetry; while their journalistic haste and propaganda basis hindered artistic competence. Yet, this active life as an abolitionist crusading for the emancipation of the slaves, as an editor fighting for the rights of the working man, and as a politician organizing reform parties benefited the poet too. It forced him into the main currents of his age away from the dream world of romance, toughened his poetic spirit, and gave him a hard-won appreciation of the values in American democracy. Despite the demands of his anti-slavery work, Whittier's affection for his own locale, which had been deepened by enforced separation and patient study, refused to lie dormant. During the 1840's and 1850's Whittier produced many regional pieces, finding in them a means of relaxation and escape. In these poems Whittier wrote of the things he knew and loved, speaking as a poet without a dedicated social or moral purpose. With maturity these interests grew as did an understanding of his art and capabilities. His mature critical creed stressed a fidelity to one's own experience, insisted on truth and realistic accuracy, and sought a style which would simply and directly reveal the man himself. Finally, Whittier saw that his art must utilize the beauty of the commonplace as found in the history and traditions of his native community. It was only then that Whittier produced his most valuable ballads.

Fortunately for Whittier, his earliest literary influences were the poems of Burns, which glorified rural life and local customs; and the romances of Scott, which centered on the heroism of Scottish warriors. His imitations of these two men, or at least his use of their themes as he saw them reflected in his own life, were the most promising verses of his early years. His first collection of poems and tales, *Legends of New England,* dealt entirely with local traditions and superstitions. They are marred by digressions and extravagant romantic phrasing and employ the typical Gothic devices of doomed lovers, ghostly ships, and hidden horrors. However, one ballad, "The Black Fox," has a sure poetic beat and adapts its subject and content to the ballad tradition of simplicity.

The introduction to the poem re-creates the atmosphere of a winter's evening in rural New England with a clearness of language and simplicity of diction that indicate Whittier's ballad capabilities:

> Around an ancient fireplace,
>   A happy household drew;
> A husband and his own good wife
>   And children not a few;
> And bent above the spinning wheel
>   The aged grandame too.[3]

The grandmother is an excellent choice as a narrator with her homespun descriptions and superstitious nature, while account of the mysterious activities of the black fox effectively conveys rural delight in the supernatural. Though the story is artificial, even sentimental in parts, it minimizes Gothic horror and eliminates moralizing—a marked improvement on Whittier's other ballad attempts.

Another early ballad was "The Song of the Vermonters" (1833). Its theme, a rallying cry for all patriotic Vermonters to defend their state during a revolutionary invasion, is an obvious imitation of Scott's border romances; while its form, rhyming couplets with a basic anapestic beat, give a martial ring to the whole:

> Ho—all to the borders! Vermonters, come down,
> With your breeches of deerskin and jackets of brown;
> With your red woolen caps, and your moccasins, come,
> To the gathering summons of trumpet and drum.[4]

The poem's local color descriptions of the countryside, boastful praise of Vermont's qualities, and defiant challenge to "all the world" are conscious attempts to present the song as an authentic ballad. In fact, Whittier predated the poem, 1779. Despite its rhetorical air, characteristic moralizing, and poetic language, many sections do accord with good ballad presentation. This poem indicates how close Whittier was to having the right medium for expressing his deep-rooted feelings about the New England past.

During the next fifteen years, Whittier only intermittently followed the path marked out by these pioneer pieces, as his abolitionist work demanded his full attention. Still, some of his abolitionistic verse show the experiments that he was making with his ballad technique. "The Hunters of Men" (1835) is a caustic satire on the newest Southern amusement, the tracking down of escaped slaves. Opening his poem in the best chivalric manner, Whittier establishes the atmosphere of a medieval chase with his invitation for all to come hunting:

> Have ye heard of our hunting, o'er mountain and glen,
> Through crane-brake and forest,—the hunting of men?

> The lords of our land to this hunting have gone,
> As the fox-hunter follows the sound of the horn;
> Hark! the cheer and the hallo! the crack of the whip.

The archaic words, the courtly adjectives, and the titling of the hunters as "lords" are all devices of olden romances; while the use of a refrain, "the hunting of men," and the conscious repetitions of similar phrases and sound patterns are part of established ballad technique. These gracious phrases and romantic images are ironically contrasted with the inhuman end of the hunt—the killing of men. With heavy-handed satire Whittier continues this romantic pretense throughout the poem: "Gay luck to our hunters," "Oh, goodly and grand is our hunting to see," and "Ho, alms for our hunters." The irony fails when Whittier depicts priests, politicians, mothers, and daughters merrily hunting the slaves—Whittier had not yet learned the restraint and understatement necessary for finished satiric art and essential to valid ballad creation.[5]

One of his first real ballads was "The Exiles," written in 1841. It shows how a decade of abolitionist work had matured him; and, conversely, how far he had yet to go for poetic maturity. Certainly his abolitionist writing had enlarged his sense of the dramatic, developed his awareness of emotional appeal, and taught him the necessity of direct statement and common words. The plot of "The Exiles" was aptly suited to ballad demands for an exciting, realistic narrative, since it was the tale of Thomas Macy's flight down the Merrimack River to escape persecution for harboring Quakers. Its theme, the dramatic struggle of one man against existing injustice, stressed the value of inner principle over outward law. Everything was within the range of Whittier's talents and interests, for he had grown up in the Merrimack valley and the greater part of his life had been spent fighting for freedom and resisting intolerance. Yet he failed to develop the poem artistically. In the first place the poem is overly long (sixty stanzas); its abounds in digressions and numerous pious interjections by the author; and finally, its labored comparisons and sentimental tone ignore the realism and simplicity of good balladry. Over half the poem deals with a wordy description of the fleeing Quaker, his being sheltered by Macy, and eventual capture—all of which distract from the central drama of Macy's courage and flight. Throughout there are numerous lapses into poetic diction, such as "plashing on its pebbled shore," "How pale Want alternated/with Plenty's golden smile," and "vile scoffer." Structurally the poem fails to preserve dramatic suspense as Whittier interjects his own personal views, like "of his bondage hard and long . . . it suits not our tale to tell" and of Macy's trials on Nantucket after his escape, "Behold is it not written/In the annals of the isle."

On the credit side is the fine ballad meter used by Whittier and touches in the story demonstrate how naturally he could portray characters and how realistically he could sketch in background settings. The inner serenity of the old Quaker is described as the covering of "autumn's moonlight," while the frustrated priest is seen with his "grave cocked hat" gone and his dishevelled wig hanging behind him "like some owl's nest . . . upon a thorn." The flight of Macy down the Merrimack is simply presented through selected scenes of nearby communities:

> The fisher wives of Salisbury—
> The men were all away—
> Looked out to see the stranger oar
> Upon their waters play.
>
> Deer Island's rocks and fir-trees threw
> Their sunset-shadows o'er them,
> And Newbury's spire and weathercock
> Peered o'er the pines before them.

"Cassandra Southwick," written in 1843, shows a considerable advance over "The Exiles" in dramatic structure and presentation. Here, too, the incident is one culled from the history of Quaker persecutions; but, instead of trying to relate the complete story behind Cassandra's imprisonment, Whittier concentrates on the attempt of Governor Endicott to have the maid sold as a slave. The early section of the poem as Cassandra waits in prison sentimentalizes her devout nature and overuses Biblical phrasing and allusion. However, once dawn breaks and she leaves for the wharves, the movement is swift and dramatic. The small details like the hoar frost melting on the walls, the laughter and idle words of the crowd, Cassandra's maiden shame under the hostile gaze of the assembled mob, and her pathetic prayer for aid convey the tenseness of the moment as she walks toward the docks. The next two stanzas show Whittier's art at its best, precise, exact, and selective. With briefest possible detail the atmosphere of a seaport town is presented:

> We paused at length, where at my feet the sunlit waters broke
> On glaring reach of shining beach, and shingly wall of rock;
> The merchant ships lay idly there, in hard clear lines on high,
> Tracing with rope and slender spar their network on the sky.
> And there were ancient citizens, cloakwrapped and grave and cold,
> And grim and stout sea-captains with faces bronzed and old,
> And on his horse, with Rawson, his cruel clerk at hand,
> Sat dark and haughty Endicott, the ruler of the land.

All the characters are generalized, but their very indefiniteness adds to the mood of suspense and uneasiness. Then, after the taunts of the priest rouse Cassandra to defend her innocence and gain the sympathy of the crowd, the sheriff solicits a boat for transporting the maid. The captains remain silent as he repeatedly asks them to gain gold by selling Cassandra; and then one defiantly answers: "I would sooner in your bay/Sink ship and crew and cargo, then bear this child away." A now aroused crowd murmurs its approval and indignantly turns on Endicott and his followers. As they leave, Cassandra is freed; unfortunately the denouement is prolonged by Cassandra's fervent thanksgiving to God. Still the nucleus of the story is well told and it does have a swift narrative movement. Whittier's use of the first person narrator gives an immediacy and interest to the whole; while the repetitions of key words, the series of "and" connectives, and the parallelisms of adjectives and nouns create a definite folk flavor in the poem. The imagery is of the simplest kind: the captain growls back his answer "like the roaring of the sea," Rawson's cheek is "wine-empurpled," and Endicott looks at the disapproving crowd with a "lion glare." Though the poem is overlong, a bit didactic and melodramatic, it is a long step from the discursive and dramatically weak "The Exiles." Whittier had found his proper subject matter and was now approaching surety of presentation.

Another ballad of the same year, "The New Wife and the Old," deals with a local superstition which Whittier had heard as a child about the power of dead spirits. Though its consciously set mood of terror is somewhat reminiscent of Gothic narrative, its excellent style holds the reader's interest:

> Dark the halls, and cold the feast
> Gone the bridemaids, gone the priest.
> All is over, all is done.
>
> . . . .
> Hushed within and hushed without,
> Dancing feet and wrestlers' shout;
> Dies the bonfire on the hill;
> All is dark and all is still.

The repetitions of similar verb patterns and the balance of phrases with their recurrence in later stanzas establishes a mood of waiting and anxiety. The resulting drama does not quite live up to this effective introduction as the young bride has her wedding ring and bracelet melodramatically stolen by the ghost of a former wife. Near the end of the story, interest switches from the terror and wonder of the new bride to an examination of the sinful conscience of the older husband. Also Whittier upsets the unity of the story by musing on the supernatural reasons for the dead wife's action. Still, the ballad technique is sure and the story does concentrate on the main incident without undue digression or moralizing.

During the next ten years the pressures of editorial and journalistic duties caused Whittier to write mainly prose and fiction; consequently, he neglected his ballads. Two ballads of this period do merit attention, however. One, "Barclay of Ury" (1847), repeats the general theme of "Cassandra Southwick" in dealing with the indignities heaped upon a former warrior for his joining the Quakers. Again the story turns on the conflict of inner conviction versus outward ridicule. The dignity of the old warrior, secure in his "inner light," is contrasted with the taunts and jeers of the surrounding mob as he slowly rides through his native town. The verse movement with its slow deliberate beat echoes the measured pace of his horse and indicates his own inner confidence. The climax of the poem occurs when a former comrade of Barclay rushes to his defense and pleads with him to fight his revilers. His bewilderment when Barclay refuses to fight serves as a dramatic introduction to Barclay's simple testament of faith. He admits that it is hard to lose friends, to be mocked by strangers, and "to learn forgiving"; but, realizing that "God's own time is best," he can endure all. Whittier could have ended the ballad with this moving speech which grows organically out of definite dramatic situation. Instead, he tagged on a moral of four stanzas which marred an otherwise good ballad.

The other ballad, "Kathleen" (1849), shows Whittier's complete mastery of ballad technique. Purporting to be a tale of old Ireland and sung by a wandering Irish scholar, the poem does not have a local theme, but its content and style are handled in traditional ballad manner. Briefly, the story relates the selling of a beautiful Irish girl to the American colonies by her cruel stepmother, a later rescue by a young lover, and a safe return to her sorrowing father. The first stanzas immediately begin the narrative with the marriage of the "mighty lord" of Galaway to another wife, while the second stanza marks out the conflict in the ballad, the new wife's favoring of her own kin to the neglect of Kathleen. A few stanzas later, Kathleen is introduced and warning is given of her coming doom. In traditional ballad fashion dialogue is used throughout to convey feeling and action; no motivation is given for the stepmother's sudden decision to sell Kathleen; and there is no plausible explanation for her triumph over the old lord's love for his daughter. The art in these following stanzas is a thing of utmost simplicity.

> He smoothed and smoothed her hair away,
>   He kissed her forehead fair;
> "It is my darling Mary's brow,
> It is my darling's hair!"
>
> Oh, then spake up the angry dame,
>   "Get up, get up," quoth she,
> "I'll sell ye over Ireland,
>   I'll sell ye o're the sea!"

This simple, objective tone is preserved throughout and the scholar's final summation, in perfect keeping with his function as a wandering minstrel, provides the desired happy ending. Noticeable, too, is the absence of sophisticated imagery; only the most conventional descriptions are given, as the girl is "fair" and "the flower of Ireland"; her arm is "snowy-white" and her hand, "snow-white"; while the stepmother is seen as "angry" and "evil." This ballad readily illustrates the progress Whittier had made from his early uneven, discursive ballads.

Whittier was now at the height of his poetic powers and the next twenty years were to witness the production of his best ballads. With the gradual absorption of the Liberty and Free Soil parties into the Republican camp Whittier's main activities as a reformer were finished. So, he began to devote full time to transmuting the wealth of historical and legendary knowledge stored inside him into distinctive American ballads. In 1827 Whittier first heard from a schoolmate at Haverhill Academy the song of Skipper Ireson being tarred and feathered by the women of Marblehead. It was a typical folk song known to all the inhabitants of Marblehead—the perfect material for a poet who knew the locale and understood the "psychology" of the people. At that time Whittier tried writing it down, but it was not to be finished until thirty years later. This gestation period proved valuable; for, when Whittier finally did write "Skipper Ireson's Ride," he produced his masterpiece and the best American ballad of the nineteenth century.

The ballad opens slowly, comparing the strangeness and wonder of Floyd Ireson's ride out of Marblehead to all the other famous rides of story and rhyme. The refrain at the end, which is repeated in each stanza with slight variations, gives the essence of the story, though it does not tell us why the skipper was driven out. The second stanza puts the reader immediately *in medias res,* as we watch the tarred and feathered skipper driven through the main streets of Marblehead by the enraged populace. The description is precise and graphic. Floyd in his tarred state is seen as "body of turkey, head of owl,/Wings a-droop like a rained-on fowl"; while the crowd, strangely consisting of women, is made up of "wrinkled scolds with hands on hips" and young girls, "brief of skirt . . . ankles bare . . . loose of hair."

Only with the fourth and fifth stanzas are we told the reason for their punishing the skipper—he had sailed away from a sinking ship that was filled with his own townspeople; he had betrayed his own kin. The brief dialogue in stanza four gives the crucial moment of the tragedy, as the drowning crew call out for Ireson to save them, only to receive his heartless reply; "Sink or swim! Brag of your catch of fish again!" Only this and nothing more. We never know his motivation, nor is the event further elaborated. One can surmise from the tone of fragmentary conversation that there was deep-rooted enmity between Floyd and the crew over a catch of fish, and for this he wrathfully allows them to die.

The horror of his act is enlarged upon by the pathetic picture of the women of Marblehead, looking "for the coming that might not be." Now we know why the women pursued the old skipper—they were the dead men's wives, mothers, sisters, and daughters, trying to wring some measure of revenge for the senseless death of their loved ones. All these things are but touched upon, as the story moves quickly back to the original scene and Ireson's shameful ride. Stanza six returns to the crowd, still predominantly women, but now joined by "sea-worn grandsires" and "hulks of old sailors."

Suddenly the mood shifts, and in contrast to the harsh voices of the jeering mob in the narrow winding streets is the picture of the road leading to nearby Salem:

> Sweetly along the Salem road
> Bloom of orchard and lilac showed.
> Little the wicked skipper knew
> Of the fields so green and the sky so blue.

As the physical setting changes for artistic contrast, so does the psychological. For the first time the skipper is allowed to dominate the scene. Here again, the action is presented through dialogue, rather than through author-narration, which helps preserve the dramatic intensity. The outward scene fades, along with the ignominy of the ride and tarring, when the inward soul of the skipper cries out wretchedly:

> "What to me is this noisy ride?
> What is the shame that clothes the skin
> To the nameless horror that lives within?"

The transition is sudden and complete, surprising the reader who is engrossed in the outward narrative and making him startlingly aware of the poem's chief theme—the inner torture and remorse of a man after his crime. The crowd in accord with their traditional New England religious heritage knows only too well the truth of the skipper's words, and their vengeful yells turn to sorrowful murmurings. With "half scorn, half pity" they turn him loose and give him a cloak to hide in, alone with his sin. In the final refrain "Old" Floyd Ireson is replaced by "Poor" Floyd Ireson, so it becomes a mournful dirge, forever accusing and dooming the man. The ballad makes the skipper live as an essentially tragic figure, a man who has betrayed the loyalties of his home and friends and the manly traditions of the sea. He towers over the drama, coming from the sea, acting without apparent justification, and then vanishing to live alone with his shame and remorse.

The ballad succeeds because of its dramatic structure, sure handling of details, definite localization, simplicity of diction, and the "psychology" indigenous to New England. The whole poem centralizes on one incident, Skipper Ireson's ride from Marblehead. Like "Sir Patrick Spens," the story is based on a conflict of loyalties and gives us no description of the central incident; the sinking of the ship is merely indicated by a brief dialogue, while its effects are seen in the actions of the women. Throughout, the author is impersonal, employing terse dialogue to keep the action objective and straightforward. And there is no moral attached; for it is organic with the story itself. The variations within the ballad, from the outward crowd scene to a flashback, then to the crowd again and to the final sudden psychological twist, are masterful; and they sustain interest. Whittier was to write other fine ballads— some more famous—but none were to equal the harmony of content and form which he achieved here.

At last Whittier had attained the artistry adequately to express his feelings for the New England scene, its history, customs, and deeper psychological traditions. And so in rapid succession followed the gems of his maturity: the lyric-drama, "Telling the Bees"; the two romance ballads, "Amy Wentworth" and "The Countess"; the more hardy ballads of Hampton, "The Wreck of Rivermouth" and "The Changeling"; and his dramatic ballads of early Quaker persecutions, "In the 'Old South'" and "How the Women went from Dover." Francis B. Gummere states in his introduction to *Old English Ballads* that spontaneity is one of the cardinal virtues of the ballad: "They [the ballads] never give us poetry for poetry's sake, but are born of an occasion, a need; they have as little subjectivity as speech itself."[6] Whittier's most famous ballad, "Barbara Frietchie," perfectly exemplifies this phase of the ballad approach. The incident—the courage of an old lady in waving a Union flag before the conquering rebel troops—was supposedly a true one. It was written in the heat of the crucial battle year of 1863 and embodied Whittier's passionate belief that fundamentally many Southern rebels loved the Union as he did. His years of abolitionist work had centered around a peaceful solution to the problem; but, when the war came, Whittier resigned himself to waiting and enduring its horrors. He knew that the Union must be preserved, and this poem was his spontaneous expression of that feeling. He saw in the image of the old lady, holding the stars and stripes, a symbol of all who loved the Union and were willing to die for it.

The story is told in the simplest of all verse forms, rhyming couplets of four beats a line, separated into stanzas. The stage for the drama is set by the few suggestive details evoking the environs of Frederick town and the luxuriant land, ripe for harvest: "meadows rich with corn," and "apple and peach tree fruited deep." The action proper begins with the entrance of the "famished rebel horde" into the town and the disappearance of the Union flags:

> Forty flags with their silver stars,
> Forty flags with their crimson bars,
>
> Flapped in the morning wind: the sun
> Of noon looked down, and saw not one.

These lines have a perfect ballad movement, and a continuing economy of detail sweeps the drama along: the ranks of soldiers are "dust-brown"; and their leader, Stonewall Jackson, is characterized by his "slouched hat" and impetuous order to shoot the flag down. Barbara Frietchie's act in waving the torn flag and her address to the rebels, "Shoot if you must this old grey head, / But spare your country's flag," are melodramatic, as is Jackson's blush of shame and order to his troops to spare the woman. Yet, the unpolished and highly emotional presentation of the scene is in keeping with the manner of true balladry, where subtlety is a thing unknown. The theatrical nature of Barbara Frietchie's and Jackson's acts heightens the climax and strikingly illustrates the theme. Her successful defense of the flag is underscored by Whittier's picture of it waving over the heads of the rebel host, and leads to the ending tribute, "Flag of Freedom and Union, wave." By means of this simple story, Whittier echoed the thoughts and emotions of an entire country. No other Civil War poem, save Walt Whitman's "Oh Captain, My Captain," was so definitely the product of an hour and so quickly recognized by the people as an expression of their feelings.

Whittier's mature ballads show many interesting variations. Two of his lesser known ballads especially merit attention. "The Sisters," written in 1871, is based on one of the traditional themes of balladry—the rivalry of two sisters for the same man—and it bears close resemblance to the original "The Two Sisters" in form and presentation. The action of the story is concentrated on a single stormy night as the sisters sleep. Annie, the younger, awakens and hears a voice calling to her. From here the narrative drives forward without a single pause. The love conflict and the impending tragedy are hinted at by Rhoda's scornful attitude toward the voices that Annie hears and by her cruel remarks about Annie's failure to have a lover. Ironically, she hits upon the truth of the situation when she ridicules Annie's insistence that she does hear the voice of Estwick Hall, Rhoda's fiancé. However, Annie claims to hear the voice again, calling her name, and the now enraged sister cries out:

> "Thou liest! He would never call thy name!
>
> If he did, I would pray the wind and sea
> To keep him forever from thee and me!"

Again Rhoda unwittingly keynotes the approaching tragedy, for Hall is dead. Only Annie, with her lover's insight, knows the truth, and in his death she triumphs as she never could have in actual life. She faces her sister and, for the first time, reveals her feelings:

> "Life was a lie, but true is death.
>
> .   .   .   .
>
> But now my soul with his soul I wed;
> Thine the living, and mine the dead!"

The whole narrative is done in dialogue with none of the before or after events included. We get only the one scene, the resulting effects of the tragedy, and must fill in the details ourselves. The presentation is bare, almost harsh, in its simplicity. Still, the story is definitely tied up with the New England coast, not as in so many literary ballads situated in the land of romance: the storm which kills Hall is a typical New England northeaster; the waves lash Cape Ann's rocky coast; and the girl's dialogue has a New England twang, for Hall's boat is the "tautest schooner that ever swam" and Rhoda's trousseau is called "bridal gear."

Another of Whittier's later pieces, "The Henchman" (1877), demonstrates his mastery of ballad techniques. Like "The Sisters," it has no moral, but it is entirely different in tone and presentation. The poem is a love song, chanted exultantly and hopefully by the lover in praise of his lady. The imagery is rich and set, heightened by a lover's exaggerations. The comparisons centralize on the joyous things of spring and summer, birds, flowers, sun, and wind, and make the lady superior to them all.

> My lady walks her morning round,
> My lady's page her fleet greyhound,
> My lady's hair the fond winds stir,
> And all the birds make songs for her.
>
> .   .   .   .
>
> The hound and I are on her trail,
> The wind and I uplift her veil;
> As if the calm, cold moon she were,
> And I the tide, I follow her.

The repetition of certain phrases and syntactical patterns enhance the tone and convey the reverence of the lover's devotion with their litany of praise. The action of the ballad is slight, though there is an undercurrent of conflict—his adoration versus her proud disdain. However, this is never developed and the lyric and decorative effects dominate.

This type of ballad is the exception rather than the rule for most of Whittier's later pieces. Some of his other ballads, like "The Brown Dwarf of Rügen," "King Volmer and Elsie," and "Kallundborg Church," also convey the charm of a foreign land and create a fairy tale atmosphere by the techniques used in "The Henchman" (in much the same manner as Longfellow's ballads). In general, Whittier's later ballads tend to take a concrete historical incident or some local tradition and to dramatize it, using actual locale for realistic background setting. These tales fit in perfectly with his critical belief that there was romance underlying the simplest of incidents and that the writer should utilize the materials within his own experience. "The Wreck of Rivermouth" is typical of these ballads. The story is based on the historical character of Goody Cole of Hampton, who was persecuted for being a witch in the latter half of the seventeenth century. Many of the supernatural exploits attributed to her were probably folk superstitions and based on unfounded popular traditions; yet, they were common in Whittier's youth. The setting is laid precisely, with an eye for picturesque detail.

> And fair are the sunny isles in view
>   East of the grisly Head of the Boar,
> And Agamenticus lifts its blue
>   Disk of a cloud the woodlands o'er;
> And southerly, when the tide is down,
>   'Twixt white sea-waves and sand-hills brown,
> The beach-birds dance and the gray gulls wheel
>   Over a floor of burnished steel.

The ballad proper begins with the boat full of "goodly company," sailing past the rocks for fishing outside the bay. The idyllic atmosphere of the summer's day is conveyed by the picture of the mowers in the Hampton meadows, who listen to the songs coming from the passing boat and who longingly watch the joyous young girls. As the boat rounds the point where Goody Cole lives, the laughing group taunts her and sails on, but only after she answers their jibes with a bitter proverb: " 'The broth will be cold that waits at home; / For it's one to go, but another to come.' " Inadvertently her prophecy proves true, as a sudden storm sweeps upon the ship, driving it to destruction on Rivermouth Rocks. In one brief moment all are lost, and the next stanzas mournfully re-echo their previous happiness; the mower still looks up from the peaceful meadows and the sea is clear, but:

> The wind of the sea is a waft of death,
>   The waves are singing a song of woe!
> By silent river, by moaning sea,
> Long and vain shall thy watching be:
> Never again shall the sweet voice call,
> Never the white hand rise and fall!

A stunned and broken Goody Cole is left behind, pathetically cursing the sea for fulfilling her wish. Her tragedy, like Skipper Ireson's, is an inner thing—the torment she will have for the rest of her life, wondering if her angry words actually caused the death of the group. The final scene in church highlights the community's silent condemnation of those who dare to transgress its conventions. This scene is overlong and marred by the needless introduction of another outcast, the Reverend Stephen Bachiler, and by the heavy moral tone of the conclusion, "Lord, forgive us! we're sinners all."

The poem illustrates Whittier's success and failures in ballad presentation. The story itself is typical and probable, and Whittier's handling of it is realistic. He places it exactly in Hampton, New Hampshire, by employing details characteristic of that locale: fishing for haddock and cod, the scent of the pines of Rye, the mowing of salted grass, and Goody Cole's use of familiar native proverbs. There is a keynote of drama in the situation, as well as good narrative appeal, that fits into ballad presentation; for, Whittier allows us to view a Goody Cole who is human and natural, and to see her as an old woman tragically destroyed by a village's narrow hate. Yet, like so many of his ballads, this one needs more concentration especially in ending before the dramatic effect is lost. Also, there is a hint here of his overreaching for sentimental and emotional effect, which is so clearly seen in his ballads, like "The Witch of Wenham" and "How the Women went from Dover."

On the whole, Whittier's ballads represent his chief poetic achievement. Like Longfellow, he was a pioneer in the development of native American ballads; yet, he understood the true function of good balladry and refused to write ballads based on European models. Whittier took moments from American history and local legends and presented them in a realistic, natural manner that was strengthened by his wide knowledge of past times and lifelong familiarity with the locale. Whittier composed these poems not for a moral or social purpose, but because of an irrepressible desire to express his feelings for his section—its history, legends, and special characteristics. And in these poems, Whittier attained the rank of one of America's finest creators of historical and traditional narrative.

Notes

1. This excludes from discussion some of Whittier's finest genre pieces and nature poems like "Snow-Bound," "Maud Muller," "Among the Hills," "The Last Walk in Autumn," and others which also depend on Whittier's New England background.

2. E. H. Cady and H. H. Clark, *Whittier on Writers and Writings* (Syracuse: Syracuse Univ. Press, 1950), p. 106.

3. Frances Mary Pray, *A Study of Whittier's Apprenticeship as a Poet* (Bristol, N. H.: Musgrove Printing House, 1930), p. 84.

4. Horace E. Scudder, ed., *The Complete Poetical Works of John Green-*

leaf Whittier, Cambridge Edition (Boston: Houghton, Mifflin, 1894), p. 509. All remaining poems and quotations will be from this edition.

5. Many of Whittier's anti-slavery poems like "The Slave-Ships," "The Yankee Girl," "The Farewell," and "A Sabbath Scene" were written in ballad meter and used ballad techniques.

6. Francis B. Gummere, ed., *Old English Ballads* (Boston: Ginn & Co., 1894), p. xxix.

Whittier

Norman Foerster*

1

Passing from Bryant to Whittier is like passing from the Old Testament to the New Testament: we are still in the Bible; the authority of the Pilot is still beyond question; the air, if less bracing, more bland and solacing, is essentially the same; the voyaging poet, as before, looks upon the spectacle of nature with the eyes of a supernatural faith. Although the perilous waters of romanticism and of modern science are dimly descried at the horizon, they are never attained—if anything, Bryant, the belated Puritan, sees them more distinctly than Whittier, the Quaker, whose fervid imitation of Christ kept his gaze fixed elsewhere. To the meditative Bryant, nature is ever in the foreground, a challenge to his imagination; to the spiritual Whittier, it is oftenest only background. Yet this contrast quite fails to suggest how Whittier loved his natural background, how he had grown out of its manifold matter and life as a boy on the farm and continued, all his days, to find joy in it. Though he lived in the spirit far more than did Bryant, he was, more than Bryant, more perhaps than any other American poet, a child of the soil.

Brought up on a farm tilled by his ancestors as far back as 1647, Whittier voluntarily spent his life of eighty-three years at Haverhill and the neighboring town of Amesbury. For the most part unhesitatingly, he accepted the religion of his fathers, the poverty of his family, the hard toil of a farm in northeastern Massachusetts, the bad food, his rather frail constitution, the long drives in the one-horse chaise to the meeting-house at Amesbury, where his teeth "could not chatter until thawed out." If there was rigor and confinement, he turned, with a happiness only the deeper, to the beauty and affection that encompassed him and meant for him "home," the dearest if not the highest word he knew; even his highest word, as we shall see, is inseparably linked with

*Norman Foerster, *Nature in American Literature.* Copyright 1923, 1951 by Norman Foerster (New York: Russell & Russell, 1958). Reprinted by permission of Russell & Russell.

the sentiment of home. To Whittier a home was a spiritual entity that had its being within a house surrounded by fields and woods—the natural frame was essential. This frame, in his case, had not a little wild beauty. Lying on a slope in the embrace of Job's Hill, the old homestead faced a brook flowing through bright meadows, with dark hills extending west and south. . . . When the wind was right, the boy could hear the distant bells of Haverhill, at other times the muffled boom of an ocean storm beating at the shore a dozen or more miles away. The ocean on one side, the mountains on the other—from the hills about the farm one can see, not only the pale waters of Ipswich Bay, but also the forms of Wachusett and Monadnock and the Deerfield range. Connecting mountains and sea, the Merrimac River flows through southern New Hampshire, imaging, in tranquil reaches, the pines and elms of Haverhill and Amesbury, and passes into the open ocean. The valley of the Merrimac, including parts of the mountains and of the coast north and south, is Whittier's country. All of it he knew and loved, and much of it he described with patient fidelity when he wrote; life itself he sometimes thought of as a voyage down a river, past snag and fall and siren-haunted islet, guided by an Unseen Pilot to a port of peace.

2

In his paper on Robert Dinsmore, Whittier made a characteristic observation concerning rural poetry: "The mere dilettante and the amateur ruralist," he said, "may as well keep their hands off. The prize is not for them. He who would successfully strive for it must be himself what he sings, one who has added to his book-lore the large experiences of an active participation in the rugged toil, the hearty amusements, the trials and pleasures he describes." This is well said, even if it has something of Wordsworth's jealous appropriation of his Cumberland mountains. The rural poet must be sincere and truthful; and Whittier was ever both, thanks to his character no less than to his environment. He was no amateur ruralist, this dark, keen-eyed, somewhat lanky countryman, who had swung axe and flail and wandered barefoot in quest of nuts and berries, who, when Garrison came to call him to the great world, was in the act of crawling under the barn after a stolen hen's nest. He knew farm life as intimately as Burns did, and he had explored the surrounding woods and meadows with an eye more observant, if not more loving, than that of Burns. Everywhere in his poetry we see the apple orchards of New England, the stone fences with their load of vine, the roads winding past small farms and ponds and glacial lakes, the brooks and placid rivers, the ocean gray in the chill fog or glancing blue under a summer sky. The scenery of a farming country and of the ocean Whittier often combined in a charmingly simple picture:

> "The slopes lay green with summer rains,
> The western wind blew fresh and free,
> And glimmered down the orchard lanes
> The white surf of the sea."
>
> [From "Channing."]

Deficient as he was in the life of the senses—he was color-blind, had no ear for music, enjoyed dully sensations of touch, odor, and taste—it is not a little surprising to find how carefully he observed and recorded the sights and sounds of the country about the farm under Job's Hill. He had, indeed, something of what he calls "White of Selborne's loving view."

Though he was not the American poet of the sea—Longfellow and Whitman both have a better claim to the title—he wrote abundantly of

> "Waves in the sun, the white-winged gleam
> Of sea-birds in the slanting beam,
> And far-off sails which flit before the south-wind free."
>
> [From "Hampton Beach."]

He watched the slow tides in their coming and going, the curved surf following the beach line and leaping upon the gray rocks of the head-land, by night the water luminous under the moon, reflecting, in the darkness beneath a bluff, the sudden shine of the lighthouse beacon; he listened to the call of the curlew across the bay, to the voices of children playing in the sand, to the cadence of miniature waves on an Indian summer afternoon, or the crash and hiss of a nor'easter bearing sheets of fine rain; he camped with Fields and Bayard Taylor, on Hampton Beach, behind them marsh, creeks, and somber oaks, before them the sea, the outbound fishing schooners, with sails aslant to the wind, the white and gray birds voyaging hither and thither; in the marshes of Salisbury he beheld the mowers sweeping down the salt hay, off Boar's Head he fished for rock cod, at the Isles of Shoals enjoyed

> "The hake-broil on the drift-wood coals;
> The chowder on the sand-beach made,
> Dipped by the hungry, steaming hot,
> With spoons of clam-shell from the pot."
>
> [From *Snow-Bound*.]

And in all of these things, particularly as he grew older, he found a subtle virtue—"the healing of the sea."

Still more closely did he watch nature in the neighborhood of the homestead above the brook. Insects, indeed, he mentioned sparingly in his poems—save the bees, whose "low hum" sounds dreamily in many of his landscapes—and he seemed to care little for the larger creatures about him, unless we except the squirrel and a number of birds. His birds are nearly thirty in number, and many of them occur several times—the wild goose floating on Kenoza Lake, the blue jay with his foolish scream, the blithe song sparrow by the river's edge. But he had apparently no favorite among the birds, nothing analogous to Lowell's bobolinks and orioles or Gilbert White's swallows, and, we may add, did not observe the ways of birds more attentively than do most country-men. General names, such as thrush and woodpecker, usually sufficed when he wished to vary his customary bird, beach-bird, sea-fowl, wood-bird, and the like. The possibility that he was unromantic enough actually to prefer these general names is, I think, removed by his evident accuracy in referring to flowers and trees.

About forty flowers blossom in his poetry, and certain of them so often that they had plainly won his esteem. Thus the "trembling hare-bells" recur five times as often as the hardhack and thistle, both char-acteristic of the Whittier country; the fragrance of clover and the luxuriant yellow of goldenrod are found frequently; the laurel and asters of the Merrimac banks and the lilies of the quiet ponds are singled out for particular praise; the violet is mentioned four times as often as the daisy, the wild rose eight times as often; and the mayflower, partly on account of its historic association, is the subject of two poems. Trees, however, are still commoner in Whittier's poetry—in all well-nigh thirty species, a number of which recur again and again. Although he was not given to mentioning the precise species—poplar, willow, and the like usually sufficed—he did so on occasion; witness his scarlet-oak and staghorn sumac. And again, whereas he had no favorites among the birds and only a conventional liking for certain flowers, he was appar-ently very fond of certain trees—the elm, the maple, the birch, the pine. He referred frequently to the elms of the village, wet with rain or gleaming with snow and ice—"a jewelled elm-tree avenue"—and to the fine fringe of elms along the Merrimac. The maple attracted him in all seasons, but especially in spring, when the little flower tassels quiver with life in the soft rain, and in the autumn, when the whole tree is aflame with color. Still oftener did he describe the birch, white of stem, dainty of foliage, a token of the purity of nature; in one of his sea-coast pictures not a birch-spray is "trembling in the still moonshine."

Yet, compared with the pine, these trees occur almost rarely. In something like sixty-five poems the pine is mentioned or described, while the birch, the nearest rival, occurs only fifteen times, the maple a dozen times, the willow three or four times. Among all the birds, flowers, and trees of the Merrimac valley, Whittier bestowed his affection first of all on the oracular pine of Emerson, the "sempiternal" and "elysian" pine of Thoreau's musings. This liking for the pine is perhaps the most striking trait he had in common with the Transcendentalists. Now the sleety wind is roaring through the pines, now the ancient pine laments with him the death of a friend with wordless moan, now he stops to admire "the storm-torn plumes of old pineforest kings," or the subtle fire of the sunshine among the delicate sprays, or the sea-coast head-land bristling with dark green, or the last sun of summer shining "through yon columnar pines"; the mountains stretch away with their massy covering of "eternal pines," and the woodland paths are overhung with "low drooping pine-boughs winter-weighed," and Chocorua is "pine-besung"; in a poem on Burns, the pine is employed as the emblem of our country, elsewhere as an emblem of "the North's keen virtue," contrasted with the languorous beauty of the Southern palm. The charac-teristics of the pine that he returned to again and again are its tenuous music when the wind touches its strings; its sturdy, steady growth, rarely tainted by decay; and its evergreen quality. The first of these brought an infinity of somberly romantic suggestions, the last two the sense of eternity. The pine retains its foliage and melancholy music when other trees are bared by autumn blasts, and it naturally became for him a symbol of sadness and survival; he, too, mourned when, year after year, friends left him for the land of fronded palms. There is something evanescent and light-hearted, even trivial, in the airy willows and aspens; and there is something "hoary-wise" and permanent in the dark and fragrant pine.

3

Like Bryant, Whittier looked to the outer and unhuman world, not for his religion, but for an ennobling recreation. He was, as I have said, lacking in the life of the senses, and we find in him none of the passionately sensuous delight of Whitman or Richard Jefferies, not even the sensuous pleasure of a normal man like Lowell. Though by no means unaware of the sheer beauty of nature, of its varied sights and sounds, he found in this beauty chiefly a moral value. "Beauty," he says more than once, "in and of itself, is good." Yet this is not the religion of beauty of which Keats and Ruskin were disciples, since the emphasis is re-versed. To Keats, if the two are identical, it is because both bring the delights of beauty; to Whittier, because both bring moral strength. Far be it from this Quaker in a Puritan land, whose main ideal was that of the home and who yet never married, to become enraptured with melancholy reverie, with the intoxication of flower meadows, with the physical charm of woman. Instead he addresses Kenoza Lake in this wise:

> "Thy peace rebuke our feverish stir,
> Thy beauty our deforming strife;

> Thy woods and waters minister
> The healing of their life."
>
> [From "Kenoza Lake."]

In "Summer by the Lakeside" there are lines that superficially resemble
those of a mystical dreamer losing himself in nature:

> "I read each misty mountain sign,
> I know the voice of wave and pine,
> And I am yours, and ye are mine.
>
> . . . .
>
> "This western wind hath Lethean powers,
> Yon noonday cloud nepenthe showers,
> The lake is white with lotus-flowers!
>
> "Even Duty's voice is faint and low,
> And slumberous Conscience, waking slow,
> Forgets her blotted scroll to show."

But, after all, this is not the mood of him who would merge himself
with nature; it is the mood of a man who places too much, rather than
too little, stress on orthodox moral values, who would therefore seek
the rest of momentary oblivion. The word "even" in the phrase "Even
Duty's voice" is significant, and it is worth remarking that Duty and
Conscience merely nod. Whittier closes the poem, not with the mystic's
yearning for union with the ineffable, but with the resignation of one
who is content that an inscrutable Creator should command his destiny—
"Unanxious, leaving Him to show."

This love of nature as a healing power . . . is still more clearly
expressed in "My Namesake." The poet is telling his namesake what
the latter should say, "when asked the reason of thy name." In the
course of his description of himself, Whittier says:

> "On all his sad or restless moods
>   The patient peace of Nature stole;
> The quiet of the fields and woods
>   Sank deep into his soul.
>
> "He worshipped as his fathers did,
>   And kept the faith of childish days,
> And, howsoe'er he strayed or slid,
>   He loved the good old ways."

As an element of style, Whittier's poetical use of nature consists
mainly in more or less labored descriptions, devoid of the witchery of
phrase, and in somewhat elaborate similies. He writes conventionally
of the analogy of the seasons and life. Although many of his analogies
are fairly well concealed, like Bryant he frequently concludes a stretch
of description with a frank "So" and a deliberate application of the

moral inherent in the description. For example: "So the o'er-wearied pilgrim," "So live the fathers in their sons," " 'So,' prayed we, 'when our feet draw near,' " "So, let me hope, the battlestorm that beats," "So from the trodden ways of earth," "So . . . be mine the hazel's grateful part,"

> " 'So, always baffled, not misled,
> We follow where before us runs
> The vision of the shining ones.' "
> [From "The Seeking of the Waterfall."]

Behind these seemingly surface analogies, however, lies a deeper meaning, an essential part of Whittier's religion. God, he says,

> ". . . Whose presence fills
> With light the spaces of these hills,"
> [From "Summer by the Lakeside."]

can surely will no harm to His creatures. Nature is fair, and it follows, in the simple but not trivial faith of this Quaker poet, that God is good and will do what is best for all:

> "Thy tender love I see,
> In radiant hill and woodland dim,
> And tinted sunset sea.
> For not in mockery dost Thou fill
> Our earth with light and grace;
> Thou hid'st no dark and cruel will
> Behind Thy smiling face!"
> [From "The Lakeside."]

So fair, indeed, are nature's forms in this world, he intimates in several poems, that they may well be "heavenly archetypes." The beauty of earth is thus not only a token of immortality, but also a token of the actual appearance of heaven itself. One analogy, however, fails, and in its failure lies the pathos of human life:

> "I go the common way of all;
> The sunset fires will burn,
> The flowers will blow, the river flow,
> When I no more return."
> [From "Sunset on the Bearcamp."]

Nature, then meant to Whittier a medicinal power, whose sovereign virtue was the sense of peace and uprightness that it imparted, and it meant further, in his contemplative hours, a source of analogies with the last mysteries of life. Much as he enjoyed the piny woods and vine-fringed river of his home country, he did not seek in nature an answer to his deepest questionings. Herein he was unlike the characteristic nineteenth-century poet; herein he was, in brief, a Quaker. Yet he had nothing of the asceticism of the Middle Ages, whose "proud humilities of sense and posturing of penitence" he repudiated more than once. In the verses entitled "To ———, with a Copy of Woolman's Journal," Whittier states clearly where the soul should go for an answer to its deepest questions. It should go, not to a ritualistic faith, not to the idle, actionless faith of the ascetic, not to "wire-worked" oracles, and not where the maiden of these stanzas goes, to nature, whose rugged features would then be falsely covered with Fancy's veil, but to the still, small voice within:

> ". . . a soul-sufficing answer
> Hath no outward origin;
> More than Nature's many voices
> May be heard within."

The same conclusion is stated thirty years later in "Monadnock from Wachusett"; it is elaborated still more in "Questions of Life," in which he turns from nature, from man's wisdom as recorded in books, from the impotence of grandiose creeds, "To the still witness in my heart"; and it is elaborated again in "The Meeting." In the last-named poem, one of the two speakers advocates worship where the slow hours "Glide soundless over grass and flowers!" The other speaker responds that the pine-laid floor of the meeting-house is not, indeed, better than "breezy hill or sea-sung shore":

> "But nature is not solitude:
> She crowds us with her thronging wood;
> Her many hands reach out to us,
> Her many tongues are garrulous;
> Perpetual riddles of surprise
> She offers to our ears and eyes;
> She will not leave our senses still,
> But drags them captive at her will."

In such passages as these, Whittier is the first important American writer to point out the perils of the "nature cult," the seduction of the spirit by the senses. In Bryant the misuse of nature was little more than hinted at, when he alluded to holy men who had spent their lives in devotion to God deep in the wilderness, and to holy men

> "Who deemed it were not well to pass life thus,"
> [From "A Forest Hymn."]

though it seemed not to occur to him to mention the votaries of Nature herself. He, for his part, would simply retire "often" to the woodland solitudes for the moral refreshment afforded by their majestic calm. Nowhere in Bryant is there the sharp distinction between inward and outward on which Whittier rests his condemnation of the quest of religion in nature, nowhere anything like

> "Oh, wisdom which is foolishness!
> Why idly seek from outward things
> The answer inward silence brings?"
> [From "Questions of Life."]

And Whittier, on the basis of this distinction, passes still farther from the worshipers of Nature when he prefers, to the silence of solitary meditation, the confraternal silence of the meeting-house,

> "For here the habit of the soul
> Feels less the outer world's control;
> The strength of mutual purpose pleads
> More earnestly our common needs;
> And from the silence multiplied
> By these still forms on either side,
> The world that time and sense have known
> Falls off and leaves us God alone."
> [From "The Meeting."]

4

Much as he loved nature, associating it, as Burns did, with the simple joys of home, he was essentially, as Burns was not, a religious poet. In his life as in his poems, God conceived as Love, and the "common needs" of mankind, are always central. What is more, they are always linked. In his humanitarian faith, the Inner Light which is the light of God is essentially the spirit of love—love of the Father and love of all His human children. A mere religion of humanity, a substitution of the love of man for man for the love of man for God, to which the nineteenth century tended both avowedly and disguisedly, would have seemed to Whittier blasphemous; when he asserts that "To worship rightly is to love each other," he implies, of course, the reality of a supernatural being, a God imagined, through the finite imagination of men, as having an abode "above" this world of the senses. Not to a democratic humanitarianism but to this supernatural humanitarianism is owing, then, that "joy of doing good" which Whittier everywhere dwells on—in his many personal poems on unselfish enthusiasts, in his various poems espousing the cause of the oppressed in foreign lands, and in his constant fiery denunciation of negro slavery, together constituting

> "A weary work of tongue and pen,
> A long, harsh strife with strong-willed men."
> [From "To My Sister."]

So dominant was this reformatory strain in Whittier that he could say,

"I set a higher value on my name as appended to the Anti-Slavery Declaration of 1833 [the early date is the point] than on the title-page of any
book." The idea of art as an end of living he could not have conceived,
much less exemplified; even art as an ideal imitation of nature he translated bluntly into "her mockery, Art." It was quite in keeping with his
view of art to assert that Longfellow's "Psalm of Life," which is certainly better morality than literature, contained more than "all the
dreams of Shelley, and Keats, and Wordsworth." Yet if his humanitarianism was excessive, it was profoundly sincere. Had he been an European
romanticist, he would doubtless have surmounted or disregarded the
obstacles to marriage; that felicity he renounced, however, along with
the simple and quiet life for which he always inwardly longed. Instead,
he dedicated himself to the abolitionist cause, soon finding, as a clerical
companion observed, that it is easier to be pious than to be good, but
continuing to face death at the hands of mobs, or personal indignities,
which seemed to him worse than death. Unselfishly responding to the
call of duty, this "silent, shy, peace-loving man," as he characterized
himself, never forgot what he had renounced:

> "For while he wrought with strenuous will
>   The work his hands had found to do,
> He heard the fitful music still
>   Of winds that out of dream-land blew."
>   [From *The Tent on the Beach.*]

What was this dreamland? Properly it was not a dreamland at all,
but the actual world of external nature and simple humanity frankly
viewed "with unanointed eyes." Much as he loved the dewy freshness
of the dreamworld of romance, of Spenser and "Arcadian Sidney," with
all its magic of beauty and melody, he loved still more the sweetly
trivial pleasures of home life in the country: the pines and wild briar,
the tinkle of sheep in the pasture, the farmer boy and barefoot girl, the
legends whose mysterious shapes haunted the land of his Quaker and
Puritan forbears. While he was writing the burning lines of "Massachusetts to Virginia" he would fain have celebrated the pumpkin glowing
under the September sun, or the delicately hardy mayflower with its
precious memories of the high-sterned ship sailing into Massachusetts
Bay. Alone and militant, he dreamed of the affections of the home circle
and of the peace of nature. Everywhere in his poems is the sentiment
of home—in the memories of "The Barefoot Boy," in the might-have-
beens of "Maud Muller," in the recollections of hearth and woman by
"The Lumbermen" of Maine, in his two finest idyls, "Snowbound" ("The
Cotter's Saturday Night" of the New World) and "The Pennsylvania
Pilgrim," the former a picture of felicity in the Quaker homestead of the
Puritan land, the latter a picture of the less austere life among the

Quakers of the Quaker land. Whittier's ocean pictures are rarely remote and forbidding—we hear everyday children playing in the sand; and his mountain pictures are not complete without "home-life sounds," such as the splash of the bucket in the cool well, the clatter of the pasture bars, the creak of the barnyard gate under "the merry weight of sun-brown children." The life of the spirit was, indeed, the great reality to Whittier; yet the spirit was incarnate, dwelling in an earthly home, which it must needs love.

Lover of home that he was, forbidden the full enjoyment of hearth and nature, Whittier looked forward with the more ardor to a home hereafter, a haven of peace amid the fronded palms of the heavenly islands, where he knew he would rejoin those whom he had loved on earth—"somehow, somewhere meet we must." In an age that was rapidly advancing, or declining, to the view that the longing for personal immortality is "the cry of unfaith," at once egoistic and sensual, Whittier cherished this hope and trust tenderly, and while the poet of his day was seeking to read Earth, he sought to read his heart. If nature is comely and human intercourse sweet, it said, God cannot be cruel; He wills what is best for insect and plant, and He wills what is best for man. Nature herself, our fair home, lost its bloom when he inwardly remembered that

> ". . . beyond this masquerade
> Of shape and color, light and shade,
> And dawn and set, and wax and wane,
> Eternal verities remain."
> [From "A Summer Pilgrimage."]

A Note on Whittier's Margaret Smith

Lewis Leary°

It is possible to be scholarly about *Leaves from Margaret Smith's Journal*, but it is not necessary to be. Like *The Scarlet Letter* it is solidly built on historical foundations; characters in it have been identified as actual people who lived then and there, and who can be thought of as acting exactly like that: the scene is right, the language, and the atmosphere. What preserves the book as a minor classic, however, is its quiet competence, not as history or antiquarian lore, but as testimony spoken with the authority of tolerant affection and muted humor about the human spirit, its failures and its possibilities, then or now or at any time. The narrative is presented as from the pen of a lively girl from Oxfordshire who from early May, 1678, to mid-June, 1679, kept a record of her visit to relatives who lived in Boston, but who summered at a plantation on the Merrimack River at Newbury. She had resolved "to keep a little journal of whatsoever did happen, both unto myself and unto those with whom I did sojourn; as also, some account of the country and its marvels, and mine own cogitation thereon." She wrote simply, claiming "no vanity of authorship"; her journal was intended, she said, for "the impartial eye" of an old friend, not for "the critical observation of the scholar."

Not too much must be expected of it, of story or adventure. One of the quite too slender threads on which the narrative is strung is the unhappy experience of Margaret's cousin, Rebecca Rawson, who rejects the strong, true love of a colonial countryman, and marries instead dashing young Sir Thomas Hale, a bogus nobleman who abandons her at last. Another is the love and selfless marriage of Margaret's brother to a pretty Quaker maiden. But essentially the journal is simply a record of what a high-spirited girl saw and heard during a visit to New England of a little more than a year: husking bees and forest rides; wild geese, humming birds, and squirrels ("striped, red and gray"); walnuts and

*Reprinted from the *Emerson Society Quarterly*, 50 (1968), 75–78 by permission of Kenneth Walter Cameron.

oil-nuts, goldenrod and asters, and "grapes, both white and purple, hanging down in clusters from the trees"—all the variety of life, its simple beauty and laughter and limitations in colonial New England. She had tales to tell, she said, "of my baking and brewing, of my pumpkin pies, and bread made with the flour of Indian corn; yea, more, of gathering of the wild fruit in the woods, and cranberries in the meadows, milking the cows, and looking after pigs and barnyard fowls."

She had an eager eye for nature, responding to its variety with wonder and delight—"the sugar-tree, which is very beautiful in its leaf and shape, and from which the people of this country do draw a sap well nigh as sweet as the juice of the Indian cane, making good treacle and sugar." Passing in spring through the woods beyond Salem, "where the young leaves were fluttering, and the white blossoms of the wind-flowers, and the blue violets and the yellow blooming of the cowslips in the low grounds, were seen on either hand," she was "glad of heart as a child": if she did not miss her friends in England so, she would "never wish to leave so fair a country." Midsummer, when "all things seem to faint and wax old under an intolerable sun," was less to her liking: "Great locusts sing sharp in the hedges and bushes, and grass-hoppers fly up in clouds . . . when one walks over the dry grass which they feed upon, and at nightfall mosquitoes are a small torment." But autumn was beautiful; the tinted foliage reminded her of "the stains of the windows of old churches, and of rich tapestry. The maples were aflame with crimson, the walnuts were orange, the hemlocks and cedars were well nigh black; while the slender birches, with their pale yellow leaves, seemed painted upon them as pictures are laid upon a dark ground." And in winter "truly it was no mean sight to behold every small twig becrusted with ice, and glittering famously like silver-work or crystal, as the rays of the moon did strike upon them." She was grateful to "the merciful God, who reneweth the earth and maketh it glad with greenery and flowers."

There in the new world of New England, "a sense of the wonderful beauty of the visible creation, and of God's goodness to the children of men therein, did rest upon me, and I said in mine heart, with one of old: "O Lord! how manifold are thy works: in wisdom hath thou made them all, and the earth is full of thy riches." Margaret quoted with approval a young man who preferred "the open fields and sky better than all the grandest churches of man's building," who thought the autumn woods and the New England sunset "better fitted to provoke devotional thoughts, and to awaken a becoming reverence and love for the Creator, than the stained glass windows and lofty roofs of old ministers." Nature was a "book always open, and full of delectable teaching."

But to Margaret human nature was even more compelling, in its strangeness of distortion and in its occasional loveliness. She wondered about the harshness of the Boston magistrate who soon after Margaret's arrival, learning that she had not been "admitted into the Church," did take "hold of my lace ruff so hard that I heard the stitches break; and then he pulled out my sleeves, to see how wide they were," and talked then "very loud against the folly and the wasteful wantonness of the times"; and she wondered particularly that his meek wife should abide such a man. She looked with dismay on one deacon who mistreated his Indian slave, with amusement on another who "had drank" so much flip that he could not keep his saddle, and with quiet mirth on the zestful, sly courtship of a third. She had a keen eye for the people who streamed into Boston from neighboring towns to hear an ordination sermon: "their odd dresses, which were indeed of all kinds, from silks and velvets to coarsest homespun woolens, dyed with hemlock, or oilnut bark," and for the young roisterers who after the service, put one of the ministers' Negro man Sam "on top of a barrel, with a bit of leather cut in the shape of spectacles astride his nose, where he stood swinging his arms, and preaching, after the manner of his master, mimicking his tone and manner."

Margaret throughout is a good-humored, wholesome girl, with a rollicking sense of fun, and not averse to innocent practical joking. Returning from Newbury from a visit to cousins on the Isle of Shoals, she and her uncle tarried overnight at a settlement known as Strawberry Bank, in the rude home of a hardworking widow. After "a comfortable supper of baked pumpkins and milk, Margaret was shown to a "dark loft, which was piled well nigh full with corn-ears, pumpkins, and beans, besides a great deal of old household trumpery, wool, and flax, and the skins of animals." Restless on her straw pallet on the floor, she chanced to touch with her foot "a pumpkin lying near the bed, which set it a-rolling down the stairs, bumping hard on every stair as it went." But let her tell the story:

> Thereupon I heard a great stir below, the woman and her three daughters crying out that the house was haunted. Presently she called me from the foot of the stairs, and asked me if I did hear anything. I laughed so at all this, that it was some time before I could speak; when I told her I did hear a thumping on the stairs. "Did it seem to go up, or down?" inquired she, anxiously; and on my telling her that the sound went downward, she set up a sad cry, and they all came fleeing into the corn-loft, the girls bouncing upon my bed and hiding under the blanket, and the woman praying and groaning, and saying that she did believe it was the spirit of her poor husband.

Margaret's uncle, sleeping on the settle of the room below, "hearing the noise, got up, and stumbling over the pumpkin, called to know what was the matter." When told that ghosts were abroad that night, he grumbled sleepily, "Pshaw! . . . is that all? I thought to be sure the Indians had come."

Margaret pitied the poor Indian, tempted and bribed to obedience by the white man's rum, driven from his lands, often made a minion. She pitied particularly the Indian mother who nursed her child in squalor, fiercely protective but gentle withal: her heart went out to the savage woman, even though the baby had "a wild, shy look, like the offspring of an untamed animal." For the Indians were not noble savages to her, though she thought they might once have been; the tales she heard of their cruelty in war were not overbalanced by what she heard from the Rev. John Eliot of their submission to his teaching. She especially liked one "very bright and pretty Indian girl, one of Mr. Eliot's flock, of the Natick people," a convert "apparelled after the English manner, save that she wore leggings, called moccasins, instead of shoes, wrought over daintily with the quills of an animal called a porcupine, and hung about with small black and white shells." She was not dissuaded by her cousins, who warned her that the Indians were a "dirty, foul people." To her they seemed "not so exceeding bad as they have been reported; they be like unto ourselves, only lacking our knowledge and opportunities." Maybe they did dance too strenuously, as John Eliot told her, and then went too quickly into the cold, so that they sickened. Perhaps they did drink too much and work too little. But to see them sold as slaves, and to see Negroes sold, tempted her to such plain speaking that it was thought by at least one leader of the church in New England, she said, "that he had lived to see strange times, when such as I should venture to oppose themselves to sober and grave people, and to despise authority, and encourage rebellion and disorder."

She reported with great interest an incident of witchcraft which came to her from the Reverend Increase Mather of Boston, about a house in Newbury so "dolefully beset by Satan's imps . . . that the family could get no sleep because of the doings of evil spirits," but she took little stock in these things: Caleb Powell, held for trial as an agent of mischief, seemed to her "a vain, talking man, but nowise a wizard"; a young girl at Hampton thought to be possessed revealed to Margaret "nothing in her behavior beyond that of a vicious and spoiled child, delighting in mischief." She was fascinated by a haunted house where there was "a banging of doors, and a knocking on the boards . . . tools flying about the room; baskets dropping down the chimney, and the pots hanging over the fire smiting against each other." Such dismal stories were told of the power of invisible demons that she could scarcely sleep at night "for the trouble and disquiet the matter causeth." She worried however about the zeal of New Englanders in attacking witchcraft. Might it not be that in "seeking to drive the enemy out of their neighbors' houses, they were letting him into their own hearts, in the guise of conceit and spiritual pride?" She avoided disputatious people. When pert, loquacious Cotton Mather came to call, she preferred to read rather than listen to him talk.

The religious complexion of New England bothered her greatly. Not only the deacons, but the clergymen also, for all their selfless dedication, lacked tolerance for any whose faith differed from theirs. Especially against the Quakers, a railing, ranting, and deluded people, much given to excess. What in their belief, she was told, "is not downright blasphemy and heresy, is mystical and cabalistic. . . . Their divinity is a riddle, a piece of black art; the Scripture they turn into allegory and parabolical conceits, and thus obscure and debauch the truth." Though honest in their dealings, making great shows of sobriety and self-denial, and abhorring "the practice of scandalous vices, being temperate, chaste, and grave in their behavior," they did thereby "win upon unstable souls, and make plausible their damned heresies." As for herself, in spite of her brother's marriage to the Quaker maiden, Peggy Brewster, "although I do judge them," she said of members of the sect, "to be a worthy and pious people, I like not their manner of worship, and their great gravity and soberness do little accord with my natural temper and spirits."

Soberness? Knowing who wrote *Leaves from Margaret Smith's Journal* and when he wrote them, and knowing also that its author was poet but also a canny propagandist with something to say, every alert reader must be aware that he is being led toward attitude by the quiet charm of Margaret's account of her visit to New England. He has been taught that Whittier was dedicated as a Quaker, but also a militant propagandist, quick to speak against those who denied rights to all men. Margaret was somehow different. Through most of her sojourn in the new world, she took great comfort in a little old-world book which "aboundeth in sweet and goodly thoughts, although he who did write it was a monk." In Thomas à Kempis's *Imitation of Christ* she learned: "What thou canst not amend in thyself or others, bear thou with patience until God ordaineth otherwise. . . . Stand with an even mind resigned to the will of God, whatever shall befall, because after winter cometh summer; after the dark night the day shineth, and after the storm followeth a great calm." She liked these words, and Whittier seems to have liked them also, and so may a reader who comes to Margaret's account unconfused by certainties that scholarship can or cannot substantiate its details. Margaret is better than a footnote; she is alive, among the first of our native heroines, and not the least attractive. The vexing question is why Whittier could not have allowed her to remain among us instead of returning her to England. Then or now, we could use such girls.

The Artistry of Whittier's
Margaret Smith's Journal

By Donald A. Ringe*

The major prose work of John Greenleaf Whittier, *Margaret Smith's Journal in the Province of Massachusetts Bay, 1678–79,* has evoked a critical response that has ranged from the lukewarm to the enthusiastic. Although most of the critics praise the accurate picture of colonial New England life that the book presents,[1] opinions about its artistic success have varied between Whitman Bennett's view that it is only "a pleasing little effort" that should not be considered "a truly notable achievement"[2] to Edward Wagenknecht's opinion that it is "one of the inexplicably neglected classics of American literature, . . . next to *Snow-Bound,* Whittier's unquestionable masterpiece."[3] Those critics who have discussed the work in detail tend to support the latter view. Lewis Leary thinks the novel a charming one and compares it briefly with *Huckleberry Finn* in the way the material is presented to the reader;[4] and John P. Pickard, in what is by far the best analysis of the work, points out the skill with which Whittier turned the journal form into a useful instrument for the presentation of his material, and praises the book for the fusion of form and theme that yielded Whittier "his one prose success."[5]

Yet for all the favorable criticism that the book has received, critics have yet to demonstrate that it is unequivocally a work of art. Some who praise it highly seem as much concerned with the content as with its mode of expression,[6] and few have approached the work in strictly literary terms. Even Pickard, who comes closest to demonstrating its artistic value, finds serious flaws in the novel. He objects to the sketchily treated "love plot centering on the disastrous romance of Rebecca Rawson and Thomas Hale and the happy marriage of Leonard Smith to Margaret Brewster," and he faults the book as well for the number of "unrelated tales," which, in his view, "expose the thinness of the plot."[7] These are serious charges to make if *Margaret Smith's Journal* is indeed the success that Pickard claims it to be, for they seem to assume that Whittier intended to write a sustained love plot which he somehow

*Reprinted from the *Essex Institute Historical Collections,* 108, No. 3 (1972), 235–43. (Copyright, 1972, by Essex Institute, Salem, Mass. 01970).

failed to realize. I wish to suggest, rather, that Whittier did not intend such a plot at all, but relied on the narrative voice to supply the focus of attention for his novel. None of the critics have treated the point of view as seriously as they should. As a result, they have failed to see that Margaret Smith is the central consciousness of the work and the means through which the various elements of the book are successfully unified.

To treat the character in any other way, as some of the critics have done,[8] is to violate the artistic integrity of the novel. Margaret Smith is the first person narrator in a work of historical fiction. As such, she provides our sole means of access to the materials through which the theme is expressed. Everything we see or hear in the book is filtered through Margaret's consciousness. She depicts the world as she sees it and reports what interests her most. To understand the book, therefore, we must understand the narrator, a unique individual whose personality and background provide the artistic control so necessary in a work that does not include a strong plot line. As an English traveler in America, she is in effect an innocent stranger, one who stands somewhat apart from the environment in which she finds herself, but who, as the niece of an important man in the colony, takes a personal interest in all that goes on about her, and who records her experience for the cousin in England for whom she is writing the journal. As a woman of twenty,[9] she is old enough to take part in serious discussions as they arise, and her sex gives her the freedom not only to associate with men in the normal course of society, but also to draw close to other women in the colony —women she could not relate to in the same way if she were a man.

Whittier never allows us to forget that Margaret is a stranger in New England, for throughout the first part of the novel, she compares what she finds in America with what she has experienced in her native land. A May morning near Agawam seems to her as "warm and soft as our summer days at home,"[10] but the American summer is hotter and drier than what she has been used to, and she thinks of the "summer season of old England" with its cool sea breezes, pleasant showers, and green fields (pp. 47–48). The colors of autumn amaze her "as unlike anything I had ever seen in old England" (p. 61), and the woods themselves are very different. The American forest, "tangled with vines" and fallen boughs, is carpeted with a "thick matting of dead leaves," whereas the English woods "are kept clear of bushes and undergrowth, and the sward beneath [the trees] is shaven clean and close" (p. 82). Through allusions like these, Whittier keeps before the reader an awareness of Margaret Smith as an intelligent visitor who looks with fresh eyes on what she sees in the colonies.

Some of what she experiences is strange and unpleasant. On her trip to Rhode Island, for example, to visit her brother and his wife, the party is forced to stop overnight at an abandoned hut, where Margaret's companions make themselves at home and soon fall asleep. The strangeness of her situation, however, keeps Margaret "a long time awake." She lies on a bed of hemlock sprigs watching the stars through a hole in the roof and the moonlight that shines in the hut "through the seams of the logs." She listens to the sound of wind and waves and "the cry of wild animals in the depth of the woods" until she at last nods off (p. 170). She cannot stomach the dried meat and the "cakes of pounded corn" on which her companions breakfast the next morning, but she buys instead two cakes of maple sugar to eat (p. 171). Most of her experience in America, of course, is not so unfamiliar to her as this, but after nearly a year away from her native land, she begins to grow homesick for her friends in England (pp. 144, 167). Though she leaves America with some regrets, she is happy when the time comes for her to go home (p. 189). To the very end of the book, Whittier is consistent in maintaining the point of view. Margaret Smith remains an observant stranger who never becomes completely a part of what she sees.

Other aspects of Margaret's individuality are more subtly presented. From the very first entry in the journal, we learn some significant facts about her. She is not a member of the church (p. 11) and thus is free to view the Puritans in a much more objective fashion than if she were one of them.[11] She dresses more gaily than an aged magistrate approves of, and she seems to be somewhat less of a religious enthusiast than her brother. As they enter Boston harbor on the day of their arrival, he lifts up both hands and cries out with a verse of scripture, whereas she merely says that she wept "for joy and thankfulness of heart, that God had brought us safely to so fair a haven" (p. 10). When she thinks that a wrong had been done, however, Margaret speaks out in no uncertain terms, as the following incident well illustrates. The aged magistrate's wife, she writes, "a quiet, sickly-looking woman, . . . seems not a little in awe of her husband," who "hath a very impatient, forbidding way with him, and . . . seemed to carry himself harshly at times towards her." When her Uncle Rawson says in his defense that "he has had much to try his temper" in the affairs of the colony, Margaret replies: "I told him it was no doubt true; but that I thought it a bad use of the Lord's chastenings to abuse one's best friends for the wrongs done by enemies; and, that to be made to atone for what went ill in Church or State, was a kind of vicarious suffering that, if I was in Madam's place, I should not bear with half her patience and sweetness" (pp. 11–12).

Because Margaret Smith is a strong and independent young woman with a mind of her own, she is able to observe intelligently the whole range of American life that presents itself to her senses and to learn from her experience. She arrives in America, for example, with certain fears and apprehensions, for thoughts of "the terrors of the wilderness" troubled her night and day. Yet when she awakens the first morning at her Uncle Rawson's plantation at Newbury, she asks herself: "Where be the gloomy shades, and desolate mountains, and the wild beasts, with their dismal howlings and rages! Here all looked peaceful, and bespoke comfort and contentedness" (pp. 19–20). A similar change in her views occurs when she meets the Indians, a change which shows her basically charitable nature. The first encounter startles her, and even to the end of her stay she can still be frightened by them. Yet Margaret needs only to meet the Indians on human terms to feel a sympathy for them as fellow creatures and to draw the appropriate conclusion. "These poor heathen people," she writes after a brief association with an Indian family, "seem not so exceeding bad as they have been reported; they be like unto ourselves, only lacking our knowledge and opportunities, which, indeed, are not our own to boast of, but gifts of God, calling for humble thankfulness, and daily prayer and watchfulness, that they be rightly improved" (p. 16).

Margaret goes through a similar experience in her other encounters with people. Her initial reaction to a Quaker girl named Margaret Brewster is to side with the Puritans against her (p. 26), but she quickly changes her mind. The gentleness of the girl and her kindness in performing acts of charity win Margaret over and probably help to influence her view of Quakers in general. To be sure, Margaret Smith is aware that some who call themselves Quakers are merely ranters (pp. 59, 180–181), and she knows that they have rudely interrupted the Puritan meetings. She does not like their "gravity and . . . staidness of deportment" (p. 172), and the "painful and melancholy look and . . . canting tone of discourse" that some of them affect (p. 179). But she notes that Rhode Island Quakers—"worthy and pious people"—were loving and kind to her when she spent some time among them (p. 172), and she cannot help but admire the "warmth and goodness of . . . heart" of Margaret Brewster (p. 179), nor does she regret that her brother married her. As she does with the Indians, Margaret Smith judges the Quakers not in terms of her own preconceptions, but rather on her own experience with them as human beings. To her mind, the goodness of Margaret Brewster and the acts of charity she has performed for others outweigh the sectarian beliefs that the Quaker girl holds.

The witchcraft excitement is the third important matter that comes to Margaret Smith's attention, and here her feelings are even more ambivalent than they are toward the Quakers. Although she believes that Caleb Powell, a suspected wizard, is only "a vain, talking man," and that a girl, supposed to be possessed, is "a vicious and spoiled child, delighting in mischief" (pp. 83–84), she does not dismiss the question of witchcraft out of hand. Though some may doubt the evidence that is presented against the accused witches, Margaret herself, as one would expect of a seventeenth-century girl, is so disturbed by what she has seen and heard at the bewitched house that she can hardly sleep (p. 101). But if Whittier maintains historical credibility by allowing Margaret Smith to be deeply troubled by the thought of witchcraft, he maintains the consistency of her charitable character by allowing her to sympathize with a condemned witch. When Goody Morse is reprieved by the governor and magistrates, Margaret writes: "For mine own part, I do truly rejoice that mercy hath been shown to the poor creature; for even if she is guilty, it affordeth her a season for repentance; and if she be innocent, it saveth the land from a great sin" (p. 187).

Margaret does not, of course, rely solely on her personal experience for the information she receives and records in her journal. She also hears the opinions of others, some of which confirm, and some contradict, the charitable attitude she usually shows toward others. These reports serve an important function in the book. The conflicting attitudes she records—and contradictory views are frequently juxtaposed in the journal—help lend an air of reality to the book and assure that the theme is presented in the most artistic fashion. Both sides of an issue are clearly presented—but presented in such a way as to confirm the views that Margaret Smith maintains. Thus, the charitable attitude of Elnathan Stone toward the Indians is strongly contrasted with his mother's bitterness toward them. He is dying as the result of wounds received in the Indian war and his suffering during captivity, yet he understands that the Indians have sometimes been provoked to warfare by the treatment they have received, and he even feels pity for them. His mother, however, "a poor widow, who had seen her young daughter tomahawked by the Indians" and is now watching her only son die, considers them simply children of the devil (pp. 28–29). Her attitude is, of course, perfectly understandable, but her son's is clearly the better one.

Other examples of the technique are found throughout the book. Margaret herself sees Deacon Dole's Indian "with blood running down his face, and much bruised and swollen" after he was punished by his master for being drunk and disorderly, yet the deacon himself says that "his servant Tom had behaved badly, for which he did moderately correct him" (pp. 49–50). When Margaret Brewster is fined for disturbing a Puritan meeting and then sentenced to the stocks for refusing to pay, some men step forward and pay the fine themselves, "so that she was set at liberty, whereat the boys and rude women were not a little disappointed, as they had thought to make sport of her in the stocks" (p. 42). There are even those who gain the reprieve for Goody Morse, the accused witch who is sentenced to death. Yet "many people, both men and women, coming in from the towns about to see the hanging, be sore disappointed, and do vehemently condemn the conduct of the Governor therein," and Goody Matson, "with half a score more of her sort," scolds and rails "about the reprieve of the witch, and [prophesies] dreadful judgments upon all concerned in it." (p. 187).

The most important example of the device, however, occurs near the middle of the book in a pair of contrasted sermons that clearly establish the theme. Mr. Richardson, a minister at Newberry, preaches against those "who have made a covenant with hell," and prays that they "may be speedily discovered in their wickedness, and cut off from the congregation" (p. 86). Dr. Russ, on the other hand, delivers a sermon on charity that urges the people to love one another. Margaret reports the second sermon at length "forasmuch as it hath given offence to some who did listen to it," and she mentions the harsh and vindictive people who find fault with it (pp. 96–97). Though Margaret herself makes no explicit comparison of the two sermons, it is clear to the reader that Whittier intended the sermon by Dr. Russ to be an important thematic statement. The great detail in which it is given provides a thematic weight that the other does not possess, and it states a view which, as we have seen, is strongly underscored elsewhere in the novel. Based on Paul's First Letter to the Corinthians, it preaches the need for Christian charity in one's dealings with his fellows and so provides the fundamental principle by which Margaret Smith, Margaret Brewster, Elnathan Stone, and others live and act.

The theme of Christian charity developed in this sermon, moreover, unifies the major elements that are included in the novel, especially the "love plot" and related incidents that Pickard objects to. Consider the most important one, the betrothal of Rebecca Rawson and Sir Thomas Hale. The particular verse on which Dr. Russ preaches states explicitly that charity is not selfish.[12] Yet the marriage is arranged for reasons of ambition and pride. Rebecca herself would seem to prefer the unpretentious Robert Pike, but her father in his pride has told this worthy young man "that he did design an alliance of his daughter with a gentleman of estate and family" (p. 39). Margaret believes at one point that "apart from the wealth and family of Sir Thomas, [her cousin] rather inclineth to her old friend and neighbor" (p. 23), but once Rebecca has made her decision, she determines to go through with the wedding no matter what misgivings she may have. Only after she has been deserted in England by the imposter and bigamist that Sir Thomas turns out to be[13] does she finally admit that she allowed herself in "her pride and vanity . . . to discard worthy men for one of great show and pretensions, who had no solid merit to boast of" (p. 193). Rebecca's experience, then, is a variation on the main theme of the book. Her tragedy results when charity is forgotten and she bases her action on vanity, ambition, and pride.

The other romances in the book provide additional variations on the theme. When Margaret is in Maine, she meets a young Mr. Jordan, who is courting her cousin Polly. Margaret learns that he is about to give up a promising career as a Church of England minister to become a simple farmer, and she twits him on what he might be doing to the social prospects of his bride. "I told him," she writes, "that perhaps he might have become a great prelate in the Church, and dwelt in a palace, and made a great lady of our cousin; whereas now I did see no better prospect for him than to raise corn for his wife to make pudding of, and chop wood to boil her kettle" (pp. 76–77). But instead of following the path of ambition like Rebecca Rawson, Jordan and Polly dismiss such prospects, prospects which, they admit, might never be realized, and turn instead to the simple life they have chosen. Margaret, of course, who always had misgivings about Rebecca's course of action, is "exceedingly pleased" with her cousin Polly's choice aud anticipates a happy life for her and her husband (p. 79).

Additional variations may be found in other romances that Margaret reports in her journal. She is much taken with the story of Sir Christopher Gardiner, who was separated from his betrothed at the instigation of her parents and who swore a vow to forsake marriage, only to encounter his beloved again in New England, where she had followed him. Margaret is deeply moved by their story, and although she never learns its outcome, she sympathizes with their plight. Whatever "their sins and their follies," she writes, "my prayer is, that they may be forgiven, for they loved much" (p. 76). In a similar fashion, she accepts the marriage of her brother Leonard to Margaret Brewster, though she would at one time have been very upset by his marrying a Quaker. She respects her brother's choice because she sees in Margaret Brewster a charitable attitude toward others that she cannot help but approve, and which she always tries to practice herself. When she learns, for example, of the sad plight of Rebecca Rawson after their voyage to England, Margaret Smith takes the unfortunate girl into her home and treats her with tender care. Each of these brief romances, therefore, develops an aspect of the theme of charity—or the unfortunate consequences that ensue when some other principle of action is followed.

Read in these terms, *Margaret Smith's Journal* is indeed a unified work of art, all major parts of which contribute to its central theme. Firmly grounded in the consciousness of Margaret Smith, who, as a consistently developed character, provides the major point of focus, the novel plays a series of important variations on the theme of charity. Margaret herself embodies a major part of this theme, for her actions and opinions well illustrate the operation of this principle in her own life. What she observes and reports, moreover, provides either confirmation of or a contrast to her view, and the interplay among the various incidents provides the major source of tension in the work. The sermon of Dr. Russ, of course, presents the Scriptural basis for the theme, and the several love affairs that Whittier includes exemplify further the need for Christian love as a basis for human action. So skillful, indeed, is Whittier in singing his series of variations, that he can stand completely apart from his novel and let it speak for itself. His artistic control, solidly based in the central character, is firmly and consistently maintained to make his brief novel what Edward Wagenknecht takes it to be—a classic of American literature that deserves to be better known.

Notes

1. That the work is indeed historically accurate has been amply demonstrated by Cecil B. Williams, *Whittier's Use of Historical Material in* Margaret Smith's Journal (Chicago: Univ. of Chicago Libs., 1936).

2. *Whittier: Bard of Freedom* (Chapel Hill: Univ. of North Carolina Press, 1941), p. 216. See also George R. Carpenter, who thought the book "too slight in substance, too sober in style" to be widely read. *John Greenleaf Whittier* (Boston: Houghton, Mifflin, 1903), p. 246.

3. *John Greenleaf Whittier: A Portrait in Paradox* (New York: Oxford Univ. Press, 1967), p. 7. See also Albert Mordell, who writes that "the book is a thing of beauty, a work of art." *Quaker Militant: John Greenleaf Whittier* (1933; rpt. Port Washington, N. Y.: Kennikat, 1969), p. 185.

4. *John Greenleaf Whittier* (New York: Twayne, 1961), pp. 127–29.

5. *John Greenleaf Whittier: An Introduction and Interpretation* (New York: Barnes & Noble, 1961), pp. 119–29.

6. See especially Mordell, *Quaker Militant*, p. 185.

7. *Whittier, Introduction and Interpretation*, p. 124. See also Lewis Leary, who, in "A Note on Whittier's Margaret Smith," *ESQ*, No. 50, pt. 2, 75 (I Quarter 1968), considers the narrative threads too slender.

8. Cecil B. Williams, for example, does not accept her as the central character in the work and considers the book disunified. *Whittier's Use of Historical Material*, p. 29. Mordell, on the other hand, transforms her into a mouthpiece for the author. *Quaker Militant*, p. 183.

9. Though Margaret's exact age is not mentioned in the book, she writes in her first entry that she is "just about" her cousin Rebecca's age, and we know from one of Whittier's letters that Rebecca, a historical character, was "about twenty-one" at the time of her marriage, over a year after the narrative begins. See Samuel T. Pickard, *Life and Letters of John Greenleaf Whittier* (Boston: Houghton, Mifflin, 1894), p. 340.

10. *The Prose Works of John Greenleaf Whittier* (Boston: Houghton, Mifflin, 1892), I, 13. Citations in my text are to page numbers in this volume.

11. There is even evidence that Margaret Smith may have High Church leanings, for in the epilogue to the story, her grandson, a curate in England in 1747, points out that Rebecca "was not . . . a member of the church, having some scruples in respect to the rituals, as was natural from her education in New England, among Puritan schismatics" (pp. 194–95). The implication is strong that Margaret and Rebecca belong to different churches at least after they arrive in England.

12. I Cor. xiii.5. The critic would do well to read the whole context of this verse, for it is very pertinent to both the sermon and the novel.

13. Although Rebecca's story reads like a bit of sentimental fiction, it is nonetheless a true one. See Williams, *Whittier's Use of Historical Material*, p. 31.

Whittier's Moral Power

Anonymous*

James Russell Lowell, in "A Fable for Critics," called in review many of his contemporary poets and touched off their characteristics, employing in each case that keen literary insight of which he was so profound a master, yet never failing to spare the sensibilities of those he was obliged to censure, by using for purposes of chastisement a switch cut from the tree of knowledge and having many leaves of good-natured humor and generous compliment still attached. There was but one author whose friends who had a right to feel that he had been too severely treated by Mr. Lowell, and that one was the author of "The Bigelow Papers." Of him, though the name was not mentioned, some rather sharp things were said; among others that he was trying to climb Parnassus with such a load of reforms on his back as would almost surely retard the ascent if not render it impossible, and that what the young rhymster most needed to learn was "the difference 'twixt singing and preaching."

It is scarcely necessary to say that though Mr. Lowell's real estimate of himself was probably as modest as this witty self-depreciation implied, yet the specific charge was rather an attempt to interpret popular criticism than to state his personal idea of a poet's function. We may be sure that if the question had been seriously put to him whether or not this criticism was just, he would have replied that whatever his faults and failures might be, and none could account them greater than he did, they did not arise from the moral earnestness that sought to smite the giant citadels of wrong with fiery shafts of verse. All the world knows that if such an endeavor is to be called preaching, he who sang of the vision of Sir Launfal in search of the Holy Grail never ceased to preach until he ceased to sing.

Seldom or never has one poet admired and loved another than James Russell Lowell admired and loved John Greenleaf Whittier. Their genius was widely different in many ways, as were their early lives and as have been their life-long careers. But in this they were and are akin:

*Reprinted from the *Boston Daily Advertiser*, 16 Dec. 1891, p. 4.

In the loftiest work of both there is always present a supreme motive transcending all care for mere literary form, or even originality and beauty of thought. This was the golden link between the sweet souled, shy Quaker at "The Knolls"[1] and the all but idolized Harvard University professor, the thrice welcome guest at the banquet tables of Old World nobles.

Whoever wishes to fittingly rebuke this pretentious froth of which we hear so much in these days, about "art for art's sake," let him cite the example of Whittier. Only try to imagine our most distinctively American poet discarding "purpose" and writing for the sake of poetry as an end and not an agent! The attempt to think of that shows how absurd the suggestion is. Study any of his best poems in order to analyze their charm. There will be found in plenty whatever belongs to true poetic art. There are brilliant imagery, chaste diction, melodious rhythm, the quintessence of meaning, the maximum of thought in the minimum of words, every grace and finish that the most fastidious literary dilettante can demand. But it is not any or all of these thing which have secured for Whittier his undisputed place as the most perfect representative which our country has yet produced of American poetic genius. In respect to them all, he has imitators, rivals, equals. Nobody cares whether, as to those things, he has superiors or not.

Whittier is what he is by means of his unmatched power to touch at the depths and stir to the height man's and woman's spiritual nature. He is the poet of the purest affections, the sublimest aspirations. He is the poet of the conscience. He is the poet of divine fatherhood and human brotherhood. He has made the family fireside glorious. He has inscribed on many a page of this work-a-day life of ours errata which, spelled out as seen through tear-dimmed eyes, take shape as follows: "For 'home,' read 'heaven.'"

NOTE

1. "Oak Knoll," an estate in Danvers, Mass., owned by three of his cousins and Mrs. Abby J. Woodman, where the poet made his home part of the year. [Ed. note.]

The Quaker Laureate of Puritanism

James Mudge[*]

It was plain . . . that the ethical was more strongly developed in [Whittier] than the aesthetical; that his hold on his readers was more because he stirred their hearts profoundly, and helped them in the battle of life, than because he gave them new ideas or impressed them with his brilliant powers of fancy. He was a seer and a prophet, a mighty moral teacher; not a theologian or a preacher exactly, but his influence on the religious thought of the American people has been far greater than that of the occupant of any pulpit. In the long run the poets prevail.

Just what did he teach? What were the main thoughts which he felt himself commissioned to communicate to the world? One does not have to read long in order to see that his productions are thoroughly saturated with the Bible. This was the one book of his boyhood days, the one with which he was most familiar all his life. He was so filled with its truths, with its language, and so intimately acquainted with every part of it, even those portions less generally perused, that he could draw at will upon all its stores of opinion and expression. The ordinary reader who attempts to trace up his Scripture references to their source will find himself driven to prolonged use of the concordance, and will emerge from the endeavor much better acquainted than before with the treasures of Holy Writ. We have noted between six and seven hundred biblical quotations or allusions in his poetical works, and doubtless the list might be further extended. But to say that he was emphatically biblical in his teaching is, of course, somewhat indefinite. What special parts of the Bible did he mainly affect? What particular truths were dearest to him, and have, through him, become most impressed upon the public? Charity, sympathy, pity, brotherly kindness, unselfishness, love—this class of sentiments all will agree, were those for which he had chief affinity. It was these qualities that he was never tired of praising. The uttermost toleration also, the very largest inclusiveness of belief, and the very mildest judgments upon others, as mind-

[*]Reprinted from the *Methodist Review*, 68 (Jan. 1908), 37–51.

ful of our own weakness, our own imperfections in conduct or creed, strongly characterized him. He was surprisingly, stupendously optimistic, with profound faith in human nature, full of hope and good cheer, enthusiasm and brightness. He sings:

> The Night is mother of the Day.
>   The Winter of the Spring.
> And ever upon old Decay
>   The greenest mosses cling.
> Behind the cloud the starlight lurks,
>   Through showers and sunbeams fall;
> For God, who loveth all His works,
>   Has left His hope with all.
>   [From "A Dream of Summer."]

There is never any doubt with him that "truth itself is strong" and shall certainly prevail; that "no seed of truth is lost, through summer's heat and winter's frost, and every duty pays at last its cost." Never any doubt, either, had he that it is perfectly safe to trust God. He constantly, clearly teaches patience under the divine discipline, faith in the Father's care— in his power, wisdom, affection; cheerful acceptance of all his allotments, perfect confidence in his all-embracing providence. It is perhaps in this more than in any other direction that he has strengthened the hearts of men to endure, and be, and do. "Before me, even as behind," he says, "God is, and all is well." "Well I know that all things move to the spheral rhythm of love." He rebukes "the faithlessness of fear." As to the "old baffling questions" which evermore send out their silent challenge and their dumb demand torturing the soul with their "riddles of the dread unknown," he says:

> I have no answer, for myself or thee,
> Save that I learned beside my mother's knee;
> "All is of God that is, or is to be;
> And God is good." Let this suffice us still,
> Resting in childlike trust upon His will
> Who moves to his great ends unthwarted by the ill.
>   [From "Trust."]

With him "nothing can of chance befall," "that is best which is," and "what is dark below is light in heaven." He is certain that "the end will tell, the dear Lord orderest all things well," that "soon or late our Father makes his perfect recompense to all," sending a fresh blessing ever to take the place of that removed. Even when our loved ones go, called to himself by the Father, "when in the shadow of a great affliction the soul sits dumb," we are not to think that any evil has been wrought, or any real loss sustained; "the good die not," "they live on earth in thought and deed as truly as in his heaven." "Life is ever lord of death, and Love can never lose its own."

While laying stress on human dignity, and the inborn right of every man to freedom and to the uttermost use of all his powers of thought and speech and act, he is not of those who idly fancy that in the universe, God-ruled, with its marvelously complicated conditions, any man can do, in the outward realm, precisely as he pleases, or is fitted to determine the course of his career.

> The threads our hands in blindness spin
> No self-determined plan weaves in;
> The shuttle of the unseen powers
> Works out a pattern not as ours.
>
> . . . .
> Through wish, resolve, and act, our will
> Is moved by undreamed forces still;
> And no man measures in advance
> His strength with untried circumstance
> [From "Overruled."]

But he is the farthest possible from diminishing our sense of responsibility or encouraging aught of fatalism or inactivity. In a very important sense "we shape ourselves the joy or fear of which the coming life is made," "the tissue of the life to be we weave with colors all our own."

> Better to stem with heart and hand
>   The roaring tide of life than lie,
> Unmindful, on its flowery strand,
>   Of God's occasions drifting by!
>
> Better with naked nerves to bear
> The needles of this goading air,
> Than, in the lap of sensual ease, forego
> The godlike power to do, the godlike aim to know.
> [From "The Last Walk in Autumn."]

Good deeds are with him ever the best kind of worship; one would think at times he meant there was no need for any other worship. He gives the highest efficacy to "the prayer of love, which, wordless, shapes itself in deeds." He would not have him called heretic "whose works attest his faith in goodness," although that faith be "by no creed confessed." In one place, defending Sumner, he seems to sneer at "frames and molds" as of little account, "the bigot's narrow bound," a mark of "cant." In another place, praising Burns, he says: "He who sings the love of many the love of God hath sung." Again he writes: "Love is one with holiness"; "beauty is goodness, ugliness is sin"; "the good is always beautiful, the beautiful is good." Perhaps he did not quite mean this. If he did, we must take some exception to it. He had the defects of his qualities. How could it be otherwise? Who has not? In stating strongly a precious and important truth, which at the time seems most needing emphasis, he could not always stop to append a counterbalancing statement or guard his sentence from abuse. We are quite certain he did not really intend to depreciate righteousness or put mere sweetness in its place. Nor was it any part of his plan to cast scorn upon the inward life. On the contrary, true to his Quaker training and the principles of the Friends, to which he was very warmly attached—he said near the close of his life: "I have been a member of the society of Friends by birthright and by the settled conviction of the truth of its principles and the importance of its testimonies"—he never tires of eulogizing the inward voice and ear, "the still witness of the heart." We must listen, he says, "through the noise of time and sense to the still whisper of the Inward Word, bitter in blame, sweet in approval heard. It is its own confirming evidence." With him the deepest test of faith, deeper than "prison cell or martyr's stake," is "the self-abasing watchfulness of silent prayer." True piety he finds stamped with "cheerful walking as one to pleasing service led, doing God's will as if it were my own, not trusting in my own, but in God's strength alone." He hears, listening with his heart, the "voice without a sound" which says: "Be just, be true, be merciful, revere the Word within thee; God is near."

Another point of doctrine wherein Whittier gives out at times an uncertain sound—although in the end he seems to emerge from ambiguity—is that which concerns the doom of the lost, or the possibility of any being finally lost. It is evident that in some moods, and at some stages of his life, he verges toward Universalism. His affections and sensibilities lead him powerfully that way; he writes some lines that can hardly be interpreted otherwise than as sanctioning that faith: "Love must needs be stronger far than sin"; "The patience of immortal love outwearying mortal sin"; "I do not fix, with mete and bound, the love and power of God"; "I know not of his hate. I know his goodness and his love." All this, if it stood alone, would surely put him with Tennyson and Browning on this theme. But it does not stand alone. There are abundant indications that in his later years, as his thought grew more mature, he saw the other side more clearly, and appreciated more fully that all could not be managed by mere softness. In 1842 and 1843 he rates the clergy roundly because they sanction capital punishment, which he crudely calls the "crime of revenge," and "the law's darkest crime," "murder by the law's command," terming the gallows a "foul devil's altar," the chaplain and hangman "two busy fiends." He favors unmeasured mercy, unlimited forbearance toward the criminal; no restraint must be put upon him for the good of society, only for his own good. This is very shallow and raw. But he speaks also of "God's hate of sin," and says: "Thy judgments too are right." "Stern-eyed duty" comes to the front in his thought no less than mild-eyed love; he seems to recognize that persons may be so inexorably, inseparably bound up with sin that they must share its treatment. He says very explicitly, replying to a letter from an inquiring friend: "I am not a Universalist, for I believe in the possibility of the perpetual loss of the soul that persistently turns away from God in the next life as in this. But I do believe that the divine love and compassion follow us in all worlds, and that the heavenly Father will do the best that is possible for every creature he has made. What that will be must be left to his infinite wisdom and goodness." He refers his correspondent to "The Answer," where he gives clearest testimony to his belief in the power of man to resist the love of God, to have gone so far in sin that his habit-bound feet will lack the will to turn—the soul prisoned in dreary selfishness and the mind unable to break the fetters of doubt or believe in the love of God; no eye left that can see, no ear that can hear; the will paralyzed by long continuance in evil. "No force divine can love compel." It would seem that all who are not Calvinists—and Whittier certainly was not such—must take this ground. In his fierce dissent from old New England Calvinism, as well as in his emphasis on the inward witness, the freedom of man, the love of God, the glory of toleration, Whittier was in close affiliation with Methodism.

. . .

His life was a consecration to all that is highest and best. Gail Hamilton says of him: "Blessed and beloved apostle! Sweetest saint in all the calendar! Worthy successor of that disciple whom Jesus loved, gentlest and tenderest of all the sons of thunder." How many hearts has he comforted, how many lives uplifted! How much we owe him for his brave stand in behalf of the despised and helpless; for lofty, weighty words of fervent faith, for tender breathings of brotherly love. In the power of the truth he assailed every form of wrong; in the name of the great Master he proclaimed the gospel of infinite mercy. We are grateful to him for Abraham Davenport, and Barbara Frietchie, and Maud Muller, and "The Eternal Goodness"—that marvelous expression of trust in the Father. The world has moved toward his positions; they must increasingly prevail. His place is secure. Even Professor Barrett Wendell, who keenly criticises him at some points, admits that "his faults are small beside his merits," and declares that "his chance of survival is better than that of any other contemporary man of letters."[1] His aims were holy. "If I ever feel like envying anyone," he said, "it is not the famous author, but some soul much like Jesus." He spoke in fitting forms those abiding principles which have been at the foundation of New England's greatness and which, if our republic is to abide, must increasingly permeate the nation. He was at once a poet of nature, an apostle of liberty, and a prophet of progress—journalist, politician, philanthropist, reformer, seer, and mystic. He has been canonized by the people, who are so deeply his debtors. His appeal was made to conscience; his work was for character, to create nobler natures and grander lives. He had a high mission, a strong message. With the soul of a child he did the task of a man. May this centennial of his birth stimulate the study of what he wrote, and thus bring to mankind an added benefit from his great example. Not too strongly did Holmes put it, as he penned his farewell meed of praise above the open grave of his friend:

> Best loved and saintliest of our singing train,
>   Earth's noblest tributes to thy name belong;
> A lifelong record closed without a stain,
>   A blameless memory shrined in deathless song.

NOTE

1. "John Greenleaf Whittier," in his *Stelligeri and Other Essays Concerning America* (New York: Scribner's, 1893), p. 200. [Ed. note.]

John G. Whittier—
The Quaker Bard

H. G. Moore*

Whittier is undoubtedly one of the finest poets in America. People do not talk much about him. He is rarely quoted by the orator of that unhewn rostrum, the stump. Nevertheless, many a maiden bends over his pages and wipes from her eye the natural tribute of a tear, while her beating heart and sympathetic sensibilities attest the magic of the lines. And many a young man on whose smooth brow time nor care has ploughed a single furrow, and on whose heart the black shadows have not as yet fallen, finds in his verses ample food for all his fond schemes of pure ambition, his aspirations, visions, hopes, dreams and virtues. And the hackneyed, cent. per cent., soulless old worlding the hey-day of whose blood is tamed and evaporated, leaving only the lees and residuum of life behind, might put a little spirit and fire in his heart, and be happy in having the purity, freshness and innocence of his youth recalled to his mind, by reading over and over again, some of Whittier's grand and moral sin-smiting conceptions, until he came to have a glimpse of their meaning.

The Yankee Bard fairly disputes the laurel crown and the ennobling palm with Longfellow and Bryant,—less learned, more passionate than Longfellow; less masculine, more melodious than Bryant.

Longfellow, like Whittier, deals roundly in ethics and didactics, but the former addresses himself to the reasoning and reflective faculty, the latter to the ever-answering moral sense; the former often needs to be explained by a little argumentation, the latter is always comprehended by the heart. There is soul, real soul, quick with the breath of God, not with galvanism, beneath the form of his verse, and by the way, of his prose also. Under the drab of a modest, straight Quaker, he hides a heart all on fire with the progressive tendencies of the times; and in quickening strains of holy and patient welcome, he sings and celebrates the advent of a more perfect humanity; counsels the suffering to abide patiently the ordained period of their deliverance, and invokes his co-workers to diligence in all their reformatory labors. There is in

*Reprinted from the *Christian Wreath*, 1 (Oct. 1847), 237–44.

Whittier such a constant mounting up to elementary principles of ethics and action, which dwell "above the smoke and stir of this dim spot which men call earth," that he really reminds us of the sky-lark which the all-sympathising muse of Shelley addressed—

> "Higher, still higher,
> From the earth thou springest—
> Like a cloud of fire
> The blue deep thou wingest;—
> And singing, still dost soar, and soaring ever singest."
>
> [From "To a Skylark"]

Whittier is the missionary and poet of Hope. He has had a waking vision of a new heaven and a new earth wherein dwelleth righteousness, and he lives, moves, thinks and acts for the sinful present, only that, Baptist-like; he may make straight the paths for the approach of the sinless hereafter, and announce the coming of Shiloh. He will not lay off his armor until that fair state of society is fully disclosed.

> Until *immortal mind,*
> Unshackled, walks abroad,
> And chains no longer bind
> The image of our God:
> Until no captive one
> Murmurs on land or wave
> And in his course the sun
> Looks down upon no slave.[1]

In such strains, akin in spirit to those of the great seers of Israel, does he celebrate the perfection yet to be revealed. Strains whose fervor stirs up the sluggish depths of our heart like the voice of an awakening arch-angel.

His love of humanity does not evaporate in generalities or common places; he singles out classes, and sets himself earnestly to the bettering of their condition. There are philanthropists who possess such a cosmopolitan or lack-a-daisical benevolence, that they love all mankind to distraction, and have a deal of feeling for the entire community, but care very little for a single old man or a little beggar boy; like one of the Poor Laws Commissioners in England, who refused alms to an applicant on the plea, that, as his duties to the poor were of a very general character, he was under no obligations to relieve individuals.

We should go to work in this matter like philosophers, begin with particulars, then ascend to generals. Whittier, however, unites these two developments of love. The chief objects of his kind feelings are

> "———— the bondmen sighing,
> By Santee's wave, in Mississippi's cane."
>
> [From "A Summons."]

Whether he is right in this selection, we cannot say. If he be right, the cause could not be extended much by his poetry. Men look not into rhymes and verses for an argument or demonstration. If he be not right, the spirit of his poems will remain the same, for the error will be only a misapplication or an over-strained application of principles good in themselves. We feel tempted to introduce here a passage from Sir Philip Sidney's quaint Defence of Poesy. Its beauty will excuse its length, and the reader will apply it to the matter in hand. We consider it quite appropriate.

"I think truly that of all writers under the sun, the poet is the least liar, and though he would, as a poet, can scarcely be a liar. The astronomer, with his cousin the geometrician, can hardly escape when they take upon him to measure the height of the stars. How often, think you, do the physicians lie when they aver things good for sickness, which afterwards sends Charon a great number of souls, drowned in a potion, before they come to his ferry? And no less of the rest which take upon them to *affirm*. Now, for the poet, *he nothing affirmeth, and therefore never lieth*: for, as I take it, to lie is to affirm that to be true which is false! so as to the other artists; and especially the historian, affirming many things, can in the cloudy knowledge of mankind, hardly escape from many lies; but the poet, as I said before, never affirmeth; the poet never marketh any circles about your imagination, to conjure you to believe for true what he writeth: he citeth not authorities of other histories, but even for his entry calleth the sweet muses to inspire him into a good invention; in troth, not laboring to tell you what is or is not, but what should or should not be. And therefore, though he recount things not true, yet because he telleth them not for true, he lieth not; unless we will say that Nathan lied in his speech to David, or Æsop lied in the tales of his beasts: for who thinketh that Æsop wrote it for actually true, were well worthy to have his name chronicled among the beasts he writeth of."—(Lond. ed. 18 vo. p. 64.)

The head may err, but as poor Burns said—

> "The heart's aye, the part aye,
> That makes us right or wrong."
> [From "Epistle to Davie, a Brother Poet."]

But we love Whittier's free spirit, and free impulses. He has a dirge for a martyr's memory, and thunder for a tyrant's ear. He has a voice

> "— for the poor man's cause,
> For labor's just reward;
> For violated laws
> Of nature and of God."[2]

As if the spirit of a Hebrew prophet possessed him, he stands and cries with the persistency of friend Fox himself:—

> "Up, then, in freedom's manly part,
>   From grey-beard old to fiery youth,
> And on the nation's naked heart,
>   Scatter the living coals of truth."
>   [From "Expostulation."]

And with the triumphant rapture of a dying patriot, just mounting from the stake to the skies, and bathed already with the purifying light flowing from off the altar before the throne, exclaims,

> "Glory to God forever,
>   Beyond the despot's will,
> The soul of Freedom liveth,
>   Imperishable still—"
>   [From "To the Memory of Charles B. Storrs."]

Whittier overflows with a kind of benevolence which the learned Dr. Barrow,[3] in one of his sermons, describes as a "universal care and complacency, making every man ourself and all concernments to be ours." With a sense of assimilation he suffers with the sufferer, and straightway his muse grasps the arrows and bolts with a flaming right hand, and becomes the avenger. He discerns the real thing beneath the masquerade of social forms. Labor and Wages, the sphinx-riddle which economists must solve for the people, or the people will solve in their own way for themselves, are shown in Whittier's poetry, dressed up in habiliments much more enticing than any ever dreamed of by Adam Smith. Not tariff or an excise, taxes, direct or indirect, representation or the elective franchise, acts of Congress or Treasury circulars, is his solution of the vexed matter, but *the golden rule and the brotherhood of mankind.*

> "By misery unrepelled, unawed
>   By pomp or power, he sees a man,
> In prince or peasant, slave or lord,
>   Pale priest or swarthy artizan."
>   [From "Democracy."]

He is a disciple of the school of Channing, and, like his gifted and amiable master, possesses but one large and absorbing idea, which overarches and underlays most of his productions. That one idea, which like Moses' rod, swallows up the others, is the dignity of human nature. Some of the modern unitarian and transcendental authors of New England seem to think that this extolled article of their creed is a waif, which they themselves have picked up—heretofore undiscovered. No such thing. "Not to call antiquity from the old schools of Greece," let them look into the tractates of John Milton, where, we hesitate not to say, the germ of well nigh every great idea which illustrates our present literature, may be found—"the originals of nature in their crude conception." Milton was, in his whole character, the greatest man ever born among the Anglo-Saxon race, the noblest citizen that ever vindicated liberty. In his "Reason of Church Government Urged Against Prelacy," he speaks of an "ingenuous and noble degree of honest shame, or call it if you will, an esteem, *whereby men wear an inward reverence to their own persons.*" There are numerous passages of like import. This thought, like many others in his prose works, is reproduced in *Paradise Lost.* It occurs in the description of Adam, going forth to welcome Raphael, his celestial visitant—

> "Meanwhile our primitive great sire, to meet
> His god-like guest, walks forth, *without more train*
> *Accompanied than with his own complete*
> *Perfections; in himself was all his state.*
> More solemn than the tedious pomp that waits
> On princes, when their rich retinue long
> Of horses led, and grooms besmeared with gold
> Dazzles the crowd and sets them all agape."
>   [From Book V, 11.350-57.]

Does that not smack of the times of the Commonwealth and Republic?

This was not a mere idle sentiment with Milton; it was the foundation on which he based his congregational plan of church organization. Expand it, and you have the doctrine of Channing and the song of Whittier.

There is a school of modern poetry, peculiarly distinct from any that has gone before it. The following, from Montgomery's *Lectures on General Literature*, will perhaps illustrate our meaning. "A poem is a campaign, in which all the marches, sufferings, toils and conflicts of the hero, are successively developed to final victory." The hero of this modern school, is *Humanity.* Its toils, sufferings, and conflicts, in the vast historical campaign of existence are developed, and its triumphs, of which stray glimpses of glory, ever and anon, break through the folds of the future, is already anticipated and heralded in songs inspired by hope. Blessed prospect! The sufferings of man have been recorded by historians; let his victory now be celebrated by the bards. Whittier shall be among the select band that shall stand on the mountain tops, to announce the flight of darkness in the west, and the dawn of an unsetting sun in the east. And while they, above, shine, transfigured by the new light, we, below, brightened by its ascending and spreading glories, shall repeat the chant, which they catch from the ancient watchers.

> Jam Fides, et Pax, et Honor, Pudorque
> Priscus et neglecta redire virtus
> Audet: apparet que beata pleno
>   Copia corno.[4]

Soon may the day-star arise! We praise and love this new school and chorus of song. They refine, elevate, purify, enlarge and spiritualize our views, kindly incline us to our fellow man, and strengthen us under the repulses and disasters of life, by fixing our contemplation on that better state of things which the coming on of time shall gradually disclose.

There is not in Whittier, a store of curious, far-fetched, diversified ideas. There is no massiveness of thought, or inexhaustibleness of illustration, no plots, or counterplots, no startling development, like the fifth act of a tragedy, nothing that hurries you along wihout breath or consciousness, and then lets you drop down ten thousand fathoms plumb, no tempest or lightnings, no rude clash of the lyre; but all is smooth, tranquil, delightful, passionate, persuasive and sweet—

> "Round an holy calm diffusing,
> Love of peace and lonely musing."[5]

Pure (not partisan) democracy, and Platonic love, are the soul of his verse, and easy melody is its graceful body. His satire cuts like a Damascus blade. His rebuke falls on the head of its victim like an old Scotch claymore in the hands of a MacGregor.

And now, kind reader, we part. Perhaps, you have had enough of poetry. If you be a dull earth-clod, electrised with a kind of nervous irritability, which counterfeits life, but excites no sentiment, no passion, no taste, it is better we should part. But if you are the man, or perchance the woman, we would fain wish you to be, it shall seem to you as it does to us, that we have been strolling through a fair garden—a vale of Cashmere, where

> "Tree, vine, and flower, in shadow meet."
> [From "Toussaint L'Overture."]

May you often turn aside from the bread-and-butter provender of work-day life, and indulge in a Feast of Roses among the sweet singing poets, where I warrant you will find no

> "—— dead sea fruits, that tempt the eye,
> But turn to ashes on the lips."
> [From Thomas Moore's "Lalla Rookh."]

Notes

1. This extract is not in Whittier's *Collected Poems*. [Ed. note.]

2. This extract is not in Whittier's *Collected Poems*. [Ed. note.]

3. Probably Elijah Porter Barrows (1807–1888), clergyman, educator, author, and editor; taught at Oberlin, Western Reserve, and Andover Theological Sem-

inary; contributed articles to *Bibliotheca Sacra*, and was an editor for the American Tracts Society. [Ed. note.]

4. Now faith and peace and honor and old-fashioned modesty
   And virtue long ignored dare to return,
   And happy plenty appears with a full horn. [Ed. note.]

5. This extract is not in Whittier's *Collected Poems*. [Ed. note.]

The Growth of Whittier's Mind—Three Phases

Harry Hayden Clark[*]

After one has analyzed Whittier's individual poems or fragments of his work, it is well to view him briefly in complete profile as a kind of man against the sky. Broadly speaking, he seems to have had three successive centers of emphasis—I say emphasis because there are of course minor exceptions which do not seriously invalidate this interpretation.

Up to 1833 Whittier was primarily concerned with the literary aspects of the sensational, the lurid, or the colorfully superstitious, usually approached from a localistic angle. The type is represented in "The Demon's Cave" (1831) in which he says there is in this actual New Hampshire cave "something to romance dear" since it is associated with "the restless phantoms of murdered men," the ghostly gibber and the demon's yell, although such superstitions have now passed "away at the glance of truth." Mary Pray's *A Study of Whittier's Apprenticeship* (Bristol, N. H.: Musgrove Printing House 1930) printed 109 of these early poems, and others have been printed by W. M. Merrill in the *Essex Institute Historical Collections*, 91 (1955), 128-54. A glance at the titles in T. F. Currier's invaluable *Bibliography of John Greenleaf Whittier* (1937) will give one an idea of his cultivation, as in his Preface to *Legends of New England* (1831), of a "new" consciousness that "New England is rich in traditionary lore—a thousand associations of superstition and manly daring and romantic adventure are connected with her green hills and her pleasant rivers." Such psychological "associationalism" of aesthetic feeling and actual historic places was in this period widespread, especially in the revered *North American Review* from 1815 on, as R. E. Streeter has shown.

Five of Whittier's early associates encouraged him in the trend suggested. Thus Joshua Coffin encouraged the boy's interest in local traditions and introduced him at the age of fourteen to the work of Burns who taught him to see the romance underlying the commonplace.

[*]Reprinted from the *Emerson Society Quarterly*, 50 (1968), 119-26 by permission of Kenneth Walter Cameron.

A. W. Thayer urged him to continue his education and to write for publication. New Hampshire's Robert Dinsmoor (on whom Whittier wrote an appreciative essay) taught him that New England scenes could provide Yankee pastorals just as well as Scotland. And in editing the work of J. G. C. Brainard in 1832 Whittier centers his long Introduction on the fact that he "prefers the lowliest blossom of Yankee-land" to far-away exotics. "New England is full of Romance; and her writers would do well to follow the example of Brainard. The great forest which our fathers penetrated—the red men—their struggle and their disappearance—the Powwow and the War-dance—the savage in-road and the English sally—the tale of superstition, and the scenes of Witchcraft,—all these are rich materials of poetry." (This Introduction and about seventy other literary comments are reprinted in *Whittier on Writers and Writing*, ed. E. H. Cady and H. H. Clark, Syracuse: Syracuse Univ. Press, 1950.) The superstitions and witchcraft of Whittier's native state were made to seem suitable for poetic treatment by the fact that (as he said in reviews of Scott and his "Demonology and Witchcraft") such a famous author had showed a "bias" toward "the marvellous and the praeter-natural" aroused by "Highland super-stition." In his review of Scott's follower, Whittier's "old favorite Cooper" and his *Wept*, dealing with a New England Indian, Cooper is critical of improbabilities and of the "females," but he praises Cooper's sea novels for "rich and rare entertainment" as well as the earlier volumes of the Leatherstocking Series, celebrating manly daring and hair-breadth escapes in the localized forests. (See Cady and Clark, pp. 26–28).

II

If up to 1833 Whittier tended to emphasize localistic sensationalism of one kind or another, from 1833[1] to 1857 he tended to emphasize out-ward reformism or abolition which after 1843 shaded into a concern for more general brotherhood and mankind's common humanity as opposed to extremism. His reformism was a response to five influences. Garrison and other humanitarians fired Whittier's imagination as he dramatized his turn from the selfish quest of literary fame to a defiance (in the poem "Ego") of "ermined robe and saintly gown" to the kind of "glorious martyrdom" for the rights of the lowly which he attributed to Garrison in his early (1833) poetic tribute. Especially important as an influence was Whittier's ancestral Quaker faith in equality and brotherhood and the stress on charity of heart associated with John Woolman whose work Whittier edited with a long eulogistic intro-duction. Milton and Puritan "defenders of English liberty, sowers of the seed, the fruits of which we are now reaping," (*Prose Works*, I, 288) were strong influences. (Milton of the great prose tracts such as

Areopagitica came closest, Whittier said, to representing his ideal man at this time.) As one who believed in relying on persuasion and on ballots rather than on bullets, Whittier cherished the natural-rights tradition of Jefferson. In his prose tract, "Justice and Expediency" (1833), Whittier responded to the Yankee spirit of practical expediency in arguing that free men, sure of the fruits of their own labor, will have an incentive to work harder than slaves will. And finally British abolitionists and the visits of their spokesmen such as George Thompson helped to inspire Whittier in his crusade.

Three poems may be cited as representing various phases of his abolitionism. Perry Miller[2] was much impressed by his poem "Toussaint L'Ouverture" in Whittier's crisis year, 1833, which illustrates the way in which his earlier romantic sensationalism erupts in an abolitionist poem: "this phantasmagoric vision of the rebellion in Haiti . . . is stark violence, massacre, and, in the climax, rape of the white planter's wife by the black demon" driven to desperation. "The sexual passion, the fire, the volcano, erupt into a terminology of orgiastic destruction." "A Sabbath Scene" tells how Whittier's "brain took fire" when a clergyman, trying to help enforce the Fugitive Slave Law, ordered his Deacon to use the actual physical "holy tome" to trip and capture a trembling slave girl who sought to escape to the supposed sanctuary of a Christian church. Temporarily at least Whittier preferred to turn from such an abuse of the Scriptures to follow the guidance of God's word "interpreted by Nature." Less melodramatic is "Massachusetts to Virginia" which recalls how the latter's statesmen such as Patrick Henry joined northern revolutionists to achieve freedom from Britain; devoted to the traditions of their First Families, Jefferson's Virginians are in this poem taunted with having become "False to their fathers' memory, false to the faith they loved." "Proem" (1847-49) was written as a comprehensive introduction to all Whittier's abolition poems. In this he modestly claims he is unable to approach the "rounded art" and "mystic beauty, dreamy grace" of poets such as Spenser and Sidney whom he loves, but he will celebrate "our common world of joy and woe" and will lay his poems on the shrine of Freedom which he loves as ardently as did Milton.[3] Elsewhere Whittier said (in "The Training," 1845) that "Milton approaches nearly to my conception of a true hero" as "the stern old republican," and "Milton's prose has long been my favorite reading. My whole life has felt the influence of his writings" (quoted in Pickard's *Life*, II, 506). Perhaps Whittier's most enduring and timely contribution to our political life is embodied in his editorial in the *Essex Gazette* for June 18, 1836, entitled "Freedom of the Press" claiming the right of dissent. (Governor Everett tried to get the legislature of Massachusetts to penalize spokesmen of abolition.) "We will yield to no laws whatever of our freedom of opinion, and the constitutional right of expressing that opinion. We are for giving Truth full play. We believe with Milton in his noble defence of the freedom of the Press." He argued that if the South managed to throttle freedom of expression and dissent, the South would enslave all white men as well as negroes, and would stagnate.

During the 1850's in poems such as "Wordsworth" Whittier holds that one can "read the world aright" who can "in its common forms discern / A beauty and a harmony," that one (like himself) whose ear is "pained / By strife of sect and party noise" finds especially welcome Wordsworth's "brook-like murmur ... of nature's simple joys." (John Pickard and C. B. Williams have described the "schism" after 1843 within the abolitionist group and the split between the followers of Garrison and of Whittier. See Pickard, *NEQ*, 37 [1964], 250–54; and Williams, *NEQ*, 25 [1952], 248–54). In "Proem" (1849) Whittier had coupled his reformist following of Milton in devoting his poems to liberty with his concern with "our common world of joy and woe." And in his "Dedication to Songs of Labor" (1850) he turns from "youth's enchanted forest" of his first period to "after-thoughts" associated with "life's autumnal lea" as he says that in his poems he seeks to "gladden duty's ways" by celebrating "the unsung beauty hid beneath life's common things." He tries to awaken not so much the reformist's unrest as "a manlier spirit of content," remembering that Christ was content to be "a poor man toiling with the poor, / In labor, as in prayer, fulfilling the same law." Remember, then, that Whittier's second period (as C. B. Williams helpfully suggests) has two phases—his Garrisonian abolition and concern with helping the helpless slave-labor, and (especially after 1843) an organic concern with the idea that "the strong hand makes strong the working brain" (cf. Thoreau) and a concern with the sanative "common things" and a manlier spirit of content with the life of the common man.

Taken as a whole, Whittier's prose essays in *Old Portraits and Modern Sketches* and *Literary Recreations* have two implications. First, wishing to give his personal reformism a broader basis, he tried to provide it with a broader temporal perspective by celebrating various now revered spokesmen of the Revolution of the seventeenth-century Puritans. Paradoxically, while he appeared to be dealing with the seventeenth-century past, he singles out those spokesmen of the past who were iconoclasts, who pioneered in leading a revolt against bondage to throne and altar. But Whittier insists that Past, Present and Future are one, centered in the Now. Second, while Whittier's primary concern at the start in his prose portraits may have been a quest for examples of reformism, the heroic figures of the seventeenth century as he studied them led him to see that for the most part they stressed the inwardness of evil and sought to make men not masterless but self-mastered. (Milton who in the Second Sonnet on the Detraction said of his more radical opponents, license they mean when they cry liberty, for who loves that must first be wise and good, having overcome individual temptations.)

III

Let us now turn to Whittier's dominant emphases during his third period, during the last thirty-five years of his life, from 1857 when Mordell (p. 178) says "the work of Whittier as the poet of freedom and the singer of the oppressed really ended." (I should prefer to say that he transcended his institutional reformism by including[4] it in a more proportionate synthesis involving the inward as well as the outward, organically related.)

As in "Skipper Ireson's Ride" on a rail while being externally tarred and feathered by the angry women whose husbands and brothers and sons the skipper had deserted, he turns in 1857 to the idea of the individual's inward conscience. Note the anguished cry of the physically tormented skipper to his persecutors:

> "What is the shame that clothes the skin (*i.e.*, tar)
> To the nameless horror that lives within?"

In his essay of 1862 introducing "Dora Greenwell" he hopes that "In the chaos of civil strife and the shadow of mourning which rests over the land, the contemplation of 'things unseen which are external' might not be unwelcome; . . . when the foundations of human confidence [in physical warfare] are shaken, and the trust in men proves vain, there might be glad listeners to a voice calling from the outward and the temporal to the inward and the spiritual" (VII, 303). In his many hymns such as "The Eternal Goodness" (1865–66) he acknowledges that past sages cannot paint too darkly the guilt and sin of which he as an individual is conscious "within." (For similar emphasis on the cause and cure of suffering as essentially within rather than outside the individual, see the Cambridge Edition of his poems, pp. 424; 433; 436; 438; 442; 448; 458; 460; 466.)

Institutional reform seemed impotent in the face of such afflictions as the death of his beloved mother in 1857, his two sisters in 1860 and 1864, and his own failing health at this time. He was also conscious of the fact that such masters as Milton and Emerson and Lowell had eventually turned from external reformism to a concern with inwardness. In 1870 he concluded, "The true life of a nation is in its personal morality, and no excellence of constitution and laws can avail much if the people lack purity and integrity" (VII, 432. See also VII, 228, where he says that "Unsupported by a more practical education, higher aims, and a deeper sense of the responsibilities of life and duty, it [women's exercise of the ballot] is not likely to prove a blessing [as a "remedy for all the evils"] in her hands any more than in man's." See also quote in S. T. Pickard's *Life*, II, 742, and VII, 356). Regardless of "outward" aids, he has become convinced that "no man his brother can redeem." In his long eulogy of Woolman he agrees with the Quaker sage that "all the varied growths of evil had their underlying root in human [individual] selfishness" (VII, 357). "There is something in the doctrine of total depravity and regeneration. We are born selfish. The discipline of [one's inward] life develops the higher qualities of character. . . . It is the [free-willed] conquering of innate selfish propensities that makes the saint; and the giving up unduly to impulses that in their origin are necessary to the preservation of life that makes the saint" (quoted in Pickard's *Life*, II, 629; see also VII, 232, 234). Whittier concluded that if the wrong-doer humbly repents breaking God's benign laws, such remorse may help to make evil educative, much as Milton did in his doctrine of the "fortunate fall" (*PL*, XII, 473–78).

During this period after 1857 Whittier urges that the Inner Light or the individual's intuition should be tested by a socially-mediated tradition such as that embodied in the Bible: The two revelations should test and reinforce one another. His "Pennsylvania Pilgrim" (1872) "read the Bible by the Inner Light." However, Whittier emphasized those aspects of his ancestral faith which accorded with other and older religious sects and he hoped that Catholics and Puritans and the Hindus would eventually come to understand that they were worshipping in the light of elemental truths at one[5] altar, just as he concluded that time is only an illusion, that past, present, and future are one.

"The Last Walk in Autumn" (1857) also illustrates Whittier's turn from the "dreams" of his earlier concern with either the luridly romantic or with utopian reform to a concern with poetic imagination which can find the universal in humble particulars, his work now being devoted to "the home and hearth" as in "Snow-Bound" (1867). "The beauty which old Greece or Rome / Sung, painted, wrought, lies close at home" and is discoverable by the imaginative "eye and ear / In all our daily walks" as well as in communion with his American friends Emerson (II, 105–112), Bayard Taylor, and Charles Sumner. He will now as a poet devote himself (in proceeding from kin to kind) to New England's "equal village schools," the "freeman's vote," religious freedom, her laborers' right to the rewards of their own efforts, and the "old home-bred virtues."

In place of his "hate of tyranny intense" and the tendency of the propagandist toward one-sidedness, Whittier in "The Problem" (1877) dividing management and labor argues that essentially "The interests of the rich man and the poor / Are one and same, inseparable evermore" and partisans of one or the other in their extremist panaceas offer but "catch-words of the blind / Leaders of the blind. / Solution there is none / Save in the Golden Rule of Christ alone," save in mediation and a peaceful recognition of the just claims of both sides in the controversy. Just as he regarded the Scripture as "a rule, not *the* rule of faith and practice," so Whittier urged his Quaker friends to find "no occasion to renew the disastrous quarrel of religion with science" (VII, 362) which men such as Swedenborg had used to show that objects in the "world of sense [are] only types and symbols of the world of spirit" (VII, 362). He also praised science as an agent of truth which had outmoded the cruel belief in witches. He praised the reverent Agassiz who was capable of prayer. Indeed, Whittier derived reinforcement for his doctrine of charity as based on the scientific or Newtonian doctrine that "in the outward world all things [such as the planets] do mutually operate upon and affect each other; and that it is by the energy of this [centrifugal and centripetal balanced] principle that our solid earth is supported, and the heavenly bodies are made to keep the rhythmic harmonies of this creation." He had faith that "a law akin to this physical law had been ordained for the moral world," sanctioning social coherence and mutual charity drawing individuals together (V, 91). Like Thoreau, however, Whittier was sceptical of "poor Etzler" as a mere technologist who prophesied the coming of a "paradisiacal state by the sole agency of outward mechanics" (V, 353). (Whittier's over-all view of science deserves much more investigation.)

If in "The Sabbath Scene" the spokesmen of slavery had invoked the sanction of the Bible and consequently Whittier had briefly preferred to rely on outward nature rather than the Bible, his more characteristic later view is embodied in "Andrew Rykman's Prayer" (1864–65) where he concluded that all the external things of nature tend to "fluctuate and flow." In "A Summer Pilgrimage" (1883) he was confident that "Beyond this masquerade of shape and color, light and shade, / And dawn and set, dull wax and wane, / Eternal verities remain."

During Whittier's last period he repeatedly emphasized the idea that "in judging of my fellow-men, I can see no other standard than that which our Lord and Master has given us, 'By their fruits ye shall know them,' The only orthodoxy that I am especially interested in is that of life and practice." (Quoted by Pickard, *Life*, I, 265.)

In "The Last Walk in Autumn," in "Snow-Bound," and especially in "The Pennsylvania Pilgrim" Whittier does not so much discard his earlier two emphases as he transcended them by including them in a larger synthesis. Thus in the latter poem, which the poet prized as among his best (Pickard's *Life*, II, 575–76), the groundwork is obviously localistic, the colonial Quaker's life being set in Pennsylvania. The prose preface uses his benign life (in which Lewis Leary finds the central figure to be that of sowing seeds which flower in reform) as an example of the way in which Quaker influence "has been felt through two centuries in the amelioration of penal severities, the abolition of slavery, the reform of the erring, the relief of the poor and the suffering—felt, in brief, in every step of human progress." But of course the primary emphasis is on the individual (Pastorius) who read the Bible—was respectful of a socially-mediated tradition—by the Inner Light, by a reverent psychological awareness and responsiveness. If in the second period, Whittier's emphasis seems to have been essentially horizontal—man's concern with his fellow-men as in "The Poor Voter on Election Day" (1848–52)—his emphasis in the third period is predominantly vertical, the Christian concern (cf. "Trinitas") for drawing one's fellow-men together being given deeper organic meaning by allegiance to the deity associated with perfection. In other words, as individuals are persuaded to approach the deity, to be responsive to the Inner Light, they will necessarily be drawn closer together in brotherhood.

In his final period Whittier increasingly deplored the divisions of secretarianism, and sought common ground between all sects devoted to the good of all predicated on making individuals not masterless but self-mastered. The extent to which his simple but not naive religious views have entered into the main stream of diverse religious groups is attested by the fact that nearly one hundred hymns have been extracted from poems (as Mr. Currier has shown in his *Bibliography*, p. 597). These hymns (some seventeen of which are still printed in standard *Hymnals* even in 1968) belie the claim of our avant-garde critics that Whittier is dead, since hundreds of thousands sing his hymns of tolerance and mercy who do not notice the poet's name.

His simple dependence on the individual's inner light safeguarded by traditional wisdom lends itself reasonably well to the uses of those who are not so much concerned with antiquarian historical facts about Christ as a person or about ritualism as with a recognition that one may think of the deity as revealed within the individual psychologically whenever he is aware of an impulse toward what generations of men have agreed to call goodness. Such an elementary belief is not likely to be outmoded.

Notes

1. Samuel T. Pickard, *Life and Letters of John Greenleaf Whittier* (Boston: Houghton, Mifflin, 1894, p. 131), says: "There was a sudden, even startling change in the character of Whittier's poetry, when he made up his mind to champion the cause of the slave," beginning (Albert Mordell thinks) when in 1832 he met Garrison and read his abolitionist propaganda. Byron, whom Whittier associated with the Greek quest of freedom, appears to have served as a kind of bridge between Whittier's two periods, leading him to glorify Garrison as venturing

close to "glorious martyrdom" as he braved "the dagger's point."

2. "John Greenleaf Whittier: The Conscience in Poetry," *Harvard Review*, 2 (1964), 8–24. (This is the first printing of an address at Swarthmore in 1957.) The most detailed account of Whittier's reformist period is found in Albert Mordell's *Quaker Militant* (Boston: Houghton, Mifflin, 1933), although the book as a whole reflects some Marxian and Freudian biases. Mordell concludes that the ardor of Whittier's "hate of tyranny intense" places him on a level with our very greatest writers whom he identifies as Emerson, Thoreau, and Hawthorne, and much above other American authors. On Whittier's political interests see also C. B. Williams, "Whittier's Relation To Garrison and the *Liberator*," NEQ, 25 (1952), 248–55, and John B. Pickard, "Whittier and the Abolition Schism of 1840," NEQ, 37 (1964), 250–54. See the bifurcated comments on Byron in the Cady-Clark volume, pp. 38–40, 93–103, and *passim*. Much as Whittier the moralist deplored Byron's licentiousness and impiousness, he could not help concluding in 1831 "We admire—we almost worship—the sublimity of Byron's genius," (pp. 70–71) for "no nobler heart" exists among the "laurel'd bards," and "he was the master spirit of his time" (p. 40).

3. In a doctoral dissertation I was privileged to direct, Lester Zimmerman (*Milton's American Reputation to 1900*, Univ. of Wisconsin 1949) has brought together Whittier's many quotations from and tributes to Milton as the spokesman of Freedom (pp. 247–80).

4. See quote in Pickard's *Life*, II, 513 and VII, 147, where he denies any "low esteem of his anti-slavery labors."

5. See V, 113–14; VII, 353; V, 310; Mordell's quotation, 297–98; and the quotation in Pickard's *Life*, II, 632.

John Greenleaf Whittier: The Conscience In Poetry[1]

Perry Miller[*]

Since I am not a Quaker, since I know the society and the spirit which informs it only from the outside as a general historian, I am not qualified to evaluate the Quaker element in the work of John Greenleaf Whittier. The sum total of his performance, both in verse and prose, is of course prodigious. It mounts, in the Riverside Edition, to seven volumes, but there are thousands of letters, reviews, verses, and articles beyond those collected, and historians are still adding to the corpus. For a man who, during most of his life, made a parade of his constitutional feebleness, who protected himself against worshipping pilgrims by the plea that he required much time for silent contemplation—for such a creature, we begin to suspect, being a Quaker eventually proved a method of self-defense. We know, for instance, that he attended General Meetings in Rhode Island, but I never can quite rid myself of the suspicion that this particular Yankee found that his role as a Quaker became, granting that much else was involved in his conviction, a wonderful convenience.

Which reflection brings me at once to the point I wish to make—perhaps the only bit of fresh light I can throw upon him, and that is simply that Whittier is a more complicated figure, both as man and as writer, than he appears in the conventional view of him as one of the five monumental "household poets" of nineteenth-century America. He possessed a fair amount of guile, which he employed most systematically in building up the legend of his guileless simplicity. Late in life he was fond of saying, "I am a Quaker because my family before me—those whom I loved—were Quakers. And also I am one because the faith pleases me. I believe in it." Yet in 1833, just as he was dedicating himself to the holy cause of Abolition, he wrote to Jonathan Law: "I have written some considerable upon Slavery & have been pretty roughly handled by the Southerners—but so long as I can entrench myself behind

[*]Reprinted from the *Harvard Review*, 2, No. 2 (1964), 8–24, by permission of Mrs. Elizabeth W. Miller.

my Quakerism, as a tortoise does under his shell, I am perfectly safe."

It would not for a moment be proper for me to suggest that he was anything but sincere in his piety and his observances. He wore the plain dark suits and broad-brimmed hats which he ordered from a Philadelphia tailor, but the very picturesqueness of his dress and speech made him so unforgettable as the author of poems that his admirers could never dissociate the image from the product. Many who visited him in the last few years at Amesbury, especially such an English admirer as Edmund Gosse, delighted to report that "it would be difficult to form in the imagination a figure more appropriate to Whittier's writing than Whittier himself proved to be in the flesh." They supposed that they were insuring the reverence of posterity; instead they did Whittier grave disservice from which his reputation now grievously suffers.

Hence in the modern revolutions of taste and fashion, the man and the poetry were bound to fall together. An age that has devoted itself to debunking or deriding all Victorian idols welcomes the suspicion that Whittier's life-long appearance was something of an act. We suspect that he, no less than Whitman, projected his sincerity into a pose. His friends and then his biographers have insisted much on the immaculate purity of his relations with women, and particularly the idyllic household where he was tended faithfully by his two sisters and by Lucy Larcom. They have made these relationships so entirely affairs of the spirit that to us they become insufferable. A few years ago Mr. John Marquand let loose a roar of relieving laughter when his novel *Wickford Point* portrayed an aged poet of Essex County, obviously meant to be Whittier, as a vain, self-satisfied egotist surrounded by a veritable seraglio of spinsters whom he exploited by methods infinitely more insidious than physical possession. Mr. Marquand grew up in the Newburyport area; as a boy he seems to have heard whispered gossip that never got into the biographies. Yet even if he, for the sake of scoring a laugh, was manifestly unfair to Whittier, we are not being vulgar when we speculate about the inner nature of his "extreme and unexplained neurotic condition," as it has been euphemistically called. We can't help wondering if it was not the manifestation of some debility more cancerous, more enervating, than the wounds left by heavy labor on his father's farm. And of course it is widely held against him today that he in righteous horror threw a copy of *Leaves of Grass* into the fire.

Problems of this sort are for biographers, and should not concern us who have neither the information nor the psychoanalytical skill to deal with them. What must occupy us is the question of Whittier the writer, or rather the poet. Has his stature so dwindled, along with those of his fellow composers for the households of the last century, that there is no longer anything worth saying about him?

It might indeed be interesting to summon him as the first witness for his own defense. In effect he took the stand in 1867 when he objected against the New York *Nation* for having attributed to him the statement that he regretted his participation in the anti-slavery movement, that he wished he had devoted himself entirely to poetry. This attribution he disowned, and then interestingly continued:

> I cannot be sufficiently thankful to the Divine Providence that so early called my attention to the great interests of humanity, saving me from the poor ambitions and miserable jealousies of a selfish pursuit of literary reputation. Up to a comparatively recent period, my writings have been simply episodical, something apart from the real object and aim of my life; and whatever of favour they have found with the public has come to me as a grateful surprise, rather than as an expected reward. As I have never staked all on the chances of authorship, I have been spared the pain of disappointment and the temptation to envy those, who, as men of letters, deservedly occupy a higher place in the popular estimation than I have ever aspired to.

At first sight, this seems merely another instance of that good-humored modesty which Whittier publicly displayed about his work. It is of a piece with the "Proem," which after 1847 he always prefaced to successive collections, wherein he announced that he could not breathe the sublime notes of Spenser and Sidney, that his words beat only with Labour's hurried time or Duty's rugged march:

> *Of mystic beauty, dreamy grace,*
> *No rounded art the lack supplies;*
> *Unskilled the subtle lines to trace*
> *Or softer shades of Nature's face,*
> *I view her common forms with unanointed eyes.*

Yet the letter to the *Nation* is written just after he has scored an immense success, financial and otherwise, with *Snow-Bound* in 1866, when he was winning another at that very moment with *The Tent on the Beach*. There was now no question that, quite apart from his Abolitionist writing, Whittier had become as firmly established in the pantheon of American poetry as Longfellow. One can understand how, out of loyalty to the old cause and to former associates, he would want to correct any rumor that he regretted his service; still, Whittier seems driven to offer some more complicated and confusing argument. He is grateful, very grateful to the cause of Negro emancipation for so engrossing him that he could escape the miseries of a purely literary exertion; hence he is protected—again, like a tortoise under his shell—against the challenge of having his work regarded as anything but "episodical." This is something considerably more devious than straight-forward humility. We are suddenly reminded that in 1853, in addressing "My Namesake" to a Vermont relative, he had then made a great point of his lack of envy for those whom Fame celebrated:

> *Let Love's and Friendship's tender debt*
> *Be paid by those I love in life.*
> *Why should unborn critic whet*
> *For me his scalping-knife?*

Whittier would seem to have been pleading all his life with the Friends Historical Library of Swarthmore College *not* to take any notice of his hundred-and-fiftieth birthday and especially not to let me, a decidedly later-born critic, whet a scalping-knife!

It seems to me that we begin to get a hint of what we are looking for in a well-known letter Whittier sent to Garrison, which was to be read at the 1863 meeting of the American Anti-Slavery Society in Phila-delphia. Whittier knew that in this hour of victory praises would be sung to him, and so he concluded once more:

> I cannot be sufficiently thankful to the Divine Providence which, in a great measure through thy instrumentality, turned me away so early from what Roger Williams calls "the world's great trinity, pleasure, profit, and honor," to take side with the poor and oppressed. I am not insensible to literary reputation. I love, perhaps too well, the praise and goodwill of my fellow-men; but I set higher value on my name as appended to the Anti-Slavery Declaration of 1833 than on the title-page of any book.

What I first call to your attention here is a shy admission that literary fame *does* have a slight attraction for him; then, secondly, that he marks 1833 as the year of the decision in which he deliberately—I am tempted to say wantonly—subordinated his desire for such fame to the concern of his conscience. How much, we may ask, was this an irresistible com-mitment to the cause of freedom, and how much was it a creative maneuvre for contriving that hereafter his literary responsibility would be limited to the "episodical"? If, as I believe, there was indeed some proportion of the second motive in the resolution, whether consciously realized or profoundly hidden, the result would be the forging of a suit of Quaker armor that would forever prevent him from again being assailed by lust for poetic fame. Thenceforth he would be liberated, a literary Antinomian, who could always obsessively insist he was outside the laws of literary competition.

We could speak more firmly about this business if we had solid information concerning the inward crisis he was passing through from 1831 to 1833. For seven months in 1829 he was editor of the *American*

Manufacturer in Boston; for seven months of 1830 he edited the *Essex Gazette* in Haverhill; he went to Hartford as editor of the *New England Weekly Review* in July, 1830, and left it, to return to the Haverhill farm, in January, 1833. We can read what he was publishing in these journals, but this gives little insight into his private thoughts, less into his emotions. It is generally assumed that in 1829 he was "in love" with Mary Emerson Smith and in 1828 with Evelina Bray. From all we can gather—and I insist, the evidence is extremely elusive—the Whittier whose character and ambitions we make out, however dimly, from the years 1827–1830 is a very different young man from the one who went with Garrison to Philadelphia in December of 1833.

For one thing, the Whittier of 1830 was a Whig, an ardent admirer of Henry Clay and of Clay's "American System," an advocate of protectionism, and an encomiast of Daniel Webster. Perhaps in the amorphous state of parties in 1830 this did not align him so strikingly on the side of business against the common man as his continued adherence to the Republican Party of President Grant did in 1870. Even so, biographers find themselves puzzled by the phenomenon, or if *they* are not, I am. When they are so puzzled, they pass over the chapter rapidly. His father had been a Jeffersonian Democrat, and he himself in 1830 deplored the rise in America of an aristocracy of wealth. Nevertheless, to him Andrew Jackson loomed, as much as to Nicholas Biddle, as a demagogue who was trying to found a despotism on a subverted Constitution. Thus, what first of all the inward crisis of 1833, the "conversion" if I may call it so, meant for Whittier was escape from a political entanglement which, had he tried to maintain it, would have destroyed him. By 1845 he was freed from all bondage to Henry Clay. Then he would smile condescendingly upon the barefoot boy in politics, explaining that Clay's "brilliant talents, his early republicanism, his splendid eloquence, excited our boyish enthusiasm and admiration." In 1845 Whittier would read Henry Clay a philippic, ending with, "Let him repent of the evil he has done to the holy cause of Liberty."

Yet *we* cannot dismiss this phase as only a youthful aberration. In so far as Whittier ever again paid attention to politics apart from the anti-slavery campaign, the radical of the holy cause seems to have been of a "conservative" disposition. He was a serious apologist for Edmund Burke, for instance, and verbally appropriated Burke's condemnations of the French Revolution; his hatred of it appears not so much Quaker pacifism as a Whiggish opposition to all revolution. Wherefore he denounced Jackson with what he termed (coming from him) only intemperance. Once Emancipation had come, Whittier advocated no more tumultuous causes. He said that he believed in women's suffrage, and he did courageously show a sympathy for labor; but even so, he was not out of place in the conservatively literary society of Boston, where "radicalism" was agreed to be a thing of the past. He scrupulously refused in 1887 to join with Howells in petitioning the Governor of Illinois to review the case of the so-called Chicago anarchists. As has often been remarked, in the years after the Emancipation Proclamation, he lived easily, though of course in no sense riotously, with the world's great trinity, "pleasure, profit, and honor."

Clearly, then, he who had still supported Clay in 1832, but who shortly was to denounce him as an enemy to human liberty, went rapidly through a transformation which provided him a quite altered view of the political scene. And all of this seems to tie up with another episode of 1832 which still remains mysterious and which even so devout a biographer as Thomas Wentworth Higginson could describe only as a "lapse." Several friends persuaded him to run for Congress on the Whig ticket, only to discover that Whittier would not reach the legal age of 25 before the balloting in November. Whittier thereupon proposed a delaying scheme, a sheer piece of skulduggery, to produce a stalemate in November, so that he might then snatch the prize in December. It is difficult to believe that this is the John Greenleaf Whittier of sanctified memory we now hear speaking, but the letter is authentic:

> The truth of the matter is, the thing would be peculiarly beneficial to me,—if not at home it would be so abroad. It would give me an opportunity of seeing and knowing our public characters, and in case of Mr. Clay's election might enable me to do something for myself or my friends. It would be worth more to me now, young as I am, than almost any office after I had reached the meridian of life.

It becomes still more astounding that our Whittier ever could have talked this way as he goes on to assure his correspondent, in the tawdry jargon of politics, that he has never deserted a friend and that "if my friends enable me to acquire influence, it shall be exerted for their *benefit.*" It is also fantastic to imagine he had not already had enough experience with his precarious health to realize that he never could have endured the pandemonium of the House of Representatives.

However, by the next May Whittier was publishing at his own expense his first Abolitionist tract, *Justice and Expediency.* This made it entirely certain that he would never be elected to any public office; his own act thus left him no option but to go with Garrison to Philadelphia. Yet, as we know, he was not thereupon entirely out of politics; on the contrary, he now became the Abolitionist *éminence grise* of Essex County. It was he who swung the election to Caleb Cushing on condition that Cushing receive petitions and work for Abolition in the District of Columbia. Whittier held his whip hand over Cushing for several years, compelling the sorry creature to do his bidding, until in 1841 President Tyler appointed Cushing Secretary of the Treasury, and Caleb thought he had escaped. He little reckoned the ruthlessness of the Quaker: Whittier made sure that Southern Senators were informed of Cushing's Abolitionist affiliations, and they three times voted him down. Later, as is well known, Whittier played an active part in supporting the two politicians who were on his side with conviction, Robert Rantoul and Charles Sumner.

No doubt the psychological implications of these events can be exaggerated, but the story itself is clear: a promising young editor, with spacious prospects both in journalism and politics, suddenly abandons his Whig allegiance, throws away his career, and goes over irrevocably to a cause which will pay him no money, which is certainly dangerous, and possibly doomed. That he calculated the cost comes through to us from the poem addressed to Garrison in this year of spiritual discovery. Because we know that slavery finally was abolished, we are apt comfortably to suppose that in his final apostrophe Whittier was simply waxing melodramatic, but if we remember the violence of Northern mobs and the fury of Southern slaveholders, we realize that Whittier honestly believed that the band were taking their lives in their hands:

> Go on,—the dagger's point may glare
> Amid the pathway's gloom,—
> The fate which sternly threatens there
> Is glorious martyrdom!
> Thus onward with a Martyr's zeal,
> And wait thy sure reward
> When man to man no more shall kneel,
> And God alone be Lord!

What fascinates me about this poem—surely one of the most memorable in the "episodical" career—is that Whittier rejects with particular scorn one charge that had been raised against Garrison:

> They tell me thou art rash and vain,—
> A searcher after fame;
> Thou art striving but to gain
> A long enduring name.

What makes this altogether striking is that just three years before Whittier had published in the New England Review a verse that at the time meant so much to him he later incorporated it in Moll Pitcher. It was entitled "New England":

> Land of my Fathers!—If my name
> Now humble and unwed to fame,
> Hereafter burn upon the lip,

> *As of those which may not die,*
> *Linked in eternal fellowship*
> *With visions pure, and strong, and high;*
> *If the wild dreams, which quicken now*
> *The throbbing pulse of heart and brow,*
> *Hereafter take a real form*
> *Like spectres changed to being warm,*
> *And over temples wan and grey*
> *The star-like crown of glory shine.*
> *Thine be the bard's undying lay,*
> *The murmur of his praise be thine.*

Here he certainly had been striving to enlist all New England in further-ing his career toward a glory infinitely more dazzling (and less Quaker-ish?) than a mere election to Congress!

Much has been written about the meagerness of Whittier's formal schooling. Those two brief terms at the Haverhill Academy, for which he so poignantly earned the pennies for his small expenses by making shoes, are enshrined in the American myth, according to which the barefoot boy makes his way by sheer force of genius, not by education. But in historical fact, this version *is* mythology. It leaves out of account how predominantly literary or rather I should say how exclusively rhetorical, the culture of the period was, how effectively it was pervaded by cheap editions of the tremendously popular English writers, and how quickly the basic ideas and conventions could be absorbed. The way Whittier acquired his copy of Robert Burns from Joshua Coffin in 1821 is an oft-told story. The obvious analogy of *Snow-Bound* to *The Cotter's Saturday Night* creates the impression that Burns was the only English writer whom Whittier studied. Whittier strengthened that im-pression by his apostrophe to his supposed model in 1854, describing his own youthful enthusiasm:

> *How oft that day, with fond delay,*
> *I sought the maple's shadow,*
> *And sang with Burns the hours away,*
> *Forgetful of the meadow!*

But recent scholarship has belatedly excavated the substantial amount of literary criticism he turned out in the journalistic years before 1832; these pieces sufficiently demonstrate that the two writers who first stimulated his vaulting ambition were, as was the case with virtually all the other young aspirants in America, Scott and Byron.

I will not delay you by long quotations from his notices of these two. He had his criticisms of them, and, like all Americans, whether Quaker or not, was distressed both by Scott's Toryism and by Byron's "immorality." But even so, of Scott he said that he had found much to admire and little to condemn; of Byron Whittier said unequivocally, both in verse and in prose, "He was the master spirit of his time." That these were deeply felt convictions is more than proved by the early poetry composed voluminously in the years when dreams of the star-like crown of glory consumed him. The project for his first collection of verses—fortunately never realized—was to be entitled "The Poems of Adrian." For a farm-boy in Haverhill to appear in print as "Adrian" was the New England equivalent of Byron's appearing before Europe as Childe Harold.

This point has not customarily been stressed, because in his later years Whittier did everything he could to expunge these early effusions, just as he systematically hunted out and destroyed every copy he could find of *Legends of New England*, originally published at Hartford in 1831. This prose effort and such pretentious verse narratives as *Mogg Megone* and *Moll Pitcher* are so palpably efforts to be a Scott in New England, to exploit the vogue for the marvelous and preternatural, to furnish his region with a legendary past, that we must credit the maturing of his critical faculties as well as the revulsion of 1833 for his subsequent efforts to suppress the lot of them. Those he could not banish entirely he skillfully locked up in the "Appendix" of the Cambridge edition, where they are seldom noticed. Biographers and scholars continue remorselessly to dig up the buried corpses.

Several aspects of these enterprises should be noted. For one, they are full of violence. "The Song of the Vermonters," for instance (published anonymously in 1833, the secret of its authorship kept until his death), is a call to action which no Quaker Meeting would approve:

> Come down with your rifles! Let gray wolf and fox
> Howl on in the shade of their primitive rocks;
> Let the bear feed securely from pig-pen and stall;
> Here's two-legged game for your powder and ball.

In *Mogg Megone*, the scalpings, declamations, slaughters, shrieks go, if anything, beyond the most clanging passages in Scott's *Marmion*. Combined with these bloody conflicts is what ever he could appropriate out of Byron's melancholy, self-pity, and demonism. As early as 1824, he hailed Byron in verse as "the boast, the pride, the shame, the wonder of his age." The poem which his sister Mary sent to Garrison in 1826, and which brought the startling trip of the editor to Haverhill to behold this genius, is called "The Exile's Departure"; it is maudlin Byronism, with an Irishman declaiming to Erin instead of a noble Lord addressing England. It makes clear that Whittier comprehended little about either of those islands, or about either sort of romantic titan. The essential fact is that he began by trying to dramatize them.

Among these verses there are still other apostrophes to Byron, and still more lush Byronic fluency; again I seek not to bore you by quoting over much juvenilia. The evidence, I assure you, is overwhelming that Whittier was ecstatically elevated by these two writers. And I should hazard that their hold upon him remained absolute at least up to the onset of the agonizing crisis of 1831–33.

But again, we know precious little of what really was working in him during this crisis, and again we must note that the later Whittier made strenuous efforts to prevent us from knowing. But I think we get a white light on the inception of his ordeal from a letter he wrote (presumably to some literary lady in Hartford in April, 1831) which Samuel Pickard released only in 1904:

> Disappointment in a thousand ways has gone over my heart, and left it dust. Yet I still look forward with high anticipations. I have placed the goal of my ambitions high—but with the blessings of God it shall be reached. The world has at last breathed into my bosom a portion of its own bitterness, and I now feel as if I would wrestle manfully in the strife of men. If my life is spared, the world shall know me in a loftier capacity than as a *writer of rhymes*. There—is not that boasting?—But I have said it with a strong pulse and a swelling heart, and I shall strive to realize it.

I find this an amazing letter. What lies behind it, I leave you to surmise. I can only remark that it does not appear to me the conventional anguish of a youth "disappointed in love." Some upheaval is commencing on a deeper level of his being, a convulsion that threatens, if it does not wreck him, painfully to transform him. For the moment the prospect, in either direction, is one of terror, of consternation. Byron could no longer shield him from it.

Commentators have usually been a bit puzzled, even more amused, by observations made about him by many among that regiment of women who sought him out as his fame grew. What we are apt to forget is that in the nineteenth century even the most genteel of feminists were fully aware of masculine vigor, though their language about it was always politely oblique. Fredericka Bremer, for instance, met him in 1850, and with implications which are unmistakable reported:

> He has a good exterior, in figure is slender and tall, a beautiful head with refined features, black eyes full of fire, dark complexion, a fine smile, and lively, but very nervous manners.

More arrestingly, in 1883 Edna Dean Proctor wrote him, "I have always been impressed by the mingled volcano and iceberg of your character."

Without attributing some superior powers to "feminine intuition," we can hardly help noting that these women (others might be cited) divined in the Quaker seer the fire, the volcano, something of the nervous strain he suffered in order to insure that only the iceberg should be exposed to public view. What I suggest is that by the end of 1833 he found a resolution which gave him, for the rest of his life, a way of living with a self which he feared he might not otherwise control. In one sweeping action he cut the complicated knot of his being; it was an act of self-confinement, I might even go so far as to say self-mutilation. Here the forces all converged: the full recognition of incurable physical debility, the craving for a Byronic success in literature, the worship of Clay, the political ambition, the drift toward conservatism. By publicly volunteering in the Anti-Slavery ranks, Whittier could come to terms with all his devils—but above all could rid himself of the incubus that most flayed him, his desire for fame. That fire was now banked: a political career was made impossible, he was an announced radical, and from now on poetry could be practised as episodical, as something apart from the "real" object of his life. Conscience had not failed him in his hour of need, had come indeed to his salvation. He could now say, in all humble sincerity, "I have never staked all on the chances of authorship." In fact, by this act he had ceased to stake anything on literature; wherefore if it should ever favor him, he could accept the benediction as an unmerited bounty, not a reward of virtue.

Thus artfully the volcano was covered over. With the result, therefore, that through the crevices it could flare episodically with terrible force but without thawing the iceberg. The stratagems of conscience are indeed wondrously subtle: it is a faculty which represses in order to release, which disavows fame in order that fame shall seek him out. By confining power—especially if one must carefully husband his every energy—conscience contrives that power gathers momentum. Within thirty years, what a tortuous road we travel from the flamboyant "Exile" of 1826:

> *Fond scenes, which delighted my youthful existence,*
> *With feelings of sorrow I bid ye adieu—*
> *A lasting adieu! for now, dim in the distance,*
> *The shores of Hibernia recede from my view.*

to the eruption of lava upon "Moloch in State Street."

> *Thank God! our mother State can yet*
> *Her fame retrieve;*
> *To you and to your children let*
> *The Scandal cleave.*
> *Chain Hall and Pulpit, Court and Press,*
> *Make gods of gold;*
> *Let honor, truth, and manliness*
> *Like wares be sold.*

> *Your hoards are great, your walls are strong,*
> *But God is just;*
> *The gilded chambers built by wrong,*
> *Invite the rust.*
> *What! know ye not the gains of Crime*
> *Are dust and dross;*
> *Its ventures on the waves of time*
> *Foredoomed to loss!*
> *And still the Pilgrim State remains*
> *What she hath been;*
> *Her inland hills, her seaward plains,*
> *Still nurture men!*

It is a bit ironical that Whittier should have slyly disowned "The Song of the Vermonters" as inconsistent with his Quaker upbringing, for that empty jingle would certainly never have incited anybody to go out and shoot two-legged game. After "Moloch in State Street," "men" nurtured in the Pilgrim State are rapidly being brought to a mood in which they will gleefully spread devastation through the gilded chambers built by wrong in Georgia and the Carolinas.

If there be any plausibility in my crude account of how Whittier emerged from his tepid Byronism, one might say that it amounts to little more than a conventional comment which all too often has been made concerning the poetic impulse in nineteenth-century America. The injunction that poetry must serve some high purpose, some exalted morality, some cause of freedom was so universally laid upon all our poets, whether their talents were great or ordinary, that they were compelled to serve a conscience which demanded precedence over sheer delight in versifying, assuredly over any yielding to sensuous gratification. Only Poe stood out against this omnipresent didacticism, and we know how America treated him. Assuredly the New England of *Snow-Bound* would have been no place for a John Keats. We can imagine how a Baudelaire or a Swinburne would have sneered at the struggles of a Longfellow or a Lowell to become poets within liberalized but still painfully moralized Puritanism, just as we all know how a D. H. Lawrence or a Dylan Thomas found in the emotional inhibitions of this country the starvation of all outgoing spontaneous creativity. If Bryant, Longfellow, Lowell, Holmes are thus blamable, then bachelor Whittier is the most pallid of the lot. His Quakerism ceases to be a factor of much importance in the story: it only made the task easier for him than for the others to divert his slight energies from a mildly sensuous but sophomoric Byronism into righteous propaganda for the bloodiest war in history.

This is not the occasion on which to defend American genius

against European attack, or even to apologize to the twentieth century for the artificialities of the nineteenth. I have no disposition to exonerate Longfellow; those who lately have tried to rescue him have been able at best to plead that he was a skillful technician. I think a case could be made that Whittier, in the variety of his verse forms, in his imagery, in his cadences, also deserves revaluation. Naturally one would concentrate on *Snow-Bound* and several poems of his maturity. To the limits of his talent, he did continue to grow, to study the craft of writing, and this fact does make the achievement of his old age a testimony to his indestructible vitality.

But all that is another story. To the extent that it is valid, the particular story I am trying to tell is the anterior condition of his ultimate success. In this story, the fact that Whittier was a Quaker, and a passionate one, makes his struggle to bring the lawless, anarchic impulse of poetry under a discipline a very different, a much more fascinating conflict than we shall discover in Bryant, Longfellow, Lowell, or Holmes, or indeed in many poets at present more highly esteemed.

Let me give one brief illustration. It is a matter of common knowledge that Abolitionists made all possible propagandistic use of the charge that Southern planters seduced Negress slaves, begot mulatto children, and sold these offspring to the rice fields and plantations. Most Southerners at the time replied that not only was this a canard, but that such Yankee obsession with miscegenation was evidence of hypocritically nasty minds. And none can deny that eventually the lurid dramatization of the sexual issue in *Uncle Tom's Cabin* became a highly effective part of the book's appeal, not only in the North but in Europe. Whittier touches on the theme from time to time, often gingerly, through unconvincing stereotypes. The lament of the Virginia slave mother undoubtedly told on the consciences of some Northerners:

> *Toiling through the weary day,*
> *And at night the spoiler's prey.*

But this is a fairly academic treatment, and about as unconvincing as the metrical reply of "The Yankee Girl" to her "Southron" wooer:

> *Full low at thy bidding thy negroes may kneel,*
> *With the iron of bondage on spirit and heel,*
> *Yet know that the Yankee girl sooner would be*
> *In fetters with them, than in freedom with thee!*

However, in 1833—the year of his crisis, of his passing from romance to Abolition and of his forecasting the martyrdom of Garrison—Whittier also composed his poem on "Toussaint L'Ouverture," which he placed at the beginning of the section, "Voices of Freedom." This phantasmagoric vision of the rebellion in Haiti streams with even more gore than *Mogg Megone,* but here the context is neither Scottian antiquarianism nor pseudo-Byronic lyricism; it is stark violence, massacre, and, in the climax, rape of the white planter's wife by the black demon. The third strophe echoes that frenzy in which the young Quaker had dabbled, but here, now that the poem will figure among the first of his "episodes," the sexual passion, the fire, the volcano, erupt into a terminology of orgiastic destruction:

> *Brief was the silence. Once again*
> *Pealed to the skies that frantic yell,*
> *Glowed on the heavens a fiery stain,*
> *And flashes rose and fell;*
> *And painted on the blood-red sky,*
> *Dark, naked arms were tossed on high;*
> *And, round the white man's lordly hall,*
> *Trod, fierce and free, the brute he made;*
> *And those who crept along the wall,*
> *And answered to his lightest call*
> *With more than spaniel dread—*
> *The creatures of his lawless beck,—*
> *Were trampling on his very neck!*
> *And on the night-air, wild and clear,*
> *Rose woman's shriek of more than fear;*
> *For bloodied arms were round her thrown,*
> *And dark cheeks pressed against her own!*

This stanza is probably one of the least constructive contributions to the cause Whittier ever made, since the implication might well be that in the South they should not emancipate such brutes but strengthen the slave-codes, that in the North sensible men, contemplating this horror, would agree. Be that is it may, this building up, through the language of turmoil, to the final bestiality of the rape makes the passage one of the few verses in which Whittier achieved an authentic intensity that none of his fellow poets ever could approximate, and which one must needs turn to the more vehement flights of Melville's prose or to the more melodramatic of Whitman's ecstasies to match. Both Whitman and Melville had their ways of saluting the Quaker culture of America, viewing it sometimes with reverence, sometimes with sympathetic amusement; but neither of them, despite the expanse of the America they comprehended, could begin to tell us wherein consists the ordeal for the Quaker striving to become an artist. Neither they nor any writer out of American experience, but only Whittier can convey to us, even though he must do it by elaborate indirection, the true ferocity of the Quaker conscience.

Note

1. This article is a talk that Professor Miller delivered at Swarthmore College, December 1957.

INDEX